CW00376076

MARKETING, SALES AND CUSTOMER SERVICES

Understanding the theory and practice of selling through service

Charley Watkins

institute of financial services

UMIST

Apart from any fair dealing for the purpose of research or private study, or criticism or review, as permitted under the Copyright, Designs and Patents Act 1988, this publication may only be reproduced, stored or transmitted, in any form or by any means, with the prior permission in writing of the publisher, or in the case of reprographic reproduction in accordance with the terms and licences issued by the Copyright Licensing Agency. Enquiries concerning reproduction outside those terms should be addressed to the publisher's agents at the undermentioned address:

CIB Publishing
c/o The Chartered Institute of Bankers
Emmanuel House
4-9 Burgate Lane
Canterbury
Kent
CT1 2XJ
United Kingdom

Telephone: 01227 762600

CIB Publishing publications are published by The Chartered Institute of Bankers, a non-profit making registered educational charity.

The Chartered Institute of Bankers believes that the sources of information upon which the book is based are reliable and has made every effort to ensure the complete accuracy of the text. However, neither CIB, the author nor any contributor can accept any legal responsibility whatsoever for consequences that may arise from errors or omissions or any opinion or advice given.

Typeset by Kevin O'Connor

Printed by Redwood Books, Trowbridge, Wiltshire

© Chartered Institute of Bankers 1999

ISBN 0-85297-511-2

Marketing, Sales and Customer Service

This textbook has been written for both students and practitioners of the subject. It has been written to a syllabus drawn up by subject experts, including current senior practitioners, which forms part of the Diploma in Financial Services Management (DFSM). This qualification is administered by the Institute of Financial Services, a wholly owned subsidiary of The Chartered Institute of Bankers and is awarded jointly by The CIB and the University of Manchester Institute of Science and Technology (UMIST). The role of UMIST in this partnership is to benchmark all aspects of the delivery of the DFSM, including this text, to first year undergraduate standard.

Though written to a syllabus specific to the DFSM it is intended that this text will serve a useful purpose for anybody studying for a business or finance-related qualification. Furthermore, this book will serve as an excellent reference tool for practitioners already working in this or related fields. All books in the DFSM series reflect the very latest regulations, legislation and reporting requirements.

Students of the DFSM will also receive a separate Study Guide to be used in conjunction with this text. This Study Guide refers the reader to further reading on the topic and helps to enhance learning through exercises based upon the contents of this book.

CONTENTS

Contents

Contents

1

Basic Marketing Philosophy

After reading this chapter you should

- Understand what is meant by the term *marketing* and the role of marketing as a management science

- Know how a marketeer must balance the needs of the market against the needs of the seller

- Understand the importance of matching profit goals with customer satisfaction

- Be aware of the reasons for setting goals

- Understand the need and the methods used to maximize scarce resource

Defining marketing

There is no precise definition of marketing. The dictionary definition is simply 'the opportunity for selling'; however, we know that there is much more to it than that! A more reasonable definition for the purposes of your study would be that used by the Chartered Institute of Marketing, which is as follows:

> *The management process responsible for identifying, anticipating and satisfying customer needs profitably.*

Alternatively the definition from *Industrial Marketing Communications*, Norman Hart (1993):

> *Marketing starts in the marketplace with the identification of customer needs and wants. It then moves on to determining a means of satisfying those needs and of promoting, selling and supplying a satisfaction.*

Whichever definition you choose, it is clear that marketing involves understanding the needs of your customers, whomever they may be, raising customers' awareness to those needs, and producing and making available an appealing solution to those needs. The marketing function is clearly an important element of the business, which seeks to identify the type and level of demand within a company's marketplace and match it with supply. It must, of course, do so at a profit to the business.

The major activities covered by the term *marketing* are:

- *Information and research* – ensuring that there is sufficient known about the customers and their needs, as well as the competition and their offerings.

- *Planning, designing, and producing products and services* – ensuring that the product and services are matched to the needs of the customer and where possible gaining a competitive advantage over other products.

- *Packaging* – ensuring that the products are packaged in a way that appeals to the customers – ensuring that they are easily understood and attractive to the target market.

- *Pricing* – ensuring that the products are competitively priced, both for the customer and for the company, taking account of costs, competitors' prices, and customers' willingness to pay.

- *Advertising and promotion* – having designed a good product and priced it accurately, the company needs to communicate the benefits to the potential customers in a way that will attract them to buy it.

- *Distribution* – having raised people's interest in a product or service, the company then has to find a way to make it easy for that customer to take the next step and buy the product. The method of distribution must reflect the needs and desires of the potential customer if it is to be successful.

Marketing starts in the marketplace. It is the use of information about the present and future needs of customers to enable the organization to satisfy those needs in a profitable way. The boundaries of the *marketplace* can be set very widely. All people could be classed as potential customers. However, from a marketing perspective, organizations need to focus on those segments of the market that appear to have the best development potential.

There are many definitions of marketing. Kotler defined it as human activity directed at satisfying needs and wants through the exchange process. According to Marsh, marketing is identifying the most profitable markets now and in the future; assessing present and future needs of customers; setting business goals and making plans to meet them; and managing products and services in such a way that these plans are achieved. It also necessitates adapting to a changing environment in the marketplace.

Marketing is a management process, in that same way that finance, staffing and production are management processes. The Institute of Marketing calls it 'the management process responsible for identifying, anticipating and satisfying customer needs profitably'. It is an integral part of running a business and should not be undertaken in a vacuum, as we shall demonstrate later in this course.

If marketing activity is undertaken effectively, customer awareness and interest in the product being promoted will be stimulated. Closing the sale, or selling the product, is an integral part of the marketing process. Selling involves leading the interested customer through to commitment. This is achieved by the salesperson demonstrating an understanding of the customer's needs, then showing how the product's features and benefits can satisfy these needs.

The marketing concept

It should not be forgotten that today's customers have ample choice. Skilful and eye-catching promotion by organizations selling financial products has made consumers more financially sophisticated and aware of the range of available options. Convenience of location and parental influence are less likely to dictate where a customer keeps an account. Greater numbers than ever before happily change from one organization to another or have an allegiance to more than one financial organization.

To succeed in the competitive world of the 1990s an organization must have a customer-focused marketing culture, and must instil this culture into all of its personnel, most especially those who deal directly with its customers. This culture is the only one on which an effective marketing strategy can be built.

The marketing concept is now about satisfying the needs of the customer. It has changed dramatically over the past 25 years from 'how can we sell what we have?' to 'what can we sell and how can we sell it?'

This modern approach to marketing recognizes that:

a) *Customer satisfaction and profit go together.* High street-based organizations must balance customer satisfaction and profit because they rely on repeat customer business as opposed to passing trade. Too high a profit could reduce customer satisfaction and undermine the long-term relationship which is so important;

b) *Customers' current and future requirements are at the heart of all marketing activity but these needs are constantly changing.* Market research enables organizations to keep abreast of these changes, and to anticipate them whenever possible;

c) *Marketing is a vital management activity.* It should be given equal priority with other management processes even when resources are scarce.

1.1   Role of marketing in the organization

The marketing department of any company is not purely a place in which the marketing activity is planned and carried out – it is an extremely important function that is an integral part of any financial services organization. Marketing is responsible for producing profit, without which the organization would cease to exist; how much more important could a function be?

Marketing, Sales and Customer Services

The activities of a fully operational marketing department may well be seen to overlap with many other areas of the organization. For example, where do the responsibilities of the sales departments stop and the responsibility of the marketing function start? The truth is that selling could well be considered to be the promotional element of the marketing mix and it could therefore be argued that sales are the responsibility of the marketing manager. In practice, however, most organizations operate separate sales and marketing departments which work closely, if not always harmoniously, together.

It is an unfortunate result of the fact that large organizations tend to compartmentalize their activities that in many of them the marketing function is seen as a stand-alone activity, rather than the truly cross-functional discipline that it is. Bear in mind the definition of marketing that we have just looked at. The purpose of the marketing function is to identify customer needs and produce and promote solutions to those needs at a profit to the organization. With this in mind it is much easier to see how the other functions of an organization are closely aligned with the roles of the other departments.

For example, the production department in a financial services organization may be the product/service design team or such things as customer services. This function would not know what to produce or what service or product to provide if the marketing department had not first discovered the exact nature of customers' needs. It may be fairly obvious but worth remembering, there would be no point in producing anything unless you know that there are customers out there who are willing and able to buy it.

Take another function common to most organizations, the finance function. In simple terms, this department is responsible for ensuring that the organization is run at a profit rather than a loss. It will make predictions of income and outgoings, project expenditure and sales revenue on a yearly and five-yearly basis. These predictions will be based on the information contained in the business plan and within the marketing plan and the marketing strategy.

Marketing contributes to the overall success of the organization by looking at the direction the company should take in the future. The marketing team looks at the market, predicts the way it will move, and the marketing strategy will ensure that the company is in the best position possible to exploit the opportunities that arise. They are therefore providing overall guidance for the entire future of the company. They are vital to the overall corporate objective, setting goals for the entire organization to work together to achieve. Such things as the research that they carry out and the SWOT analysis they conduct will enable the organization's management team to make informed strategic decisions. There will always be alternatives for the company to consider and the marketing department will help them to make the right choice.

The other function performed by marketing on behalf of the entire organization is that of keeping a focus on customers, understanding what they need and how those needs are changing – the kind of things that it would be easy for the other departments to forget.

Unfortunately, especially in new or small businesses, marketing can be seen as a 'nice to have' area of a business rather than an essential area of any thriving and developing business.

To properly understand the important role that the marketing department plays for any management team we must remember the following:

- In many businesses, the marketing function focuses the management team's attention on the customers and what they want.

- Marketing ensures that the management team can concentrate on satisfying the needs and wants of the selected, specific target markets.

- The marketing function supplies managers with a great deal of their planning capacity.

- Marketing also helps them to monitor and control their activity.

- Marketing helps managers to achieve their business plans by providing their customers with tailored solutions and thus giving customer satisfaction.

Marketing is a very complex area of the business; it combines both the concepts and the philosophies of business together with the actual practice of attracting customers, making sales, and producing profit. The marketing function therefore provides management with both a planning capability as well as a functional unit of the business.

The most successful financial services companies are therefore those that believe that marketing is a fundamentally important part of their business, a basic philosophy and way of working that needs to run right through the organization, forming the cornerstone of everything they do. In order for the marketing to be effective, the marketing concept must run right through the company and feature in everything they do. We can start to see that if the marketing is to be successful it must have the support of management at all levels. Senior management must be willing to run a business that is customer focused and considers both the needs of the market as well as the needs of the organization.

1.2 Needs of the market versus needs of the seller

For any financial services company the needs of the market, i.e. the consumer, must be paramount. The purpose of the company's existence is to provide products and services that the customer requires. Therefore it could well be argued that the needs of the seller must always be second to that of the customer.

However, the organization will have goals and objectives that it wants to achieve in order to continue to prosper and grow. In order to meet these goals there will be certain things that the company needs to do. There will therefore have to be some very careful balancing between the needs of the consumer and the needs of the organization that the marketing manager will have to consider.

Although the marketeers are part of the organization and therefore working towards the company's objectives, their role is to ensure that the products and services they offer meet the needs of the consumer. They will know that the sale of those products is the aim of their role within the company, and should always work to the principle that the needs of the company can be paramount only in as far as it is necessary to improve the benefits for the consumer. However this is often easier said than done!

Let us consider some of the areas where the needs of both the market and the seller may have to be carefully balanced.

The need of the consumer for the best possible price

V

The need of the seller to make the maximum profit

The need of the consumer for the best possible service standards

V

The need of the organization to maintain low servicing costs

The need of the consumer for tailor-made products that exactly match individual needs and requirements

V

The need of the seller to produce mass-market products that appeal to a wide audience

The need of the consumer for individual attention from branch staff

V

The need of the seller to reduce staffing levels and become more efficient

The need of the consumer for a local branch network for easy access

V

The need of the organization to rationalize the branch network

The need of the consumer for advice rather than hard-sell sales tactics

V

The need of the seller to make sales and therefore income

Whereas there are various legislative measures in place to ensure that the needs of the consumer are properly taken account of, often the balance between the market requirements and the company's objectives is a balancing act that must be carried out by the marketing function. Although they will want to see the company thrive and prosper, they will always remember that their function in the team is to ensure that the consumer needs are met.

Balancing the needs of the market against the needs of the seller will be covered in more detail in Chapter 18.

We can see from the examples given above that the main area of conflict is likely to arise around the subject of cost, i.e. the amount charged to the consumer in order to make profit for the company, and we will therefore look at this aspect in more detail.

1.3 Importance of matching profit goals with customer satisfaction

At the very start of this text we looked at the different definitions of marketing, and they all involved the satisfying of customer needs. However in the Chartered Institute's definition, we also saw that this must be done 'profitably'. Financial services organizations are, after all, businesses. They are not charities and they cannot afford to operate each year making a loss; they need to make a profit.

Financial services companies are owned in one of two basic ways: they are either mutual or they are owned by shareholders. If a company is owned by shareholders, those shareholders expect to see some return for their investment. They will expect the company to make a profit and therefore declare a dividend. In the longer term they will want to see the continued profitability of the company leading to its increasing value and therefore the value of their share rising. Many companies' corporate plans involve primary objectives that relate to the 'increased shareholder value' they wish to deliver, and most are focused on the need to deliver good returns to their investors.

Mutual companies do not have shareholders. They are owned by the people who have invested in their products, and all profits are returned to those people who do business with them. This does not mean however that they do not need to make a profit. People who have invested and saved with a mutual insurance company often have invested in the *with-profits* fund of that company. (This means that the money invested in the fund relies on the profits of the business for its growth.) These customers are reliant on the profits of the company for a return on their investment. The company will also be reliant on being able to show good returns on its with-profits fund in order to attract new business. We can see that whichever way a company is owned it needs to make a profit if it is to stay in business.

For this reason most companies set themselves primary objectives and goals that relate to the production of profit in one form or another. This is a necessary part of the management of a successful business and we shall look in more detail at the structure and purpose of a corporate plan in Chapter 4. They could include such things as:

- A desired level of profit for the company in that year;
- A certain level of *return on investments* (ROI) or *return on capital employed* (ROCE);
- A desired level of increase in share price, or a target level of dividend;
- Growth of the business;
- Any combination of these.

Although each and any of the above objectives would be appropriate in different circumstances, the company will inevitable have one or more of these measures within its major corporate objectives.

This said, a company must balance its desire for profit with the needs of its customers and the satisfaction it provides for those customers. Although creating a profit, expanding the company and providing shareholders with an acceptable level of return on their investments is obviously important, the management should never lose sight of the fact that such profits will be derived from their dealing with new and existing customers.

The obvious way to increase the amount of profit made would be to increase the prices charged to customer, or reduce the costs incurred by the company by offering a lower standard of product or service. However this would obviously have the effect of displeasing customers. It would therefore be expected that some of the customers would see the increased prices and/or reduced quality and take their business elsewhere. This would probably have the effect of reducing the income to the company and therefore the profit, the opposite of what it was designed to do.

The opposite end of the spectrum would be to supply the maximum possible level of customer satisfaction by providing the best possible products and service at market-beating prices. However it is fairly obvious that this strategy would be unlikely to meet the organization's goals regarding profitability.

We can see that simply having a goal or objective to make money and increase profits will almost certainly fail. We can also see that to simply aim to provide the utmost customer satisfaction will also fail. For the organization to succeed, the management must carefully balance the two desires and objectives. Their goal should be to make profit *through* customer satisfaction.

Figure 1.1: Profit versus customer satisfaction

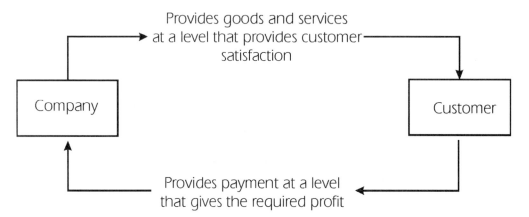

The balancing of customer satisfaction with the profit goals of the company is a complex but extremely important function of the marketing manager's role. This can be achieved by the careful management of the elements of the marketing mix, such as product and price. The job of the marketeer is to ensure that the right products are offered at a price, and with a level of service, that will both ensure satisfied and loyal customers, as well as bringing the required level of income and profit to the organization. The marketing mix will be examined in more detail in Chapter 2.

1.4   Reasons for setting goals

A goal is something that we want to achieve. When quantified, goals become objectives, for example:

I want to have sold 6,000 new personal loans by the end of March.

Everybody sets goals in everyday life, often without really realizing they are doing it. All throughout life we set ourselves targets of where we want to be and what we want to achieve (I want to get home by 6 o'clock; I must finish the ironing this evening; etc.) and we should apply this discipline to our business lives.

Everybody within the organization needs to have goals, and therefore the need to set goals applies throughout the company – from the managing director and the senior management team, through the middle managers and through each department's manager. It applies equally to each and every person who works within the company, who should set themselves individual goals, outlining what they personally want to achieve.

The benefits of setting goals and actually taking the time to think about what we want to achieve has many benefits.

- It forces individuals and senior managers of a company to take the time to think about what it is they actually want to do. What is it that they are trying to achieve and where are they hoping they will be in the future?

- This thought process ensures that all the senior managers are in agreement with the reasons they are working together. Any differences in what they hope to achieve will be highlighted and ironed out. From that point forward everybody will be working together with a common purpose, and therefore conflict should be reduced.

- The goals of the company can be cascaded throughout the entire workforce so that everybody can see what is being achieved. This will ensure that all the staff can see the purpose of the job that they are doing and will give them the satisfaction of knowing that they are contributing to the overall goals of the company.

- Having goals set for the company as a whole will ensure that as each department and individual sets goals, with the overall objectives in mind. This again will help to enable everybody to work towards a common goal, and ensure that people are not heading off in different directions and wasting effort.

- Having clear goals set and actually stating what you want to achieve is the beginning of the planning process. It enables people to make plans for themselves and their colleagues in order to achieve these stated goals. (We will look in more detail at the benefits of planning in Chapter 10.)

- If the organization, or indeed the individual, actually knows what it wants to achieve and what it wants to do, it is far more likely to achieve the aim.

- Having a goal is the only way that a company or individual can measure success. If there is a stated goal, something that people want to achieve, this is the base against which progress can be measured and people can see what they have achieved.

- Having set a goal and planned how to achieve that goal, actually doing so will give the people involved an enormous sense of satisfaction. This will then give them the enthusiasm to go on and set themselves more challenging goals and achieve those. This will benefit both the individual and the company as a whole.

Goal setting, and then turning these goals into real objectives, is important at all levels of an organization and for everybody who works there. The organization as a whole will have goals and objectives and these will be included in the corporate plan. These will then be interpreted by the individual department managers, who will be able to see what they need to achieve in order to have the organization achieve its goals. These managers will then set themselves and their staff goals and objectives to achieve.

The marketing manager will state these goals and objectives at the start of the marketing plan, and the activities of the marketing department will be aimed at achieving these goals. We will see throughout this book that goal setting and objective setting are important for not only the managers and the marketeers, but also for the branch managers and the individual salespeople, who will all contribute to the overall success of the business.

1.5   Maximizing the use of a scarce resource

Resources are often an issue, particularly for major projects. In the current environment where the need to be competitive is becoming more and more important, profit margins are thinner and the organization is likely to be running with the minimum number of staff in order to complete its business. Because of this, when a major project that is resource intensive is introduced, the company needs to plan very carefully the amount of effort that is required from each area within the business, and the times that this resource is needed for.

If the company cannot find the required number of employees to carry out the tasks, it should not mean that the project is cancelled or de-prioritized. The company could outsource some of the work in order to ensure that the project goes ahead.

The company can call upon the services of one or more of the following for assistance, all of which can be employed for just a pre-agreed period of time.

- *Market research agencies* – They can advise on the use of market research, plan and carry out the research and help a company to understand the results and how to use them

- *Product design agencies* – These product specialist bring to a company new ideas for the design of products to suit the company's customer base or help it to gain a competitive edge and win new customers.

- *Advertising agencies* – These agencies can provide creative input into the best way to advertise a product, what the message should be and how to communicate with customers. They can also help with the planning and execution of the campaign.

- *Media buying agencies* – These agencies advise on the best newspapers or magazines to advertise in or the best poster sites to use, etc. They will also take the responsibility for negotiating prices and booking the space.

- *Contract and freelance workers* – There are many marketeers who, rather than work for one company, work for themselves, taking on specific marketing tasks for a number of companies when required. They are usually paid on a daily rate for the time that they are needed.

- *Training companies* – These companies will, for an agreed fee, come into a company and train their sales or admin staff on new products or new processes.

All of these organizations will bring with them their specialist knowledge and experience as well as an overall market view rather than just seeing things from a company viewpoint. They will, of course, charge for their services and these costs will have to be included in the cost of any project.

Of course resource may not necessarily mean individuals and their time. There may also be resource issues in terms of budget. Most financial services companies are extremely conscious of all monies spent and the need to show a return on all capital outlay. This means that the marketing department will have only a limited budget for any particular year, and is likely to have a number of projects that it would like to carry out.

This being the case, it will need to asses the spend for each one and prioritize them in order to decide the best possible way of using the resource. When there are a number of initiatives all requiring money to be spent, the marketing function will need to have some formalized method of ensuring that the money is spent only when and where there is a real need and a real benefit to be gained. The best way to do this is to ensure that a limit of spending is set. Any level of spending above this would need to be approved by the management team.

This would be done only following the documentation of the idea, how it would be carried out, the benefits it would produce, and the corporate or marketing objectives it will help to achieve, together with a detailed analysis of the costs and other resource implications. Shown below is an example of a template for the type of document that will help a marketing manager to ensure that the resources are used only where there will be real benefit for the company.

Figure 1.2: Resource documentation

Resource approval document

Section A Project description

Xxxxxxxxxxxxxxxxxxxxxxxxxxxxxxxxxxxxxxxxxxxxxxxxxxxxxxxxxxxxx
Xxxxxxxxxxxxxxxxxxxxxxxxxxxxxxxxxxxxxxxxxxxxxxxxxxxxxxxxxxxxx
Xxxxxxxxxxxxxxxxxxxxxxxxxxxxxxxxxxxxxxxxxxxxxxxxxxx

Section B Corporate/Marketing objective supported by the project

Xxxxxxxxxxxxxxxxxxxxxxxxxxxxxxxxxxxxxxxxxxxxxxxxxxxxxxxxxxxxx
Xxxxxxxxxxxxxxxxxxxxxxxxxxxxxxxxxxxxxxxxxxxxxxxxxxxxxxxxxxxxx
Xxxxxxxxxxxxxxxxxxxxxxxxxxxxxxxxxxxxxxxxxxxxxxxxxxxx

Section C Project deliverables

Xxxxxxxxxxxxxxxxxxxxxxxxxxxxxxxxxxxxxxxxxxxxxxxxxxxxxxxxxxxxx
Xxxxxxxxxxxxxxxxxxxxxxxxxxxxxxxxxxxxxxxxxxxxxxxxxxxxxxxxxxxxx
Xxxxxxxxxxxxxxxxxxxxxxxxxxxxxxxxxxxxxxxxxxxxxxxxxxxxxx

Section D Alternatives considerations and reasons for selecting the recommended actions

Xxxxxxxxxxxxxxxxxxxxxxxxxxxxxxxxxxxxxxxxxxxxxxxxxxxxxxxxxxxxx
Xxxxxxxxxxxxxxxxxxxxxxxxxxxxxxxxxxxxxxxxxxxxxxxxxxxxxxxxxxxxx
Xxxxxxxxxxxxxxxxxxxxxxxxxxxxxxxxxxxxxxxxxxxxxxxxxxxxx

Section E Manpower resources required (both marketing and other departments)

Xxxxxxxxxxxxxxxxxxxxxxxxxxxxxxxxxxxxxxxxxxxxxxxxxxxxxxxxxxxxx
Xxxxxxxxxxxxxxxxxxxxxxxxxxxxxxxxxxxxxxxxxxxxxxxxxxxxxxxxxxxxx
Xxxxxxxxxxxxxxxxxxxxxxxxxxxxxxxxxxxxxxxxxxxxxxxxxxxxxx

Section F Costs involved

Xxxxxxxxxxxxxxxxxxxxxxxxxxxxxxxxxxxxxxxxxxxxxxxxxxxxxxxxxxxxx
Xxxxxxxxxxxxxxxxxxxxxxxxxxxxxxxxxxxxxxxxxxxxxxxxxxxxxxxxxxxxx
Xxxxxxxxxxxxxxxxxxxxxxxxxxxxxxxxxxxxxxxxxxxxxxxxxxxxxx

Section G Benefit analysis

Xxxxxxxxxxxxxxxxxxxxxxxxxxxxxxxxxxxxxxxxxxxxxxxxxxxxxxxxxxxxxx
Xxxxxxxxxxxxxxxxxxxxxxxxxxxxxxxxxxxxxxxxxxxxxxxxxxxxxxxxxxxxxx
Xxxxxxxxxxxxxxxxxxxxxxxxxxxxxxxxxxxxxxxxxxxxxxxxxxx

Section H Management sign off

xxxxxxxxxxxxxxxxx————————————————————————

xxxxxxxxxxxxxxxxx————————————————————————

xxxxxxxxxxxxxxxxx————————————————————————

xxxxxxxxxxxxxxxxx————————————————————————

The completion of such a document will enable the manager to see exactly what resources he or she has committed to each and every project that teams are undertaking. It also indicates clearly which objectives are being worked towards. If there is a shortage of resources, either financial or manpower, the manager will be able to see the cost benefit analysis for each case and make reasoned and informed decisions about the best use of that resource.

2

THE MARKETING MIX

After reading this chapter you should:

● Know the components of the marketing mix

● Understand the importance that each element plays in the marketing of financial services

● Understand how each of the elements interacts with the others

Marketing mix had traditionally been made up of the four Ps, Product, Price, Place and the Promotion. More recently People and Processes have extended the mix to the six Ps. These are the elements that the marketing manager must manage in order that he or she can meet the requirements of the business in terms and sales and profits, as well as ensuring customer satisfaction.

The marketing manager will not only have to manage each element of the mix to ensure the best possible benefits are gained from it, but will also have to ensure that each element of the marketing mix works with the others. The elements must complement each other in order to bring to market the best possible package, i.e. the right product at the right price, advertised in the right way and available through the right channels.

2.1   Product

The product, which can in many cases be a service, is plainly an important part of the marketing mix. The product is the thing that satisfies the customer need, the thing that provides the benefits they needed or wanted. The product is one of the ways in which the company can differentiate itself from its competitors. For example, there are many providers offering home contents insurance and their core products may be very similar and priced at similar levels. In order to create differentiation and attract additional customers and therefore additional profit, a company may choose to offer an augmented product, i.e. one with additional features. This could be in the form of an extra service such as a free 24-hour help line or free legal cost cover, etc. Obviously such things are a benefit to the marketing mix only if they are appealing to the customers that the organization is trying to attract, and therefore research is essential to verify this.

Figure 2.1: Augmented product

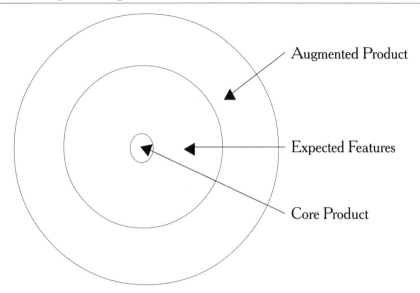

Augmented Product

Expected Features

Core Product

The market for and the appeal of any product changes over time and it is essential that products are monitored and updated, or closed and new products developed to take their place where appropriate. Let us look at some of the product management tools used by the marketing teams when changing the marketing mix.

Product life cycles

In the past the financial services industry has offered the same products over a number of years. It was not commonly accepted that a product had a 'life cycle'. However, the nature of the market at the present time, with increasing customer awareness, the increased use of technology, and the high level of competition have all meant that the idea of a product having a life cycle is now widely accepted within the financial services industry.

Products are seen to go through four stages in their life cycles. These are:

● Development and introduction;

● Growth;

● Maturity;

● Decline, and possibly elimination.

Figure 2.2: Product life cycle

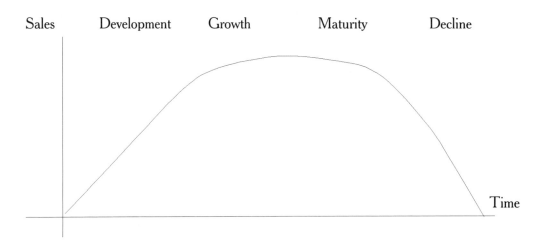

We will now look at these stages in more detail and consider them in terms of product management activity.

Development and introduction

Although there are exceptions, development time within the financial services industry is ideally short due to the intense competition and the element of copying that often occurs. During this stage competitor information is extremely important, especially if the product is designed to be an improved version of something currently available elsewhere, with the intention of gaining market share.

Even more important is information about the customers and their needs, and so the research department plays an important role both prior to and during the early stages of product development.

Once the customers' needs have been researched, the product manager can draft an initial product design which will then be discussed with all other areas of the business. These discussions will focus on the feasibility of the product and ensure that the proposed design can be built, administered and sold by the business. There will also need to be discussions with the finance area of the business which will examine closely the proposed costs and charges. They will be checking that the charges within the product and the predicted sales volumes will lead to a profit for the company once the development and sales costs have been accounted for.

The majority of product launched into today's market will require a great deal of technological support, and there will therefore be a need to ensure that the proposed design can be built and administered on the systems that the business currently has. If not additional systems will need to be bought or built, or the design amended.

Once the product and pricing is agreed, the design goes through the building and testing phases and, if successful, is then launched for sale to the target market. Around the time of launch the marketing activity is focused on raising the customers' awareness to the existence of the new product and promoting its benefits. This could take the form of any or all of the following, as covered in Chapter 5:

- TV, radio or newspaper advertising;
- Poster campaign;
- PR;
- Branch campaigns if the company operates through a branch network;
- Mailings;
- Magazine and newspaper inserts.

In order to reach the expected and desired levels of business the promotional activity needs to be carefully planned and executed. Because of the nature of this stage of the product's life cycle, the company will experience a period of expenditure rather than profit making.

Growth

Assuming the launch is successful, the initial phase will be followed by a period of growth. The sales volumes will increase and the company will start to recoup the money that was spent on the development and launch. If this was a totally new product, then it is likely that during this stage, competitors will launch similar products into the market, and will have attempted to improve upon the product design and features. It is therefore important to both continue to research the competitors and to promote your own product in order to ensure that there is no loss of market share. During this stage the marketing activity is likely to focus on promoting the benefits of the product in comparison to the competition.

Maturity

Maturity is the stage at which sales, and therefore revenue, are at their highest. It is also a time of intense competition, and therefore the company may find that in order to maintain market share it needs to cut costs or introduce special offers. Marketing spend may well be cut back in favour of other products which are in the launch or growth stage and therefore give a better potential return on the outlay. Any promotional activity undertaken at this stage will be done with the aim of delaying the product's entry to the next stage of the life cycle.

Decline

Eventually, as new and improved products are launched which more easily meet the customers' needs, the sale of the product will move into the decline stage. During this stage the sales will gradually fall, as will the profits, and therefore little or no money will be spent on promotion.

The decision of the marketing and product manager is whether to maintain the product with little or no expenditure, or whether to eliminate it.

The Boston Consulting Group (BCG) Matrix

In order to make reasoned decisions as to a promotional strategy for any product, the product manager will need to be aware of where the product sits in terms of market size and any growth in the market. One technique used to do exactly this is the Boston Consulting Group (BCG) matrix as shown below.

Figure 2.3: Boston Consulting Group Matrix

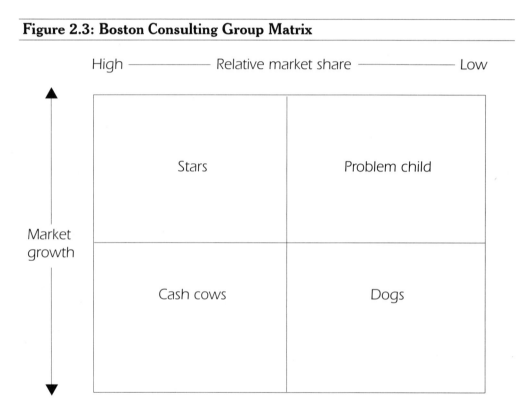

The way the matrix works is by classifying products according to the share of the market they hold, relative to competitors, and the growth that the market may undergo. The products are placed into one of four categories as follows.

Problem child

A product the product manager would class as a problem child is one which is currently attracting only a small share in the current market, but is in a market which has potential. The product manager will need to make some tough decisions about such a product, because he or she will be keen to gain a better position in a growing market. The manager is therefore likely to undertake some development enhancement or promotions work in an attempt to improve its position. Alternatively the decision may be taken to eliminate the product and develop a new one along lines similar to that of more successful competitors.

Stars

Stars are products that are achieving a good market share in a growing market. The product manager will be pleased with the performance of this product but cannot be complacent and cannot simply sit back and hope the success continues. Such a product will no doubt attract the attention of competitors who will want to copy or improve upon the product in the hope of taking market share. Therefore continued marketing activity will be required to protect the sales and income provided by the product. The manager will need to monitor the competition and be ready to react quickly to any new ideas.

Cash cows

These are products that sell well but that are in a market that is experiencing little or no growth. If the market is stable the company may choose to undertake some promotional activity in order to consolidate its market share. However, if the market is in decline, it may decide that any money spent would provide insufficient return. It will instead spend money on other products, ensuring that it has an alternative profit stream built up to provide the revenue it will need if this product's sales volumes dwindle.

Dogs

Dogs are products with a low market share in a market with little or no growth potential. If the product is profitable despite the low sales volumes the product manager may well decide to continue with the product. Otherwise it should be considered for deletion.

The BCG matrix should be considered alongside other marketing techniques when deciding on a product marketing strategy.

Directional policy matrix

The directional policy matrix is a development of the BCG, as some product managers found it difficult to accurately measure relative market share and market growth. Because of this the BCG matrix was evolved into the directional policy matrix, as shown.

Figure 2.4: Directional policy matrix

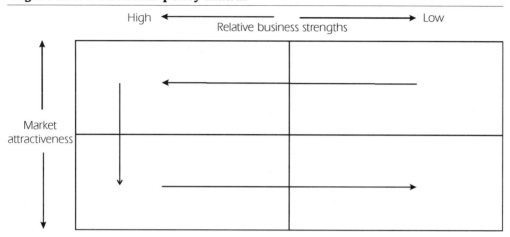

In the directional policy matrix, relative market share and market growth are replaced by business share and market attractiveness. Market attractiveness is not only the size of the market but such things as the potential for growth, the profit margins, the lack of competition, or any favourable market conditions. Business strength is such things as number of sales, the company's and product's reputation, service levels and pricing relative to the competition. These are all very practical attributes and very specific to the organization. When using the directional policy matrix it is probably most useful if considered alongside the product life cycle as follows:

Upper right-hand quadrant

There would be little point in developing a product unless there was a market for it and the company felt it could do well there, and the product manager will have carefully studied the attractiveness of the market before taking a decision to develop the new service. When a product is first launched its sales volumes and market share are likely to be low and therefore any new product is likely to appear in this box when it is introduced.

Upper left-hand quadrant

Following launch, and with the right promotion, the sales will increase and the product will become a strength to the business as it starts to generate increased revenue and increased market share. It will therefore move to the upper left-hand quadrant.

Lower left-hand quadrant

As existing customers' needs are met and as new products with greater appeal are introduced by competitors, the growth in sales will slow. If the market becomes saturated, providers may well cut charges and therefore profit margins. This in turn means that the market attractiveness reduces and so the product is now in the lower left-hand quadrant.

Lower right-hand quadrant

If sales diminish due to lack of customer appeal, decreasing market or competitor strengths, the product manager may well reduce or even withdraw completely marketing support and promotion. If not achieving a good market share or turning in good revenue and profit levels, the product is now placed firmly in the lower right-hand quadrant.

Using the product management techniques

By considering the product life cycle and placing products into the BCG and directional policy matrix, the product manager can predict how sales will evolve and therefore develop a suitable product strategy. They will enable the manager to forecast future revenue and costs and therefore assist in the management of resources. He or she will be able to see which of the products would provide the best return following investment in such things as advertising.

These techniques rely on having good quality, up-to-date information about the market and the competitor products, hence the importance, once again, of the need for market research.

In order to get the best use from these techniques, the product manager will also need a good understanding of the market conditions and be able to predict future trends, etc. This will enable the manager to plan for any product changes or new products that may be required.

2.2   Price

The next element of the marketing mix is the price charged for a product or service.

Price represents the cost to the seller of producing and distributing the product, and to the buyer it is the cost of consuming the product. Within financial services the price can often be referred to in different ways such as charges, interest rate, premium, etc. Price is an obvious way in which one product provider can differentiate its offering from the other products on the market. If all the products are fairly similar, but one is priced lower than the others, all things being equal it is the cheaper one that will attract most customers.

Alternatively, setting a higher price is the way in which the company can maximize profit. Provided the margins are large enough, large levels of profit can be achieved even with a relatively small market share. What the organization must be careful of is that in attempting to maximize profit they do not price themselves out of the market. We can see from this brief look at pricing what a complex matter it is and how carefully the two things, maximizing profit and attracting customers, need to be balanced. Of course the pricing needs also to complement the other elements of the marketing mix in order to present an overall package to the customer.

Pricing has become a much more important element of the marketing mix for financial services marketeers in recent years as the competition to attract new customers increases. Many of the products are highly regulated and therefore the scope for differentiation in product design is more limited than in other industries. Because of this, many providers are looking more and more to price as a way to achieve a competitive advantage.

Although other areas of the marketing mix, e.g. product or distribution method, can be changed in order to create a competitive advantage, by far the quickest thing to amend and therefore probably the most flexible element of the mix, is the price.

However, we must also consider the effects of pricing on the overall marketing of the service. The price can be used by many customers to judge the quality of a product, and therefore being the cheapest may not always automatically lead to an influx of new business and new customers.

Also, when considering price, there must be a great deal of consideration given to the brand values and the overall positioning of the products and services. If the brand values are ones of quality and reliability, these values are unlikely to be enhanced by becoming the lowest in price. When considering a pricing position, the marketing manager must look back not only to the marketing plan, but also to the corporate plan and the strategies contained therein.

All pricing decisions must also be considered in terms of the impact they will have on revenue, and therefore on the profits of the business. We can start to see from this brief overview that any decision on pricing is an extremely important one, not only to the customer, but to the organization as well.

Making the pricing decision

The price-setting process must always begin with the marketing objectives, which will state the marketing department's strategy on pricing. These will in turn reflect the company's objectives as set out in the corporate plan.

The pricing needs to be set in a way that will enable the marketing team to meet their objectives. These objectives are likely to fall into one of two main categories:

- Attracting new customers to the organization and therefore increasing the company's market share.

- Making the maximum possible profit for the organization irrespective of actual volume of sales.

If the objective is to attract large volumes of new business, then the pricing may need to be set at a low enough level to attract customers in volume. In order to do this the organization may well need to accept that the price it is charging will simply cover costs and not make huge amounts of profit. The organization with the largest market share is not always the most profitable.

On the other hand, if the objective is to maximize profits, then the company may have a strategy of higher pricing. While not attracting volume business, the organization will make a profit on each and every product and service it sells.

Of course these two objectives are not mutually exclusive, and in an ideal world the company would like to achieve both market share and maximize profitability. However, when it comes to actually setting a price, the organization's objectives should give a clear indication as to which of the above it considers to be of more strategic importance.

Once a pricing strategy is determined, then the actual process of setting the price can begin. The process adopted must involve all of the following considerations:

● Cost;

● Profit;

● Competitor prices;

● Customers' willingness to pay.

Cost

For many organizations, the first step in setting a price is to assess the costs of the product. For a financial services company the costs involved are likely to be such things as:

● *Design and development costs.* How much the company spends in building the product that they are to sell.

● *Marketing costs.* Such things as the documentation, the cost of the promotional activity both throughout the launch period and ongoing throughout the life of the product.

● *Sales costs.* These will include the cost of any new technology required to sell the product, or such things as salesperson's commission or salary.

● *Administration and ongoing service costs.* Once the product or service has been sold, the company will need to administer it and provide an ongoing service to the customers. The company will need to estimate the average lifespan of the product and how much it will cost to provide these services.

Profit

Once the costs of the product are determined, the company needs to determine the level of profit it wishes to make from the sales. This will be influenced heavily by the objectives as discussed above. Thecompany will need to make an estimate of the level of sales it expects to make, and therefore how much profit it needs to make from each product.

Competitor prices

The amount it is able to charge will also be influenced by the charges being levied for similar products offered by the competitors. If the product offered by them is exactly the same and offered in exactly the same place, through the same distribution methods, there will be little scope to do anything other than match their prices. However, if there is some differentiation in any of the other aspects of the marketing mix which would justify a higher charge, then this could be considered.

Customers' willingness to pay

One of the most important considerations when setting charges must be the price that the customer is willing to pay for the product or service he or she is to receive. If the other aspects of the marketing job have been done particularly well, then price becomes almost irrelevant. For example, if the company has produced a fantastic product that satisfied exactly their customers' need, and it has promoted and distributed it in such a way that customers are actively trying to buy it, then they will be willing to pay whatever is asked. In reality price will always play a part in the buying decision, but how great a part it plays will need to be understood and factored into the pricing decision.

There are three basic methods the product manager can use to determine the price he or she wishes to charge for the product or service being sold. Theses are:

- Cost-based pricing;

- Value-based pricing;

- Competitor-based pricing.

With cost-based pricing the manager will base the price charged to the customer on the cost of producing and selling the product. He or she will take account of the fixed costs, such as initial design and development, as well as the variable costs such as production and sales commission. The manager will then add the required level of profit and the result will be the price that is charged to the customer.

Figure 2.5: Cost-based pricing model

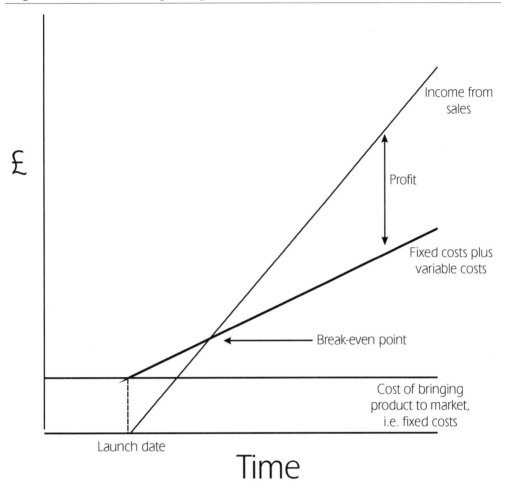

With value-based pricing the product manager will set the price of the product or service based on the customer's perception of the value of that product rather than on the seller's costs and profit. He or she will need to determine exactly who the customers are likely to be and what value they will place on the product. From this the manager will be able to judge the price that can be charged while still maintaining the desired level of customer satisfaction, and the customer's feeling of value from the product.

Once this price is determined the manager can deduct both fixed and variable costs, and whatever remains will be the profit to the company.

Figure 2.6: Value-based pricing

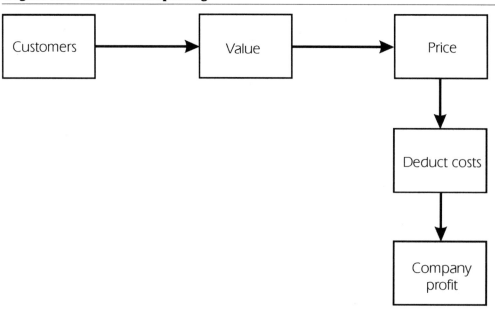

A strategy of competitor-based pricing will involve the manager setting the price of the product or service to be competitive with the other similar products in the market. The level of profit enjoyed by the group will be the difference between this price and the costs involved in the production and sale.

In reality the marketing manager will probably use a combination of these three pricing strategies to determine the amount that the customer is charged. For example, he or she could use the cost-based pricing, but asses the price against the competition, and amend it slightly depending on the customers' willingness to pay.

Once a price is set, particularly for a new product, there will need to be regular reviews of sales figures and customer feedback to ensure that the right decisions have been taken, and if necessary the price amended.

2.3   Place

The third element of the mix is place.

Place relates to the distribution of the product or service, i.e. where the products are sold and how are they sold. Before an organization can decide on a distribution strategy it needs to consider the answers to such questions as

● What is the nature of the product?

● Who are the customers?

- Where are the customers?

- How do they like to buy?

- What distribution methods do they find acceptable/preferable?

- How are the competitors' products distributed?

It may be that the organization distributes through a third party rather than direct to the customers, which is often the case for such things as motor insurance, etc. where the products are sold via a broker. If this is the case these questions are still relevant in deciding which brokers they should sell through and where these should be.

2.4 Promotion

Let us now look at how financial services products are promoted. The term 'promotion' relates to the manner in which the organization tells the buying public about its products and services. The method selected is likely to depend again on exactly who the customers are and the nature of their need. The diagram below gives an example of the different methods of promotion available.

Figure 2.7: Routes for the promotion and sales of financial services business

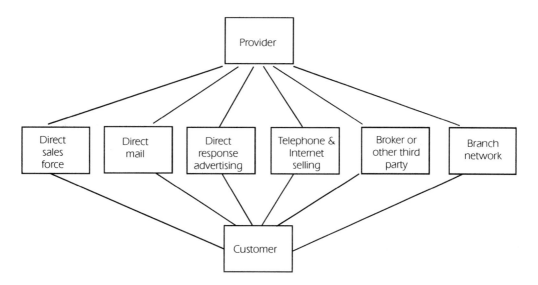

Direct sales force

A large number of retailers, particularly insurance companies, still sell the majority of their products through a *direct sales force*. This phrase is used to describe a team of highly-trained sales professionals who work for one company to sell that company's range of products and services to the public. The company commands the salespeople's total allegiance and they can work for no other company as long as the agreement exists. Salespeople have a duty to inform customers that they represent one company only, and that they can therefore recommend only that company's products. In return for selling the company's products, the salespeople receive a salary, a commission, or a mix of both.

The sales force occupies a unique position as the link between the customer and the provider company. As far as the customer is concerned, the sales force is the face of the company. This position is made difficult by the fact that salespeople have to work in the interests of the company, but also have a duty to act in the best interests of the customer. In the financial services industry, recent adverse publicity has meant that, in order to be successful, the salesperson must be able to obtain the trust of his or her customers. Because of this, the recruitment, training and motivation of the direct sales force are crucial, and these are examined in more detail in Chapter 13.

The direct sales force has traditionally been a very successful way of selling financial services products. The industrial insurance companies used their door-to-door premium collectors to sell further products to the family and friends of their original customers, thereby ensuring a stream of new business. Many insurance companies also use large direct sales forces to sell their products by means of prospecting and home visits. Here the salesperson uses anything, from electoral rolls and telephone directories to personal recommendations, to find suitable customers. The salesperson then interviews the prospective customer and completes the sale in the customer's own home.

The number and size of direct sales forces in operation has increased in recent years due to the increase in home ownership. As the mortgage market has increased, direct sales forces have been used to sell accompanying endowment products. The decrease in the number of *independent* advisers offering their services to the public (as a result of the costs and difficulties of complying with stricter regulation) has also tended to increase the direct sales forces.

While it is usual to associate the phrase 'direct sales force' with a team of full-time salesmen and women who visit customers' homes, we must remember that in many financial situations the sales force will in fact be members of the branch team. These members of staff have dual responsibilities, both to service business and customer queries but also to act as the sales point for further products.

Many banks and building societies now have their own direct sales forces to promote their insurance products. However, these have tended to be based in their readily accessible branch network rather than making home visits.

There are many advantages in choosing a direct sales force as the distribution method. For example:

● They can be used to sell more complex products, because the competent and highly-trained salesperson will be able to explain features and answer queries;

● They offer the customer the individual, personal approach and develop a level of rapport and trust with the customer;

- Because of their depth of discussions with customers, salespeople can give valuable feedback on customer needs and input into future product development.

However, there are also drawbacks to this method. For example:

- A direct sales force is extremely expensive to operate; the recruitment and training of these sales professionals involves a large financial commitment for a length of time before any return is shown; ongoing costs can also be high, involving such things as salaries, provision of cars for home visits and ongoing training.

- The regulatory environment in which most sales forces operate means that the supervision of the salesperson can be both time-consuming and costly. Any rogue salespeople can damage the company's reputation and lead to severe punishments for both the individual and the company.

Telephone-based sales operations

The growth of the telephone as a method of distribution of financial services products has already been discussed. The costs involved in the operation of a direct sales force make telephone-based sales an attractive alternative. The use of the telephone is now common practice for the purchase of general insurance, such as motor and household cover. Companies such as Direct Line lead the way, but have been closely followed by many of their competitors. Similarly, First Direct led the market in telephone banking, allowing customer access to the usual banking services without the need to visit a branch. First Direct have been followed by a large number of other companies and banking by telephone is now commonplace.

Although it was initially felt that this distribution method would prove popular only with the more sophisticated end of the market, the public's general acceptance of the use of the telephone for the purchasing of financial services had led many companies to consider it as a viable alternative for other products within this sector.

Some building societies now offer mortgages by phone to customers who prefer not to visit a branch for an interview. Also, insurance companies and bancassurers now use the telephone as a method of selling supporting endowments and other insurance and investment products to the public. This market, that of telesales for life assurance and pension products, has yet to experience the successes described above, but is considered to be a growth market and is seeing many new entrants keen to exploit this potentially lucrative new distribution channel. The sale of life and investment products via the telephone can be done in one of two ways.

1. The provider can offer products for sale to people who telephone knowing exactly what they want. An application can be completed over the telephone and, in some cases, the first premium can be paid by debit card. In the case of life assurance products cover can, in some cases, be granted instantly.

2. The provider can offer advice over the telephone. The regulatory requirements are the same as for giving advice face-to-face, and details must be forwarded to the customer to sign. Again, some customers can be offered cover instantly.

Some providers offer a service that combines telephone and direct sales force selling. The customer makes initial contact with the company using the telephone; then, if the case is complex, or more personal contact is required, an appointment is made for a salesperson to visit. This method of combining the two sales approaches has yet to achieve any major success in the industry.

There are both advantages and disadvantages to the use of the telephone as a distribution method for financial services. Some of these are described below.

Advantages of telephone-based sales

Costs are much lower than those of a 'face-to-face' sales force. The salesperson that sells via the telephone can do so for a very large proportion of his or her working day because they are not required to travel to customers' homes. Also, calls that prove to be inappropriate do not waste several hours of the salesperson's day – he or she simply answers another call.

The customer has access to financial services outside office hours. Many telesales centres are open until 10 o'clock in the evening, allowing customers to deal with their financial affairs at a time that is most convenient to them, and from the comfort of their own homes.

It allows the organization to reach a segment of the market that would not have otherwise bought from them. Many of the people who buy via the telephone do so because they do not want to visit the branch and do not want a salesperson to call at their home.

Disadvantages of telephone-based sales

The service offered via the telephone must be efficient, and therefore the use of technology is imperative. This can mean large initial costs for any company considering setting up a telephone-based sales organization.

The personal contact and development of a trust-based customer relationship is much more difficult for this type of distribution, as compared with the use of a direct sales force.

Direct mail and direct response advertising

The use of direct mail as a retailing tool for financial services products has increased substantially in recent years, and financial institutions are among Britain's leading users of such facilities.

Direct mail is often used to solicit sales of a particular product from a specific marketplace. For example, it may be used to achieve the sale of credit cards to high earners, or life assurance to families with children.

Direct mail can, for example, take the form of a mailshot included in a magazine or newspaper whose readership is known to be made up of the target market. More usually, direct mail is sent to existing customers of the organization who may require further products. The customer responds by completing the form, either to receive further details about the product, or to apply for the product itself.

The success of a direct mail campaign depends largely on the choice of the customers to be mailed. Improvements in technology have made it possible for banks, building societies and insurance companies to target their mailshots more successfully by segmenting their huge customer databases. Whereas traditionally such segmentation was based only on geographical or demographic factors, many customer databases can now be segmented by such things as habits, attitudes, lifestyle factors or profession. The more accurate the segmentation, and the more tightly defined the recipient customers are, the greater the level of response. Selecting the customer in this way also allows the material mailed to be designed with that specific target group in mind, rather than having to adopt an approach to suit everybody. If mailshots are properly targeted they become highly cost effective.

Any direct mailing will have one of the following objectives:

● To provide customers with information about the products and services the retailer has to offer

● To stimulate sufficient interest from customers to encourage them to contact the company and request more information

● To help customers recognize that they have a need, and that they require advice, therefore arranging for an appointment with a member of the sales force

Direct response advertising is a phrase used to cover both direct mail and press and leaflet advertising. In direct mailshots the customer is usually provided with sufficient information to be able to purchase the advertised product, usually by completing an enclosed application form. In press and leaflet form, the product is usually sold using a two-stage process. The customer is generally required to respond to the advertisement by requesting further information. The provider company then sends an information pack and the customer responds in a similar way to that outlined above.

Generally, the use of direct mail and direct response advertising means that the customer buys the product without the involvement of a salesperson, either employed or independent. If successful, this method of distribution is very cost effective. Some companies also use a combination of the distribution methods. For example, a customer who reads a direct response advertisement may be able to request an appointment with an adviser rather than receive an information pack.

Although a wide variety of products can be sold by this method of distribution, those that are sold most successfully tend to be the simpler products that customers feel comfortable buying without the need for advice.

There are advantages and disadvantages to this method of distribution. Some of these are described below.

Advantages of direct mail and direct response advertising

The lack of involvement of salespeople means there are no commission payments. Thus the costs of acquiring the business can be kept very low.

The use of direct response advertising can generate a huge database of customers who prefer to deal direct. These customers can then be mailed with other product offerings, so achieving low-cost cross sales.

The Financial Services Act has placed many restrictions and much regulation on the information that must be given to a customer in any advertisement for a regulated product. The use of direct mail allows a greater amount of information to be given to the customer.

Financial services products can be very complex, and customers' knowledge of them may be fairly limited. The use of direct mail allow customers to read and re-read the information if they choose to, and also allows them time to come to a decision on what to do. It may therefore prove a success with people who are nervous of moving too quickly into buying.

With direct mail, the message can be personalized, sometimes merely by adding the customer's name, on other occasions by targeting them with something known to be of particular interest. The more personalized the sales message is, the more powerful it is as a sales tool.

Even if the customer does not respond to the mailing by purchasing another product, there will be additional benefits that come from regular customer contact; in other words, those of relationship building.

The results of a direct mail campaign are relatively easy to monitor. The provider simply measures the number of customers who respond and buy a product, against the numbers and costs involved in the mailing.

Direct mail is very controllable. The provider has ultimate control over who receives the mailing, what is included in the mailing pack and when it is sent.

IFAs and brokers

Many companies rely on other firms to distribute their products to the end customer. In other industries it is common practice for manufacturers to distribute their products to wholesalers, who in turn distribute to retailers and then on to the ultimate customers. Although financial services products have very different characteristics, and therefore require different sales methods, it is still common for a third party to be involved in sales. These third parties do not purchase the goods and sell them on, but simply bring the customer and the provider together. They receive a commission payment for doing this.

These third parties are known as *brokers*. Before the emergence of the telesales market in recent years, this method of distribution was the method by which most motor insurance was sold, and it still accounts for a large proportion of the general insurance market. The customer details his or her need to the broker, and the broker recommends a product and a provider. In exchange, the broker is paid a commission by the provider company.

This method of distribution is also used to sell life assurance, pensions and investment products. Since the Financial Services Act and the polarization requirements therein, brokers are required to act either solely for one company or as an independent financial adviser.

These IFAs are individuals or companies who are free to enter into agreements with any number of provider companies to sell their products. This means that when a customer is seen by an IFA and explains his or her needs, the IFA must consider and recommend not only the most suitable type of product, but the best available in the whole marketplace. The IFA must recommend the product and provider that most clearly meets the customer's need. Such decisions can be based on criteria such as:

- Price;

- Investment performance;

- Claims paying history;

- Product features;

- Service offered;

- Financial security of the provider company.

With this method of retailing, the company depends heavily on the broker for its business, and therefore usually employs salespeople to ensure that the best possible service is offered by the IFA.

Because the IFAs are independent (that is, not employed by any of the provider companies) they are responsible for their own expenses and the costs of such things as training and complying with the regulations. This has meant that, as the regulatory requirements have become more stringent and the competition from other retailing methods has increased, the number of IFAs has decreased.

Although IFAs still represent a large proportion of the business of insurance companies, their customers tend to be at the more sophisticated end of the market. IFAs typically deal with the large cases and corporate clients as well as individuals. This is likely to be exacerbated if the market for selling life products direct increases. This would mean that many of the simpler products would be dealt with directly, leaving IFAs to concentrate their efforts on the complex customer needs.

There is also a trend for IFAs to ask for the commission they would have earned from a product sale to be reinvested in the product, or rebated to the customer. Instead of receiving this commission, the IFA charges the customer a fee for his or her advice. This method of doing business is intended to increase the impression of the professionalism of the broker, who offers services in a similar way to an accountant or solicitor. It also means that the IFA earns an income even if the customer decides not to buy. Often this means that the customer who does buy a product is better off financially. However, the introduction of fee paying to IFAs means that in years to come independent advice may be available only to those who can afford to pay for it and, more importantly, who are willing to pay for it.

There are a number of advantages and disadvantages to selling financial services products through brokers. Some of these are described below.

Advantages of IFAs and brokers

Selling through IFAs and brokers means there is only a cost where a sale is made. Although the company will pay commission for each sale, there are no salaries to pay to the brokers, because they are independent of the provider company.

There are fewer regulatory requirements. Many of the regulatory requirements surrounding the sale of life assurance and investments relate to the time of the sale and the customer contact at the time of the recommendation. This is the responsibility of the IFA rather than the provider company.

Disadvantages of IFAs and brokers

The company is reliant on the third party to introduce business. If the broker decides to favour another provider, business is lost.

There are no cross-sales opportunities. The majority of IFAs require a company to agree not to cross-sell other produces in their range to the customer, before they will agree to introduce business to them. This means that every sale requires a new customer.

Branch network

For many financial services providers their main method of distribution continues to be a branch network. Although the competitiveness of the market and the recent mergers and acquisitions have led to a decrease in the number of branches, for most banks and building societies they remain an excellent method of reaching the customers.

In the past, the availability of a branch and the ease of access to that branch has proved to be a major influencing factor in a customer's selection of financial services provider. Having a branch network will therefore attract a large volume of new customers. It will also enable the company to be in an excellent position to cross-sell and up sell to those customers because they will have access to them every time they visit the branch.

The branch will also be able to provide vast amount of data about their customers and their transactions, thereby helping the marketing department to build a more accurate picture of customers and their buying behaviour.

Advantages of a branch network

Branches will attract new customers who find the location appealing.

Branches provide excellent marketing opportunities, especially the new branch designs with large window spaces, which will again attract new customers.

Constant contact with the customer via the branch will help to develop and deepen the customer relationship and therefore increase loyalty.

The branch environment provides the company with excellent opportunities to speak to customers and attempt to interest them in further products and services each time they visit the branch.

Disadvantages of a branch network

They are very expensive as a method of servicing business. New telephone banking methods prove much less expensive to operate and the cost saving can therefore be passed on to the customer, making it very difficult for the branch-based companies to compete.

The branches can be open for only a limited period each day, and customers are becoming more and more demanding of financial services companies. Many customers wish to speak to their bank during out-of-office hours, and a company that operates only a branch network will be unable to provide such a service.

2.5 People

The marketing manager must consider carefully the interaction between the public and the employees of the company. For some products and services it may be vital that there is face-to-face or telephone contact with an individual from the company before the product can be sold, and the selection of these people is of the utmost importance.

Even if the marketing process means that the customer buys the product directly from the company without the involvement of a salesperson, there will still be several interactions with members of staff. The people selected for these roles must be considered as an important part of the marketing mix.

Obviously the selection of the marketing staff is important. They need to have excellent marketing skills and experience as well as being creative and innovative. On top of this, ideally they will have an excellent knowledge of the financial services industry, and customer behaviour when buying financial services products.

Having ensured that the marketing team has the right mix of knowledge and skills, we need also to ensure that the other staff involved in the marketing process have the correct attributes. These people will include the following:

Data managers

These people need to fully conversant with the needs of the market and be able to select, and manipulate data, as well as understanding results in order to build propensity models for future campaigns.

Print and media buyers

These people are responsible for ensuring that print is purchased at the best possible rate and that the most suitable and reliable printers are used. They also need to book the most suitable advertising space for the product and target audiences, and ensure the best deal possible is achieved.

Creative staff

Creative staff are responsible for the ideas generating and need to understand the market and its preferences as well as being able to produce effective and innovative ideas.

Call-centre personnel

Call-centre personnel need to be selected and trained in order that they portray the correct image for the organization when they deal with customer enquiries and requests for service information. They need to be knowledgeable and efficient while being friendly and welcoming if they are to gain the maximum impact for the company.

The sales staff

The staff in the branches who deal with sales also need to be equally well trained, efficient and knowledgeable. They should be helpful and friendly, but also need to be sales focused and be motivated to meet the sales targets they have been set.

The administration staff

They deal with the applications and need to be efficient and effective both in processing the business, and in dealing with the customer queries they receive.

Any person involved in the marketing process needs to be carefully selected to ensure the maximum benefit is gained from all activity undertaken. They must all be focused on the needs of the customer as well as the needs of the company, and dedicated to providing excellent service, especially when in direct contact with potential customers.

2.6   Process

Another extremely important element of the marketing mix is the process used. Although initially it would seem that the process used has little to do with marketing, if we start to think about the operation of a marketing campaign, we can see how important the process can be.

Let us take as an example an advertising campaign that also includes direct mail. The bank is going to sell its new flexible current account to new customers and also to existing customers who do not have a current account with them.

Of course in order to make the campaign a success the bank will need to ensure that the product is right for the target market and that it is correctly priced. It will also need to ensure that the promotion it uses and the distribution methods selected are suitable. But it will also need to ensure that the processes they have in place for dealing with the campaign are suitable and robust.

So what exactly do we mean by process? Well, such things as:

- How do customers respond to the advertising?
- Who deals with their queries?
- Who send the customers the information they need?
- Who keeps records of these enquirers?
- How are these enquiries recorded?
- What follow-up action is required?
- How does the customer actually purchase the product?
- Who is going to be mailed?
- Who will actually carry out the mailing?
- How will responses be dealt with?
- How will the management information on the campaign be collected and presented.

All of these things need to be considered and processes put in place before the marketing activity can take place. Let us take a very high-level view of the process that could be put in place for the bank's current account campaign (please turn to page 38).

Figure 2.8: Campaign process for newspaper and magazine advertisements

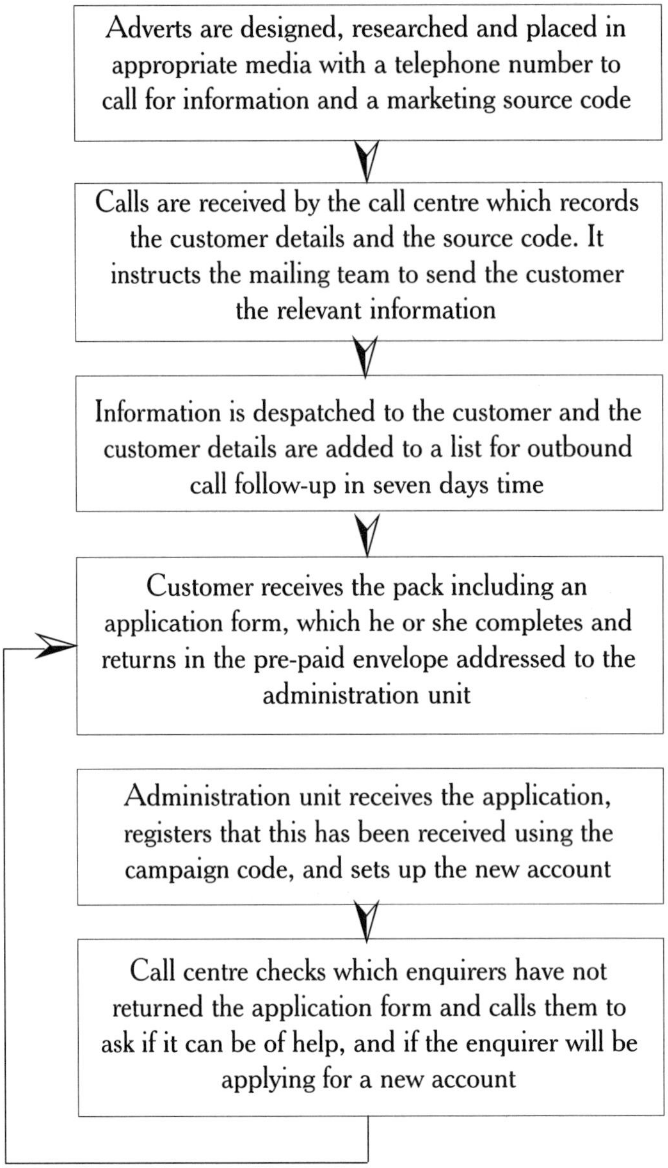

Adverts are designed, researched and placed in appropriate media with a telephone number to call for information and a marketing source code

Calls are received by the call centre which records the customer details and the source code. It instructs the mailing team to send the customer the relevant information

Information is despatched to the customer and the customer details are added to a list for outbound call follow-up in seven days time

Customer receives the pack including an application form, which he or she completes and returns in the pre-paid envelope addressed to the administration unit

Administration unit receives the application, registers that this has been received using the campaign code, and sets up the new account

Call centre checks which enquirers have not returned the application form and calls them to ask if it can be of help, and if the enquirer will be applying for a new account

Figure 2.9: Process for direct mail campaign

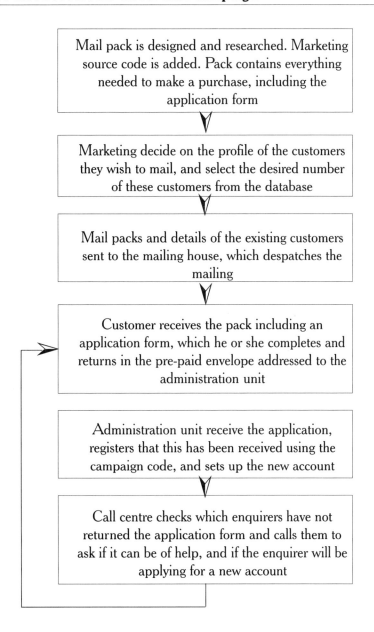

It is very important that sufficient thought is given to the issues of process before the marketing activity starts. If the process is not properly thought out and documented as well as tested before the marketing activity starts, then a number of issues could arise and the company could lose the business it is trying to attract. For example:

- The customer queries could be mishandled when they come in and no information issued.

- The wrong set of information could be sent out.

- There may be time delays while people try to find out how they should handle these enquiries.

- There may be insufficient management information to be able to decide if a campaign was successful, e.g. if it is not possible to track the actual number of sales resulting from a campaign.

- The customer could receive no follow-up mailing/call, or could be called even though he or she has submitted an application.

- There may be insufficient tracking to be able to see the commercial value of the activity, i.e. how much did it cost to attract each piece of business?

Any of these consequences of poor processes could lead to customer dissatisfaction, and could mean that they will end up not buying the product they have been offered, or worse still, taking their existing business elsewhere. It could also lead to problems for the marketeer who will be unable to analyse the value of the work that he or she is doing and the benefit going to the organization. We can now see that as part of any marketing mix, the processes involved in the marketing activity are very important.

2.7   How the elements of the marketing mix interact

Now we have looked at each element of the marketing mix we need to look at how each of them interact and how we can manage the different elements to produce one single customer proposition.

When we decide to offer a product or service to a customer, whether it is an individual or a business customer, that customer does not see the offer as being segmented into these particular elements, i.e. he or she does not look at the offer and consider it in terms of the product, then the price, then the promotion, then the distribution. The customer sees it as one whole package, one proposition. It is this whole proposition that he or she will find either attractive or not.

If we are to be successful at marketing our products and services we need to view our offerings in the same way as our customer will and ensure that the elements fit together to become that overall customer proposition. If we are to do this then we need to not only consider each singular element of the marketing mix, but also how they look and feel when they become that singular proposition.

Let us look at some examples of how this can work. It may be that the product that has been designed by the product manager is a truly excellent, leading-edge, revolutionary new product, but if the design of the product means the costs will be high, then the customers may well reject it when it reaches the market. Obviously this is not always the case, and sometimes the customers will be willing to pay more for a product they deem to be offering them more, but this will need to be tested, and there must be a strong link between the product and the price.

Once the product and the price are aligned, these need to be matched with the appropriate promotion. The way in which the product is promoted and distributed will need to be considered in line with a number of other issues such as

● The nature of the product and therefore the profile of the customer who is likely to be attracted to it.

● The price, and therefore the margins within the price available for promotion and distribution.

There is little point in promoting a child's savings account in a newspaper or magazine read only by young, single students. The marketing manager will need to examine the features of the product and see what needs this product satisfies. From this he can see the type of customer that the product will appeal to and target the promotion at those people.

There will also need to be some consideration as to the profit level of the product. If the product carries only a small loading, i.e. it is a price-sensitive offering, then the method of distribution selected will need to be low-cost so as to fit within the pricing structure. Remember the cost of the potential distribution method will need to be discussed during the pricing of the product and built into the costs. For example, a product with high loading could be distributed by a salesperson who takes time to discuss the matter with the customer and then makes the sale. However where there is little margin, the product may need to be sold off the page, or by direct mail in order to keep distribution costs low. This said, there would also need to be some consideration of the nature of the product, as some of the more complex products do not lend themselves to direct distribution.

There will also need to be some interaction between the processes used and the other elements of the mix. The processes will always need to be efficient, but there may well need to be cost considerations where the price is being kept to a minimum. There will also need to be some consideration of the promotion and distribution methods when deciding on the process to be used. For example, if a product is being distributed via the Internet to customers who have expressed this as their preferred method of contact, then this factor will need to be built into the both the sales and the servicing processes.

We can see that what is becoming clear is that it is no use getting each of the elements right in isolation, they must also be right when they come together as an overall customer proposition. The role of the marketing manager is to ensure that this happens. Often when a marketing campaign fails or does not achieve the results expected of it, it can be corrected by simply looking again at the overall proposition and ensuring that there is harmony between the different elements.

3

THE PRINCIPLES OF MARKETING FINANCIAL SERVICES

After reading this chapter you should:

- Be aware of the importance of both understanding customers and being able to identify buyers

- Know what is meant by 'customer segmentation' and why and how this is done

- Be aware of the sources and the use of customer data and customer research

3.1   Understanding and identifying buyers

Marketing starts in the marketplace with the identification of customer needs and wants. It then moves on to determining a means of satisfying those needs and of promoting, selling and supplying that satisfaction.

If we follow this definition and agree that we must start in the marketplace with the identification of customer needs, we can start to see how important it is that we understand exactly what and who our marketplace is. What we mean by 'understanding our market' is the ability to understand our customers and their needs, wants and preferences.

An organization will be successful only if it directs its efforts into providing the right customer with the right product at the right time and in the right manner. Having seen this it is obvious that the organization must focus on the customer and that the first step is to find out exactly which customers make up our 'market' and how we can identify them.

It would be extremely naive of any organization to consider its market to be simply everybody outside the organization. People are different and have different needs. The key for the company is to recognize those needs and satisfy them. Therefore the key to success must be for the company to take the following steps.

- Understand its own organization's capabilities, and the environment in which it operates (SWOT).

- Identify the opportunities that exist for the organization.

- Identify the potential customers and fully understand their needs and their buying behaviour.

- Investigate and understand what will satisfy those needs and how the organization can accommodate their purchasing preferences.

- Having successfully identified customers and met their needs profitably, it needs to be able to identify those customers' qualities, and find more customers with similar properties and qualities.

Identifying buyers

The understanding of buyer behaviour relates to the acts of anybody who purchases goods or services, and to ensure that we make the most use possible of this information we must bear in mind the following.

- The desires, needs and opinions of the customer are of paramount importance and a marketeer will ignore these at his or her peril.

- With the proper research we can gain a reasonable understanding of customers and how they behave in the buying process.

- Our marketing activity should then use this knowledge and understanding of their behaviour in order to influence what they buy.

Most people will buy a financial services product at some time in their lives. These days it is almost impossible to survive without them. Most people have a bank account usually either as a teenager or when they first start work. An increasingly large proportion of people will buy their own home and require a mortgage to help them to do so, and it is increasingly common for people to have not just one, but a number of credit and debit cards.

With the reduction in the welfare state and the increasing need for private provision many people will turn to financial services companies for such things as pensions and medical care cover.

We can see from this that almost everybody will at some point be a buyer of financial services. In order to identify who may buy what product or service at any point in time we need to understand more about why people buy such services, and how they go about making the purchase decision.

Because the nature of the products of financial services companies is that they are one-off major purchases, they involve the consumer in a fairly high degree of decision making and selection. This decision is of much greater significance than that needed when purchasing things such as food or toiletries for example, and therefore the behaviour customers display during this purchase also differs.

The following flowchart illustrates the stages that a customer will go through and the behaviour he or she will display when making a purchase that involves a large amount of money or with significant impact. We will look at each of these in turn in more detail and try to determine what influence, if any, we can have on the customer's behaviour and decision making.

Figure 3.1: Buyer behaviour

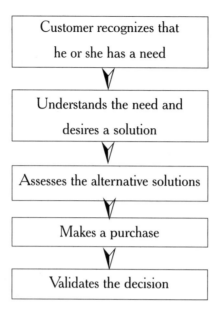

Recognizing the need

The first stage of any major purchase must be the customer's recognition of the fact that he or she currently has a problem. The problem is usually one of a gap between what the customer has at the present time, and what he or she would like to have or need to have. This recognition can often be triggered by a change in circumstances that will highlight that the present situation is inadequate.

Marketing efforts can play a part in helping the customer to recognize that there is a problem and many companies have used advertising to attempt to do this. However the only really successful way for this stage to be influenced by the organization is via personal contact with the customer, i.e. with branch staff or salespeople spending time with the customer and examining the current situation.

Understanding the need and desiring a solution

Once the customer has reached the point of being dissatisfied with the gap in circumstances that that has been recognized, he or she will begin to think about the consequences of that gap. Depending on the perceived effects seen the customer may well decide to take some action, and improve the situation.

Assessing the alternative solutions

This follows next. During this stage of the customer's behaviour he or she is looking at all the alternatives that are available for satisfying the need. This will involve looking at the different products that would be suitable and comparing their benefits.

Having decided which product will best suit their needs, the customer may then look at the offerings of different providers and compare their features and price.

It is during this stage that they marketeer can have most influence on the customer's behaviour, and where the marketing activity he or she undertakes can be of most success in influencing and indeed changing the behaviour. All elements of the marketing mix can help to influence the decision. Advertising the product and its features or its price may be central in persuading the customer to make a purchase. Alternatively, the method of promotion or being in the right place, somewhere that is convenient for the customer, may be the factor that gets the business.

Making the purchase

Having decided which product or service best satisfies the need the customer will go ahead and make the purchase. Customers will choose to buy in a way which suits them; some will buy remotely, i.e. over the telephone or through the post, and others will want personal contact and therefore visit a branch or salesperson. The marketing manager will need to note their preferred buying method, because this will be useful later when the organization tries to sell them additional products.

Validating the decision

When a customer makes a purchase which is large in terms of financial commitment and the effect that it has, he or she is likely to require some sort of reassurance that they have done the right thing. This will be apparent in the fact that customers may ask questions following their decision to buy regarding the product and its benefits. It is important that the company does not lose any of the sales it has made and therefore the after-sales service it offers, and any mailing it does to new customers, must offer them reassurance that they have made a good decision.

Influences on buyer behaviour

There are a number of factors that influence the consumer's buying behaviour and it is worth looking at these to see how they may effect the marketing and sales of the organization's products.

The family unit is an important factor in a customer's buying behaviour, as it will effect both the volume and type of products consumed and will also influence attitudes and desires. It is also important to consider how the consumer behaves as part of a family unit because such units account for a large proportion of the population. The needs of the family and the way in which it chooses to satisfy those needs will depend on whether they have children and if so how old they are, whether there are two parents or one, and whether both work, etc.

The *social background* of the customer is likely to have an influence on buying behaviour. This explains why segmenting customers into socio-economic classes is such common practice. Their social class will influence their taste and preferences and so must be considered when marketing.

Culture is another influencing factor that must be considered. A person's behaviour is influenced by his or her geographical location, by nationality, by ethnic background or by religion or educational background. It is important to remember these cultural differences and the way in which they effect the customer's buying behaviour if we are to avoid making expensive marketing blunders.

3.2   Applying the knowledge of buyer behaviour

Once we have an understanding of how our customers and prospective customers may behave, we need to use this to ensure that our marketing activity is directed to the areas and the behaviour where the organization believes it can be most effective in influencing that behaviour. For example, in an industry where the customer is likely to want the product rather than actually need it, the marketing manager may feel that there is little point spending time money and effort attempting to help customers with the 'recognizing the need' stage of the behaviour patter. Instead he or she may feel that the customer will recognize the need and therefore the organization would be well advised to concentrate its efforts on the 'assessing the alternatives' stage. If this is the case, the promotional activity will be focused on highlighting the product benefits and making comparisons with other offerings in the market.

Within the financial services industry, for many of the products sold the above situation will apply. For example, a customer will decide himself or herself to buy a car, and with insufficient funds to do so, will recognize the need for a loan. This means that the customer will progress on to the next stage of the buying behaviour, i.e. looking for a solution, and then approach a financial services company, usually a bank or building society. This means that the marketing manager in charge of personal loans will concentrate his or her efforts on ensuring that the product is competitive and easily accessible. The manager will advertise the competitive elements of the product through channels felt to attract and be seen by people in this kind of situation.

On the other hand, the marketing manager in charge of life assurance products will know that advertising the product is unlikely to attract many customers. This is because most people who need life assurance are unaware, i.e. they have not gone through the first stage of the customer's buying behaviour. He or she is therefore likely to spend more of his time and resource to try to show people the need that they have, i.e. help them to recognize their problems, and then show them the solution.

We will look in more detail at buyer behaviour and how sales activity can be matched to it in Chapter 12.

Life stages

One way in which a financial services company could try to identify who may currently be a possible financial services customer, i.e. looking to make a purchase, is by identifying the kind of people who will typically buy a particular kind of product. Alternatively it could look at the different stages customers go through in a typical life-time and try to identify the products and services they may therefore need. Many financial services marketing departments have done such a life-stage exercise to help them to understand who the buyers of each product are likely to be, and therefore help them in their marketing.

3.2: A typical life-stages exercise could produce the following results

Life stage	Needs	Products or service requirements
Student	Money	Bank account Student loan
Young singles just starting work	Savings Borrowings for car etc.	Savings account Credit/Debit cards Personal loans Personal pension
Married couple	Finance for new home Savings	Mortgage Home insurance etc. Will-writing service Investments
Young family	Finance for a larger home Cover for income if sick or on death Children's savings Borrowing for holidays etc.	Mortgage Life cover Health insurance Savings accounts Personal loans
Older family/ Empty nesters	Savings and investments	Pension provision TESSAs/ISAs Unit Trusts etc. including advice
Retired	Investment of retirement money Medical cover/care	Investments products and advice Long-term care

This type of exercise will help the marketing manager to identify the types of customers who may be potential buyers of products and services. The next stage is to divide the population and the customers of the organization in to the different groups or categories in order to try and see what their needs may be.

3.3 Segmenting markets

Segmentation: what is it?

We have just seen that not all of the customers of any organization are the same, and therefore they do not all have the same needs. Nor do they all have the same behaviour or buying patterns. For example, insurance companies sell pension plans to both individuals and to companies, and these two sets of people have very different needs and buying methods. Organizations recognize this is the case and therefore they attempt to divide the market into a number of small groups who have similar needs and similar behavioural patterns. The reason for doing this is that it focuses the requirements and enables the company to design solutions to their specific needs and to promote those solutions in a place and a manner that will suit the customers within that segment.

A good definition of market segmentation is 'The subdividing of a market into distinct and increasingly homogeneous subgroups of customers, where any subgroup can conceivably be selected as a target market to be met with a distinct marketing mix' (Kotler).

Why use segmentation?

Remember that the basic purpose of the marketing function is to match the products and services offered by the company with the needs of the customer. With this in mind we can see that segmentation will benefit the organization in the following ways:

- By identifying the needs of customers within the group, the organization can design products and services specifically for them.

- The company can select target markets whose needs are closely aligned with the strengths of the organization, i.e. an area where the company is most likely to be able to become market leader.

- By understanding who the target groups are, the marketing function can focus its promotional activity on attracting more customers whose characteristics resemble those of its profitable customer base.

- If all of the target customers have similar buying behaviour as well as similar needs, this will allow the marketing promotion to be much more focused, and therefore it is much more likely to be successful.

3.4 Approaches to segmentation

There are many different ways that a market can be divided and subdivided, and the criteria used are likely to depend on the nature of the organization and the products and services they sell. We will now examine briefly some of the more commonly used segmentation variables.

Sex

This is commonly a factor used to divide the market because in many areas the needs of men and women are different. Even in cases where the basic need is the same and therefore the same product can be sold, often men and women display different buying behaviours. If this were the case, the company would want to use different promotional methods or different marketing messages, for example, when promoting to these two groups.

Age

This is also a useful criterion for segmenting markets. Often people have similar needs and similar buying patterns to other people of the same or similar age.

Customer's income

A person's income also dictates what type of products he or she can afford to purchase and so it may be that people of a similar income level will have very similar needs and wants as well as similar preferences as to the way they like to be sold to.

Socio-economic groupings

These are commonly used to determine a target market. This method of division has proved to be a reliable way of predicting people's needs and indeed their behaviour, and is therefore likely to be included in most segmentation exercises. People are categorized as A, B, C1, D or E. These are defined as follows:

A   *Upper middle class.* High-ranking managers and professional people

B   *Middle class.* Middle management and administrative occupations

C1   *Lower middle class.* Junior management, and administrative clerks

D   *Working class.* Semi-skilled and unskilled manual workers

E   *Subsistence level.* Unemployed and those on state benefits.

Geo-demographic segmentation

This technique classifies and groups people depending on where they live. The underlying theme is the belief that two people who live in the same or similar neighbourhood are more likely to have the same characteristics than are two people chosen completely at random. It also therefore implies that each neighbourhood can be categorized in terms of the type of person that lives there.

By using this technique the marketing manager can more accurately target his promotional activity and/or place salespeople. He or she will identify the characteristics of the people who have purchased existing or competitors' products, and then target areas where the people display similar characteristics. This should greatly increase the take-up rate of any direct mail etc. and therefore increase profitability. One of the most commonly used methods of geo-demographic segmentation is the ACORN classification method. There are 17 different classifications such as:

Wealthy achievers, in suburban areas

Well-off workers in family areas

Better-off executives in inner city areas

Affluent greys in rural areas

Lifestyle segmentation

Another way of segmenting the population is to divide it into groupings depending on lifestyle. This works on the assumption that people who live similar lifestyles and are at similar stages in their life cycle will have similar needs and wants. They should also display similar buying behaviour and similar dislikes. This is a popular method of segmenting and there are several models available to enable marketing managers to apply the technique and therefore more clearly understand both the existing customer base and potential new customers.

One model available is VALS produced by SRI International, which identifies nine segments. Here are just a few examples:

- *Achievers*. These people are self-confident and ambitious, often materialistic. They see themselves, quite rightly, as running the show. They will view their homes and their offices as a symbol of their success.

- *Socially conscious*. This type of person is acutely aware of social and environmental issues. Many of them will choose a simple, non-consumerist lifestyle.

- *Sustainers*. These people are under economic pressure. They are seeking to sustain, and in time, improve their position. They are insecure and will be nervous of experimenting or taking unnecessary risks.

It is easy to see that the marketing manager who is trying to sell high-quality, expensive home office furniture would do well to target the achievers, but would be wasting time, effort and money if he targeted the socially conscious category. However the opposite might be true for someone attempting to recruit membership for a green charity.

Segmentation in practice

Having looked at a variety of different segmentation methods available to a marketing manager, what we do now is to have a look at how these methods could be applied and how they could be used.

Let us take an example of a marketing manager of a company that sells household and motor insurance. He or she is launching a new product that insures household appliances against breakdown and wants to know which of the customers on his very large database he should mail with the introductory offer.

The first thing he needs to do is to divide the database into segments. To get the best results and to have the clearest picture of the customers who make up the database, he is unlikely to choose one method alone, but will select a number of different criteria in order to carry out the analysis. In this case he decides to segment by age, sex, geo-demographics and lifestyle, and combines the information to come up with a total of 10 different categories or segments he could choose to mail to. Let us have a look at a few of the segments he has to look at.

Borrowers

The people in this segment are typically young married or co-habiting couples, many of which have both partners in work to pay substantial mortgages. They are aged between 25 and 44 and have a household income of between £20,000 and £35,000. They are active users of debit and credit cards and are usually good payers. They are most likely to live in the counties of Berkshire, Buckinghamshire or Wiltshire.

Experienced investor

These are an equal mix of males and females, often couples whose families have left home. Their typical age is between 45 and 64 and they have a household income in excess of £35,000. They are comfortably off, are readers of such publications as the The Guardian, The Times and The Daily Telegraph and may be inheriting money from their parents. They are most likely to live in London, Surrey, Avon or Hertfordshire.

Spenders

This group of people tends to be young, around 20 to 30, and are mainly single, often living in rented accommodation, probably sharing. They have an average income of around £12,000 to £20,000 but spend this rather than save. They also use credit cards and personal loans. They are likely to read the The Sun and live in East Sussex, Berkshire, or Hertfordshire.

The manager can now see the type of customer he has and he will also know the number he has that fall into each segment. What he needs to do now is to select one or more segments that he believes will have a need for his product, ensure that the product fills that need, and that the marketing material is suitable for the customers in that segment.

Selecting a segment

Once the segments and their characteristics have been identified, the next step is to select which of them will be targeted. Before deciding on a segment or number of segments he wants to market to, he will need to answer the following questions.

- Is the segment large enough? Are there enough people from this grouping within the database for there to be a large enough number of sales to generate the required profit?

- Can he reach the customers within this segment? Do the preferred buying methods of this segments fit with the current promotion and distribution methods of the organization?

- Can the selected segment be reached profitably? Can they be reached through the distribution methods they prefer at a profit to the company or will the promotional costs be more than the sales revenue?

● Is the segment stable? This is extremely important if the company is going to commit large amounts of money up-front to such things as product development. They will need to successfully market the product for some time to recoup the up-front costs and therefore the selected segment must be stable, and not likely to change dramatically or even disappear in the near future.

The marketing manager will then go on to use this information in his marketing plan and in his promotional plan for this particular activity.

3.5   Database marketing

A good database helps to improve the quality of marketing and management decision making and is particularly useful for storing information about customers and in helping to segment them. A database is a method of storing, organizing and managing large volumes of information, and for retrieving, searching and analysing this data. The extent to which this data can be useful depends on how comprehensive it is, how it is stored and how accessible it is.

The database of a major financial services organization will be held on computer and will contain information including the customer's name and address, age, sex, marital status and income. It will also include information regarding the products and services bought from the organization. In order for the database to be a useful marketing tool it must be kept as up-to-date as possible, with any change of address and all new product sales being meticulously recorded.

Databases can, if used efficiently, be an excellent direct marketing tool. The goal of direct marketing is to sell a product or service that a customer needs. For example, it would be useless to attempt to sell a lawn mower to a person who lived in a flat, and therefore the more the company knows about a person, the more likely it is to get the offer and the message around it to be suitable to the recipient. This targeting can be done only with a thorough understanding of the customer segment you are hoping to sell to and an understanding of both their needs and their buying behaviour.

Because existing customers, having bought from the organization previously, have displayed that they will accept the company and their brand values as a supplier, this is one less hurdle to overcome when attempting to sell. Because of this, direct mail is often more successful if mailed to existing customers rather than to the general public. For this reason, mailing to customers from the database is a common direct marketing activity. As we have just discussed, this will stand a much greater chance of success if properly targeted, and so the marketing function is likely to use the sophisticated segmentation techniques we saw earlier to select the customers it wants to communicate with.

For example, company A decides to carry out some direct mailing activity to promote its credit card. The company knows that it has successfully promoted its card to several categories of customer, but wants to be sure that this mailing will be as successful as possible. Therefore before the mailing is designed the company use the database to check which type of people have typically responded well to their previous direct mail activities.

The database shows that socio-economic groups A and B have previously responded well, particularly males aged between 25 -45 and 55- 65. The database is then checked to see if there is any crossover between these people who have shown a propensity to respond to direct mail and the type of person who has previously applied for the credit card. It is found that the typical user of this card is a male, class A, B or C1 and aged between 35 and 55. Having checked the records it is clear that the 35 to 45 age group are more likely to default on their payments than any other group and therefore the company decides to mail males aged 45 to 55 who are As and Bs and earn over £35,000 p.a. The database can then be asked to produce a list of people who fit these criteria and who do not currently have its credit card, and the company can mail them with the offer.

We can see from this brief example that when the database carries comprehensive up-to-date information, and this is used to its full potential, the a customer database is an extremely useful marketing tool. It can help with research and improve enormously the chances of the marketing activity being successful. It has numerous advantages over traditional marketing methods. Below are a range of applications for a marketing database:

- Focusing on prime prospects

- Evaluating new prospects

- Cross-selling related products

- Launching new products to potential customers

- Identifying new distribution methods

- Building customer loyalty

- Increasing the frequency with which customers use available services

- Targeting niche markets

4

THE LOGIC OF A CORPORATE PLAN AND THE MARKETING PLAN CONTAINED THEREIN

After reading this chapter you should:

● Be aware of the structure of a corporate plan and the type of information contained within it

● Be aware of the structure of a marketing plan and understand how it is constructed

● Understand the interrelationship between the two plans and the elements in each

4.1   Structure of a corporate plan

Different companies take different approaches to constructing their corporate plan, and tailor the plan to suit their business needs. However, this said, the basic structure of a corporate plan is as follows.

Figure 4.1: Development of the organization's mission statement

Statement of objectives

Situation analysis

Strategy development

Specific plans

Implementation

4.2   Mission statement

Usually the corporate plan will start with the company's mission statement. A mission statement is simply a statement of what the company is aiming to achieve through the conduct of its business. In a sense, it could be thought of as a statement of the organization's reason for existence. The purpose of a mission statement is to give the company some focus and direction, and to ensure that all activity carried out within the business is done in a way that will contribute to the purpose of the business.

The corporate mission statement depends on a variety of factors. Corporate history often influences the markets and the customer groups that the organization states it wishes to do business with. An example of this would be in the banking sector where Credit Agricole has maintained strong links with the farming community, while Coutts continues to concentrate primarily on high-net-income customers for its retail banking activity.

If mission statements are too narrow they tend to blinker management thinking and it may therefore fail to take advantage of new opportunities or recognize and act upon threats to their market. This can ultimately hinder the profit making ability of the company. British Rail were accused of getting their mission statement wrong when, for decades, they saw themselves as being in business in order to 'run a rail network'. It could be claimed that their image of their business resulted in their failure to respond quickly enough to the development of new motorways and a domestic airline network. Arguably it would have been better for them to see themselves as being in the business of 'Transporting people and freight throughout Britain' since this may well have led them to consider more seriously the threats to their business that the motorways and air network were posing.

On the other hand, a mission statement that is too broad will lead to insufficient focus for the management team and for the employees of the company, rather than efforts being focused on areas in which the company could be successful and profitable.

Thus it is insufficient for a bank to identify its mission as being purely 'banking'. It would be far better to broaden the purpose of the organization. For example it could be something like 'meeting the customers' needs for financial transactions'. A mission statement should offer guidance to the managers as to how the business should be developed and in which direction the company is heading. A clear mission statement enables future growth strategies to develop what are regarded as key competencies and aim for synergies by dealing with similar customer groups, similar customer needs or similar service offerings.

A good mission statement is concise, and clearly answers the question What business are we in? Financial and profit dimensions need not appear in the mission statement because they will be covered more specifically in the corporate objectives.

A mission statement could therefore read something like:

To be a the first-choice provider of all financial services products for our customers.

Statement of objectives

Objectives are part of any planning process both at corporate and at marketing level. Corporate objectives define specific goals for the organization as a whole. They may be expressed in terms of profitability, returns on investment, growth of asset base, earnings per share, etc. These will permeate the planning process and be reflected in the objectives for the marketing department and other functions of the business. Clearly the objectives specified for any marketing plan will need to be a subset of those in the corporate plan.

An important element of the marketing planning process is to translate the corporate objectives, which are most often financial, into market-specific marketing objectives. This will involve targets relating to the size of the customer base, growth in the usage of certain facilities, gains in market share for certain product groups or customer categories, etc. Any objective must conform to three criteria: it must be consistent, it must be clearly stated and it should be quantifiable.

Objectives are clear statements of what the business intends to achieve. They will be written in hierarchical order. The lower objectives contribute to the achievement of the primary objectives.

Primary and secondary objectives

In the hierarchy of objectives, a primary corporate objective is more important than a secondary objective. Both types need to be restricted by the constraints on corporate activity. The secondary objectives may well be strategic issues that will ensure the achievement of the overall corporate objective.

If a company sets itself a primary objective then it needs to develop a strategy to ensure that the objective is achieved. Conversely, an objective must be set for each strategy. Many secondary objectives are simply targets by which the success of a strategy can be measured.

Trade off between objectives

When there are several key objectives, some may need to be achieved only at the expense of others. For example, a company's objective to achieve a good level of profit and growth may well have an adverse effect on the quality of the service it offers to its existing customers.

There may well also need to be a trade off between long-term and short-term objectives. Most managers are measured against their short-term objectives, for example:

- Middle managers are criticised if they do not stick rigidly to the budgetary constraints set.

- The board of directors of a public company are expected to achieve a certain level of growth in profits each year. Failing to do so will lead to criticism of the company by the market analysts and a reduction in the share price.

This emphasis on short-term achievements creates pressure for managers to sacrifice longer-term objectives in order to achieve short-term goals. Ideally an organization tries to control the short-term to long-term objective trade off, in order to ensure that the most suitable decisions are taken in each situation.

The company objectives could therefore look something like this:

'To create real growth in profit year on year'

(primary objective)

In order to do this the company would need to:

Increase the market share of personal loans in the UK

Make significant cost savings across the branch network

Improve the cross-sales of life and pension products to our banking customers

Introduce more ATMs across the country

Double the number of customers subscribing to the on-line banking facility

(these are all secondary objectives)

Once the corporate mission statement has been agreed and the objectives formulated, this information – along with further detailed analysis of the environment – provides the input for the next stage in the planning process.

Situation analysis

Environmental factors will have influenced the company's mission statement and its objectives, but a much more comprehensive analysis is necessary as a basis for both overall and market-specific objectives. Situation analysis involves a thorough study of the broad trends within the economy and society. It also involves a comprehensive analysis of markets, customers and competitors. In particular, the nature and extent of the market segments the company is intending to target should be investigated. There will also need to be an investigation of the company's internal environment to find its particular strengths as well as any factors that may hinder the company's progress.

Market research and external data will provide the majority of the information relating to the external environment. An audit of the company's activities and capabilities will provide the information required about internal environment.

The most common method of making a check on the company's current situation is to carry out a SWOT analysis.

4.3   Internal health check (SWOT)

One of the most important factors relating to a company's success is that it should understand its own company inside out. One of the best ways of doing this is to carry out a SWOT analysis. SWOT stands for

● Strengths

● Weaknesses

● Opportunities

● Threats

A SWOT is generally depicted as follows:

Figure 4.2: SWOT analysis

Strengths	**Weaknesses**
Things that the company is good at	Things that it could improve or that the competition does better
Opportunities	**Threats**
Attractive parts of the market or new markets	Things that may negatively effect the market

Before undertaking any new project or sales or marketing initiative, a SWOT analysis will help you to see how viable the project is and what are its chances of success. It will also highlight what you will need to alter and improve if you are to be successful, and what you already have which will enable you to succeed.

Strengths are those things at which the company excels or the things that set the company apart from the opposition. Identifying and understanding these will enable the marketing manager to play to these strengths when planning marketing campaigns. It is these strengths which will enable him or her to develop a USP (*unique selling proposition*) for the goods or services on offer and help to set the product above that of the competition.

Weaknesses are the things at which the company or its products currently perform poorly when compared either to the competition or to customers' expectations. It is important that these are highlighted and understood so that action can be taken to reduce them and reduce their impact on the project, otherwise competitors will be only too pleased to point them out.

Opportunities include anything that could be beneficial to the company or to the project. While not exclusively so, these are most often external factors such as closing down of a competitor, legislative changes, or economic factors. Recognizing these opportunities can greatly shape the marketing plan and could be crucial in planning such things as timings of advertisement campaigns or product releases.

Threats are anything that could hurt the business or disrupt the plans or the project. For example, it could include such things as a major competitor launching a new product at the same time. It is essential that the marketing manager understands the threats in order that he or she can minimize them. The manager will also need to ensure that there is a contingency plan for any eventuality considered to be a major threat.

Case study

The A&B Bank has stated in its mission statement that it intends to be a leading provider of deposit-based investments. One of its primary objectives is to increase the size of its market share of deposits, and in order to do this, one of its secondary objectives is to launch new versions of deposit accounts. The new account will have an excellent rate of interest and the plans are to sell it by direct mail. The bank has undertaken the necessary research and believes that there is a substantial market for this product and that the product and literature designs they are considering will suit their target market. The SWOT analysis could contain such information as this:

Figure 4.3: SWOT analysis case study

Strengths	Weaknesses
● The brand of A&B Bank ● The bank's reputation as a deposit taker ● The size of its customer base ● The amount of information held about each customer ● The product design ● The company's ability to produce mailing material	● The bank's inexperience of marketing via direct mail ● Restricted administration capability for handling postal accounts ● Lack of understanding about competitors' capabilities
Opportunities	**Threats**
● Falling interest rates make guaranteed rates attractive ● Currently no other providers offering similar products to the market. ● Launch of cash ISAs will lead to customers' considering deposit-based investment.	● Interest rates. The company must take a view on the future rises or falls in interest rates and this may prove to be incorrect ● A competitor may enter the market at the same time offering a better rate/ product

---

4.4   Using the SWOT analysis

Once you have completed the SWOT analysis, the findings can then be used to ensure the success of the corporate and marketing plans. The way to do this is to ensure that the objectives and the strategy match the strengths of the company with the opportunities that are presently available in the marketplace. Recognizing an opportunity in the market is only advantageous to the company if it has the required strengths to take advantage of it and fulfil those customer needs. Similarly, a company strength should not become the focal point of the company strategy unless there is a corresponding opportunity currently available in the marketplace.

A alternative strategy that a company may decide to take would be to spend time and effort converting its weaknesses to strengths in order to be in a position to capitalize on opportunities that currently exist, or may arise in the future.

Strategy development

The next element in the corporate plan is the section that details the organization's strategy. This section outlines the strategies the business will adopt in order to achieve the objectives it has set itself. For example, the organization may have set itself an objective of becoming a top ten financial services company. The strategy will determine the way in which this will be achieved. Corporate strategy is the most general level of strategy and is concerned with such things as the type of business the organization as a whole will be involved in and such things as diversifying the activities of the organization. It outlines any plans the organization has to expand into new markets or any plans for merger or acquisition of other businesses.

The business strategy discusses how the business will approach particular markets or outlines the business activities for certain areas within the overall organization. It may, for example, outline certain key products that the company will develop and market. It may be concerned with a particular segment of the market that the company believes it will be able to successfully target for increased business levels in the coming year.

Specific plans

The strategy that is outlined in the previous section will then carry through to this section, that of specific plans. If the strategy was one of diversification, for example, the plans as to how this should be achieved will be contained here. This element of the plan would contain the information relating to the new markets the company intended to diversify into, the new products or services it would need to develop in order to be successful in this new market, and how it would promote and distribute into this new market.

Implementation

The final section details the way in which the plans to implement the strategy and meet the objectives will be carried out. It outlines such things as the resource requirements and time-scales, including the progress that will be made by the end of this particular planning period.

4.5   The marketing plan

It is clear that the construction of the corporate and marketing plans and their control is essentially a management task, and input is required from managers at many levels. However these planning activities cannot be undertaken in a vacuum. Although the construction of a marketing plan may seem a relatively simple task to carry out on paper, there must be an acceptance of the plans at all levels of the organization before it can turn from a plan to a working document.

Initially the planning process will be driven by senior management if the plan is to be used as a working process in an organization. Ideally a system will need to be established in order that all functions within the organization – from branch level to head office – can provide information to be inputted into the plan. All levels must be made aware of the type of information they will be expected to contribute. For example, senior managers will be expected to contribute at a 'macro' level, but a contribution from a branch manager would be expected at the 'micro' level. This ensures that not only is everybody working together, but also that everybody is supplying information from his or her own field of expertise.

Managers at regional offices and branches have the responsibility of delivering the organization's services on a daily basis. Therefore they have, even if they do not realize it, valuable and meaningful information regarding customers, trends in the market and the company's strengths and weaknesses. Branch managers need to be trained on the planning concept and the processes involved in order that they see the marketing planning as an integral and important part of their role. Contributing to the overall marketing plan will also help the branch manager when he comes to develop his own branch plans and strategies.

This method of gathering information at all levels of the distribution chain is known an 'bottom-up' planning and we will look at it in more detail when we go on to look at sales planning. A process involving bottom-up planning can be very motivational to managers, who feel that they are contributing to the direction of the organization, and that their views and knowledge are considered important. However this will only be the case if the information they supply is seen to be included and appreciated, and copies of the final plan are then shown to those people who have made a contribution.

4.6   Structure of a marketing plan

Before a marketing plan can be constructed it is essential that the marketing manager understands some of the fundamental issues of the organization. He or she must know and fully understand the mission statement as stated in the corporate plan because this will state the overall strategy of the company and what it aims to be. The manager will also need to understand the corporate objectives. This is because the purpose of the marketing plan is to show how the business will realize these objectives.

The marketing plan must therefore fall out of the overall corporate plan of the business. The corporate plan will outline the company's mission statement and a brief overview of what will need to be done for the company to realize its aims. The aim of a corporate plan is to ensure that the senior management team thoroughly understands its own business and who its customers are. It will also identify exactly what the company wants to achieve and what it needs to do in order to get there.

Before the marketing plan can be constructed there will need to be a marketing audit. The purpose of the audit is to determine how well equipped the organization is at present and therefore decide if the objectives are realistic, or show what additional work will need to be done before they can be achieved.

A *marketing audit* should consider the following:

The marketing environment

- What are the company's major markets, and how are these markets segmented? How are these segments likely to change?

- Who are the organization's customers? What is known about their needs, desires and behaviours?

- Who are the company's competitors and what is known about them?

- Have there been any developments in the broader environment that will effect the company's marketing?

Marketing objectives and plans

- What are the organization's marketing objectives with respect to both products and services, and how do these relate to the overall corporate objectives?

- Are the resources being committed to marketing sufficient to enable it to achieve the stated objectives?

- Is the expenditure allocated to such activities as direct mail, advertising etc. appropriate for the objectives to be pursued?

- What procedures are in place for formulating marketing plans and exercising management control of these plans?

- Is the marketing department and its personnel operating efficiently and effectively?

Marketing activities

The audit of marketing activities will include the following:

- A review of pricing by looking at supply and demand, customers' attitudes and the use of temporary price reductions.

- A review of each product, its competitiveness, and the product mix as a whole.

- A critical analysis if the distribution systems.

- A review of the size and efficiency of the sales force.

● A review of the effectiveness of all advertising and sales promotion activity.

Before we look at the exact content and structure of a marketing plan it is worth remembering that there are different types of plan for different purposes. A *tactical marketing plan* would generally have a time frame of around one year and would deal with marketing mix issues using existing products and services. A *strategic marketing plan* will span a much longer time frame, possibly five or more years. It will define new markets and products and match opportunities in the market with the strengths of the organization. This said, a strategic marketing plan would generally follow the following general pattern.

Figure 4.4: Structure of a marketing plan

4.7 Interaction between the stages of the marketing plan

Most companies and most marketing managers follow this framework when writing their plans. This is not because there are any rules or regulations governing how they are written, but simply that each section impacts on the others, and therefore there is a natural order in which they will need to be completed. For example, only when the audit and analysis have been completed, can the objectives be set. Only when the objectives are known can the marketing manager decide on the strategy he or she will undertake in order to achieve those objectives.

Once the strategy is decided, only then can the detailed planning be carried out, showing the resources needed and the timescales involved. Again, only when the resource plans are completed can the budgets be decided, and once all this is complete, then all parties can sign up to the plans. Let us look at each for these in more detail.

Executive summary

Although this appears at the start of the plan it will usually be written last. It provides a brief summery of the content of the plan and is designed for those managers who do not need to know all the detail contained in the plan, but simply require a brief overview of the marketing objectives and what will be done to achieve them.

Situation analysis

In this section there will be the results of the SWOT analysis and the projections as to what is expected to happen in the marketplace affecting the organization, its competitors and their customers. It will be carried out in a similar way to that which is in the corporate plan, but concentrating on the strengths and weaknesses of the marketing facilities as well as those of the company as a whole.

Objectives and goals

The marketing objective is the overall aim towards which all marketing activity is directed. It must be very closely linked to the overall business objective and does in fact form a link between the organization's goals and its actual activity in the marketplace.

The marketing objectives are an important communication that must be understood by the marketing department, the management team and the rest of the organization. Therefore the manner in which it is expressed is very important. When writing marketing objectives it is wise to follow some basic rules applicable to all objective setting.

Objectives should be *precise*. They should state very clearly exactly what is expected including, for example, amounts and dates. If the objectives relate to new markets, these need to be clearly defined.

Not only do they need to be precise but they also need to be *measurable*. There is little point in setting objectives if you are then unable to measure whether you have achieved them or not.

They should also be *realistic and achievable*. While it is important that the objectives are challenging and test the marketing function to push boundaries, setting unrealistic, unachievable objectives will lead to certain failure and is likely to waste the time, effort and resource of the organization. It is also possible that a failure to deliver set objectives will lead to a lowering morale among the marketing personnel.

They should also be *known and understood* by the people who will be expected to have any part in the delivery of them. It would also be useful if all the staff within the organization knew the objectives. This would enable them to feel part of what the company is trying to achieve.

The marketing objectives are usually expressed in terms of product and market. Unlike the organization's mission statement which will be very short and to the point, and the corporate objective which is likely to be singular, there are usually a number of marketing objectives. It is usually necessary to write an objective relating to each market that the organization currently operates in and intends to operate in within the timescale of the plan.

Below are some examples of the kind of marketing objectives an organization may set.

- We will become a top ten provider (by unit sales) of personal pension plans in the UK by January 2003.

- We will increase the number of credit card holders by 20% over the next five years.

- We will develop a motor cycle insurance policy, to be available by 1.1.2000, and to have 1% market share by 1.1.2001.

- We will double the volume of sales through the call centre over the next three years.

- We will investigate the possibility of selling our products via direct mail, and if viable, to have plans in place to commence this activity within twelve months.

Once the objectives have been written, it will then be necessary to prioritize them so that everyone is clear where resource should be dedicated first. The work that has been carried out investigating the market opportunities and competitor activity, for example, will prove useful when deciding which of the objectives should be viewed as priority 1, etc. When prioritising the objectives it will be useful to consider such things as the long-term and short-term objectives. Many managers are judged each year on their annual achievements and therefore there may be a tendency to prioritize short-term objectives above longer-term goals in order to see earlier benefits, even if the long-term goals are more important to the company.

There may need to be a trade off between objectives – for example the quality of the product against the level of profit that is required. The marketing manager may need to refer back to the corporate objectives before deciding which of these should be sacrificed for the sake of the other.

The objectives will be set at the time the *marketing strategy* and marketing plan are constructed but will need to be constantly monitored and, if circumstances require it, there will need to be updates. It is therefore important that there is some degree of flexibility in mind when objectives are laid down. In an environment that is subject to the level and frequency of change that we see in the financial services industry, the monitoring and revision of objectives becomes essential.

Marketing strategy

There are many different definitions explaining exactly what is meant by the term *marketing strategy*, such as Kotler's:

> *Marketing strategy is the logic by which the business unit expects to meet its marketing objectives. Marketing strategy consists of making decisions on the business's marketing expenditure, marketing mix, and marketing allocations in relation to expected environmental and competitive conditions.*

Put simply, the marketing strategy states the ways in which marketing will use the tools available to it to achieve the objectives. The marketing objectives tell us what the marketing wants to achieve, the strategies tell us how it will achieve them.

The first decision that will need to be made is whether the strategy is to be defensive, developing or attacking. Probably the best way to communicate the strategy is express it in terms of the four elements of the marketing mix, i.e. product, price, promotion, and place/distribution. Below are some examples of marketing strategies.

Product

- We will have simple, straightforward products that will meet the needs of 95% of our target customers.

- We will ensure that our products are comparable with the best our competition has to offer.

Price

- We will be price proximate with the major competitors in each market segment.

- We will always be in the top ten when compared to our competitors on price.

- We will charge a fair price that reflects the additional services we offer our customers over and above that offered by our competitors.

Promotion

- We will promote our product directly to the customer.

- Our promotional messages must always reflect our brand positioning of 'The customer's friend'.

- We will always promote our brand and our services rather then the individual products themselves.

Distribution

- We will have a variety of distribution methods suitable for each of the customer segments we target.

- We will expand our sales force to ensure that we have national coverage within the next five years.

- We will concentrate on distributing through electronic media only.

Action plan including resource estimates

Once the objectives have been set and the strategy for achieving those objectives has been decided on, the next step is to carry out some detailed planning of how this will be achieved. Each strategy is broken down into a series of tasks, and for each task there needs to be a series of actions tied in to certain timescales. When this piece of work has been done for each task needed to achieve each of the strategies, they can be put together to show the year's operating plan. There will need to be a check at this point that there is sufficient resource within the marketing area to conduct all of the activities stipulated. Resource may also be required from other areas of the business, particularly areas such as finance, sales, IT, etc. and these will need to be stipulated in the plan, and the plan agreed with the managers of those areas.

Budgets

When identifying all of the tasks it is important to outline all of the costs involved. The reason for this is twofold. Firstly there needs to be a check that the overall spend planned for the coming year and five years is within the amounts budgeted for. Also each task will need to show that the activity is beneficial for the business before it is carried out, i.e. that the benefits outweigh the costs.

If the cost of carrying out the plans is greater than the profit that will be gained by the success of the plans, then you may as well give up and start again. The aim of the budgeting process can be related back to our original definition of marketing, in that we need to produce the products and services that meet the customers needs, and we need to do so while making a profit for the organization. Put very simply, there needs to be some payback for the money spent. The next stage therefore is to look at the activities within the marketing plan and

- Assess the costs involved in carrying out the planned activities. The scale of the project will dictate the kind of budget that will be required, and if the objective is a major increase in business or, for example, the introduction of a completely new distribution channel, then major capital investment may be required. A new distribution channel may require new personnel and such things as cars, and technology to be introduced, all of which will need to be budgeted for.

- Assess the expected profit from the increase in business that will follow the implementation of the plan. In order to do this the marketing manager will need to make predictions regarding how many sales will be made, what will be sold, what revenue those sales will generate and what the costs of making those sales will be. It will then be possible to see the estimated profit that will be generated.

- Compare one to another and ensure that the activities are still attractive to the business and that the priorities are still reasonable. This will depend largely on how important the project is in relation to the overall company strategy. For example, a minor product enhancement may get the go-ahead only if the costs involved in its development can be recouped by the increased sales in a six-month period. However, if the company's introduction to a major new market or method of distribution is of strategic importance to the organization, it may do so even if the profit does not immediately compensate for the capital spend required.

- Ensure that the required resources (financial and otherwise) are available at the required time. This will include not only budgets but also the people in each department who will be required to give some time to helping to implement the plan.

Signatures

The plan and it implementation will need to be controlled and will require the support of senior management, both from within the marketing function and the rest of the business. By signing the document they are giving their support of the objectives and strategies, and committing the resource and the budgets outlined.

4.8   Relationship between the corporate plan and the marketing plan

We have examined in detail the construction and the content of both a corporate plan and a marketing plan. It is important now to understand the relationship that exists between these two documents. The diagram below aims to represent pictorially the way in which the corporate plan feeds the marketing plan, and how in turn the marketing plan will feed the sales plan.

Figure 4.5: The relationship between corporate and marketing plans

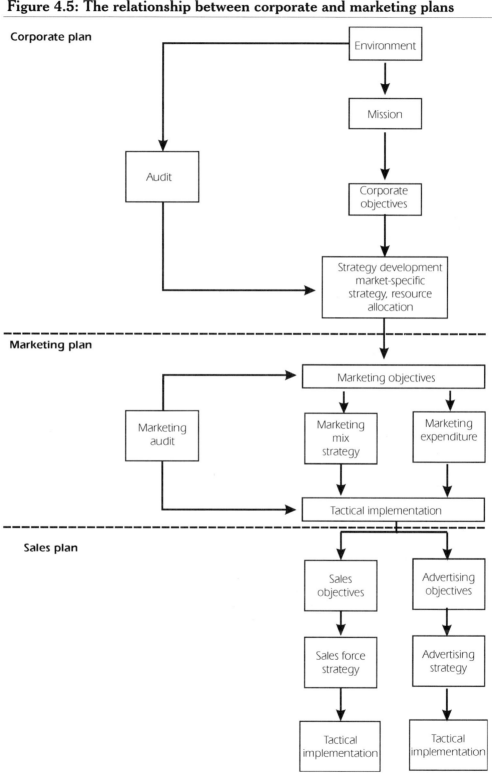

A marketing plan cannot be devised in isolation. The very purpose of a marketing plan is to outline how the corporate plan will be achieved.

Everybody should plan their work and decide how best to allocate the resources they have available in order to achieve the objectives they have been set. As a result of this, people at all levels of an organization will have objectives, strategies for achieving those objectives, and tactics. This goes part of the way to explaining the interrelationship between the corporate plan and the marketing plan. The corporate plan is the senior management document, the marketing plan is the similar document used by the middle management, namely the marketing manger, to achieve the objectives he has been set.

The corporate objectives will have been set by senior management following their construction of the corporate plan. The corporate objectives we saw were then transformed into a strategy and from there into actual plans and tactics in order to achieve those objectives. It is those specific tactics and plans that become the objectives of the marketing manager and therefore the start of the marketing plan as shown below.

Figure 4.6: Relationship between the corporate and marketing plans

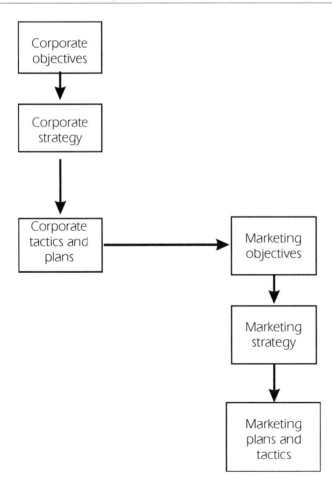

We can see from this that the corporate plan and the marketing plan are inextricably linked. Everybody who works on either the corporate or the marketing plan is ultimately working towards the same objectives and the same ultimate goal. The difference is that people are simply working at different levels of detail. The marketing plan may well deal with only sections of the corporate plan. There may be elements of the corporate plan that do not involve marketing and therefore are not contained in the lower-level details of the marketing function. However we can see that the construction of a good, robust and complete marketing plan depends on the marketing manager having a clear and full understanding of the contents of the corporate plan and the objectives of the company as a whole. From this he or she will be able to see marketing's part in that plan and ensure the marketing plan is built around the need to achieve the marketing objectives that fall out of that corporate plan.

5

RELATIONSHIP BETWEEN PROFIT, SERVICES AND CUSTOMER SELECTION

After reading this chapter you should

- Know the commercial factors that influence customer selection

- Understand the issues relating to cost versus profit

- Be aware of the effects of reachability and timescales

- Understand how the customer's needs and customer selection influence the design of the product features

- Understand the difference between transactional selling and relationship marketing

Introduction

In Chapter 1 we looked at the importance of matching the profit goals of the company with the service requirements and the needs of the customers. In this chapter we will take that discussion further. We shall look at how this balancing of needs and profit affects the commercial decisions made by the marketing manager. We shall consider such things as the influence it has on the type of customer the company chooses to sell to, the segments of the market it chooses to target and nature of the products it chooses to produce.

5.1   Customer selection

When a marketeer is considering the market for a certain product or service, he or she is well aware of the fact that one cannot simply try to sell to everybody. Organizations often have huge client databases with millions of customers recorded on them. They select from these millions of people the customers that they are to target with their product or service offering.

We looked in Chapter 3 at the principle of segmentation – that is, dividing the customers on the database, or in the market as a whole, into groups. The customers are grouped according to the qualities they have, e.g. sex, age, marital status, family status, socio-economic group, income, wealth, occupation, product holding, buying patterns, etc.

The level to which the market or the database is segmented depends on the amount of information held and the nature of the product or service being promoted. It is possible to segment in some detail if enough is known about the customers.

The purpose of this segmentation activity is to divide the customers into smaller groups so that the marketing manager can select which of these groups to target with certain product and service offers. The next step is therefore to consider which of these segments to select.

This decision is based on a variety of factors including the following:

- The potential profit that will be derived from those customers

- The size of the segment or segments

- The cost of marketing the products to those particular segments

- The accessibility and reachability of the segments

- How the features and benefits of the product match the needs of the customers in the segment.

Potential profit

The most obvious criterion for selecting a segment to target with marketing activity would be to select the group of people who are most likely to bring profit to the organization. One way in which they could bring profit to the company would be to buy high-margin products. However, with the increasing customer awareness of the charges made for financial services products, and particularly following the government's introduction of the CAT standard (*charges, access and terms*), and the increasing competitiveness of the industry, companies are under pressure to cut margins.

The other way in which customers could be seen as having the potential to bring profit to the organization is if they have the ability to either buy multiple products, or through the size of the product they buy. For example, if marketing ISAs, there will be more profit from a customer who can invest £5,000 than from a customer who has only the means to invest £500.

The way to select such a segment would be to ensure that the criteria for selection include either a minimum income level or a minimum level of wealth. Shown below is the kind of information the marketing manager would require to see which segments are likely to contain such customers.

Figure 5.1: Socio-economic groups' share of income

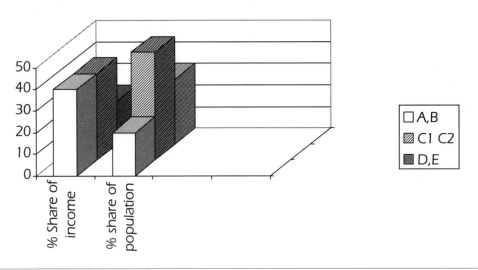

Figure 5.2: Socio-economic groups' share of wealth

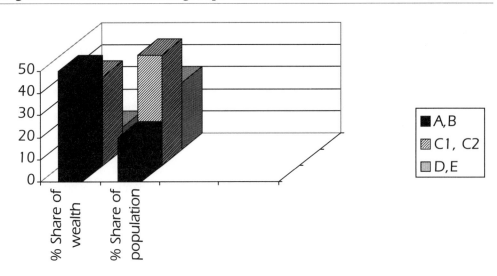

Before deciding that such segments are the ones to target, it should be borne in mind that all other financial services companies will be carrying out similar research and selecting segments of the population to market to. Whereas these customers will have the greatest potential for profit, they will also be the most sought after – the customers for which there is the greatest competition.

Size

Although the ideal situation would be to find a segment of the market with huge potential for profit that none of the competitors were successfully targeting, there are other considerations.

The segment must be big enough to warrant the time, effort and money that will be spent in marketing to it. If there are targets set for the number of cases to be sold or the number of new customers that will need to be attracted by the particular piece of marketing activity, the segment will need to have the potential to achieve these targets.

Costs

The costs involved in marketing to that particular segment are also a major consideration when selecting potential customers. While there may be enormous potential for profit from a particular segment, if the costs involved in attracting them are great, the decision may be taken to market to a segment with slightly less potential profit but at vastly reduced costs.

For example, the marketing manager may have to make a decision between marketing to two different segments of the market as shown below.

Table 5.1

Segment 1	Segment 2
Male	Male
Age 45-60	Age 35 – 60
Working	Majority working
Income range £40,000 - £200,000	Income range £15,000 – £39,000
Minimum account balance £50,000	Minimum account balance £2,000
Minimum property value £150,000	Minimum property value £35,000

Initially Segment 1 looks far more attractive than Segment 2, and certainly has greater potential for profit. However when we look at the costs involved in marketing to these two groups the situation changes. This is because

- The competition for these customers will be greater and they will therefore have received other similar offers. Because of this, the response rate may be much lower. This in turn means that the company would have to approach a greater number of potential customers to get the targeted number of sales, thereby increasing costs.

- The customers in this segment are far more likely to shop around, that is they will compare the offer made to that available from other providers. Therefore to attract this customer, the organization may need to increase or enhance the benefits offered by the product or reduce the price. Each of these options will involve cost to the company.

- Because the customers in Segment 1 could be considered as 'high-net-worth' customers they will expect a certain quality in the material that they receive. Anything that is sent to them in the post will need to be of excellent quality if it is to attract their attention and persuade them to buy.

- The customers in Segment 1 are likely to be far more financially aware and far more demanding of the service levels they receive in exchange for the charges they pay. In order to attract and retain these customers the organization may need to change or improve the aftersales service it offers, and this will involve costs.

- The customers in Segment 1 may well want additional distribution methods to those the company has in place already. For example, they may want a home banking facility with any current account they use. If this were the case, then marketing a current account that relies on a branch network would have little response. The introduction of such a facility would, of course, be extremely costly.

- It may be that the customers in Segment 1 would be less likely to show loyalty than those in Segment 2. Research shows that the more financially sophisticated the customer is, the less likely he or she is to buy all products and services from one provider. If the company is looking for loyal customers who will buy, over time, a number of products, Segment 2 may look more attractive.

We can see that simply having the potential for profit does not make a segment the automatic first choice for marketing purposes if there would be considerable costs in doing so. On the other hand, the company could well decide that the costs involved in carrying out a successful marketing campaign to a particular segment would be money well spent if the segment was large enough and the profit potential great enough.

Accessibility and reachability

We have already touched briefly on the accessibility of certain segments and how this may make them more or less attractive as a potential market. There is little point in targeting a segment, no matter how profitable it would be, if it is inaccessible.

There are several reasons that a particular segment could be considered to be inaccessible. For example, the company may not have the products or services that satisfy those customers' needs. If this is the case, the only way in which the company will be able to do business with those people is to design and launch new products. If it cannot do that, then those customers will always be unreachable.

Customers will only be accessible to an organization that has the distribution methods to suit their purchasing behaviour. For example, a company that deals solely over the telephone may want to target additional segments to attract new business. There would be little point in them targeting people whose buying pattern showed a strong desire for personal service in a High Street branch. No matter how good the offer, if the people in the segment do not like using the telephone, then they will be inaccessible to a telephone-based operation.

Another reason that customers may be inaccessible is because of a company's brand or brand values. There are some brands that appeal only to certain segments of the market. Other segments would simply not consider purchasing anything from them as their brand values do not appeal. If this is the case, then again, no matter how good the offer, the customer is never going to buy from them.

These situations are not irreversible, and sometimes companies decide that a segment is so attractive they will take the necessary steps to access the customers that are currently unreachable. They could launch new products, invest in new distribution channels or even launch a new brand with the values that would appeal to the segment they wish to target.

All of these things would of course require a great deal of money and represent a major investment for the company. However if they wish to target currently inaccessible segments of the market, this may be a strategy the company wishes to adopt.

5.2 Product design and customer selection

This could be considered to be bit of a chicken and egg situation, i.e. which comes first, the product design or the customer selection? Does the marketeer

1. Design a product that he or she feels there is a market for and which the company can produce, service, promote and sell at a profit, and then look for the appropriate customer segments to sell it to?

2. Look at the customers the marketeers can sell to, examine the needs they have, and then design, manufacture and promote a product that satisfies those needs?

The reality is probably a mixture of the two. The product manager would be stupid to design a product without first ensuring that there was a market for such a product and that it had the desired features. On the other hand he or she would not design a product that is totally focused on the needs of a particular segment of the market without ensuring that it can be serviced, administered and promoted by the company at a profit.

The series of events leading to the selection of a product design and market would probably therefore look something like this:

Step 1   Initial product idea, spawned either from a change in legislation, spotting a gap in the market, or from something offered by the competition.

Step 2   Research the market in order to see the scale of the opportunity and to assess the type of customer who would have a need for such a product.

Step 3   Assess in detail the exact nature of the customer's needs including the customer's willingness to pay for the satisfaction of those needs.

Step 4   Design the product including the features and benefits, pricing, promotion and distribution. The packaging is also designed at this point.

Step 5   Once the product has reached the launch stage, the marketing manager will then examine in detail the needs that the product can satisfy and the type of customer that will have those needs.

Step 6   Using the segmentation techniques the manager will then carefully select the type of customer to offer the product to.

For example, if the product is an investment product that benefits from investment in the stock market and has a high minimum investment, the manager will select customers who will have needs satisfied by those criteria. He or she will pick a segment or segments in which the customers have a high attitude to risk (i.e. are willing to risk capital in exchange for the possibility of higher returns) and have the desired level of wealth.

If the product being promoted is a re-mortgage product with a high loan to value (e.g. 100%) which allows payment flexibility, these features will determine the selection of the target audience for the advertising. Such a product would be marketed to people who currently own their property and have a mortgage on it. It would be marketed to those people who live in areas where property prices have not risen sharply in the past and therefore will not have equity in their property and therefore need to borrow the full value.

If the segmentation techniques are sufficiently advanced, the manager may also be able to select from these groups, for example, the people who have jobs with irregular income such as contract workers etc. who will need the flexibility of payments that this product has to offer.

The manager will also need to consider the features of the product that will not appeal to certain types of customers. While the basic benefits of a product may appeal to a certain target audience, if there are particular features that they will not want or need, this will also influence customer selection, particularly if these benefits are charged for within the costing.

It is not only the features and benefits of the product that will influence the selection of the customer, but also the methods by which the products can be promoted and distributed.

If the product can be distributed only through the branch network, then the marketing manager will need to select customers not only on the basis that the product satisfies their needs, but also on the basis that their buying behaviour matches the promotion and distribution.

It would be pointless promoting such a product to a consumer who wanted to make the purchase over the Internet or over the telephone because they did not have access to a branch. No matter how well the product features match that customers needs, the organization will never make the sale.

5.3 Transactional selling versus relationship marketing

The customer is the focal point of any financial services business, as without the customer there would be no one to buy and use the products and therefore there would be no business. For any organization to thrive it has to understand the importance of its customers and hence the phrase 'the customer is always right'. Of course we know that customers are not, but the phrase has sprung from businesses that understood the value of a satisfied customer and the problems that can be caused by a dissatisfied one.

The business wants to make as much profit as possible; the way to do this is to sell as many products as possible. Obviously there are only a limited number of people in the market and a vast number of suppliers all attempting to attract their custom. This means that once an organization has managed to attract a customer, it needs to ensure that it does everything possible to make that customer happy in order to keep the business. The benefits of a satisfied customer are easy to see. Satisfied customers will:

- Continue to use the product or service that they have purchased, therefore ensuring continued custom for the business.

- They are likely to buy further products or services from a supplier that they feel happy dealing with, ensuring further sales with a lower acquisition cost than that of attracting a totally new customer.

- They may well tell other people of the excellent products and services they have received and therefore attract more business for the organization.

- They are much less likely to be tempted to switch their business to another provider if they are satisfied with their current company, even if the competitor is offering a slightly better price.

- Satisfied customers, especially those who have customers for a considerable length of time, are more likely to be open and honest with the company about their needs, thereby providing a good source of customer research.

Customers who are, on the other hand, dissatisfied with the products they have bought or the services they have received will have the opposite effect on the business, that is:

- They will discontinue with the product or service they have purchased. This is a particular problem for financial services providers for whom most of the cost of the product is experienced up front in the setting up etc. and recovered throughout the term of the contract. This means that for many products and services, the customer needs to remain a customer for a specified time before any profit is made.

- They are unlikely to purchase a further product, meaning that to attract new business the organization will need to go to the trouble and expense of attracting a totally new customer.

- Unhappy customers will tell people of the problems they experienced, and will tell far more people than will the corresponding satisfied customer. Also people are far more likely to take notice of and be influenced by a poor-service story than a good one.

Looking at this information we can start to see the benefit of customer loyalty and what loyal customers can mean in terms of profit to the business. Any good salesperson knows that it is far easier to sell to a satisfied existing customer than it is to a new one. This fact has not escaped the notice of the marketing managers of financial services organizations. They have also found that when carrying out their marketing activity that the response from a 'warm' customer database, especially where those customers have shown a willingness to develop a relationship with the company, will be considerable better than that of a mailing sent to totally new prospects.

Figure 5.3: Ladder of customer loyalty

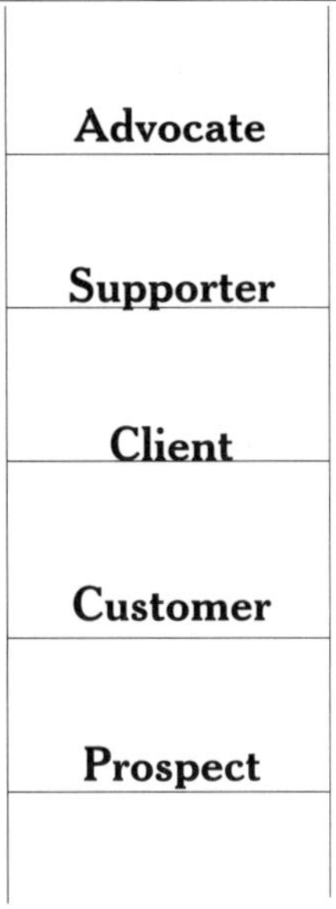

Advocate
Supporter
Client
Customer
Prospect

This is the basic knowledge that has led the majority of financial services organizations to move from a basis of transactional selling to relationship marketing. With transactional selling the organization attracts a new customer, carries out the transaction (sale), and that will be the end of relationship. With relationship marketing, the organization attracts the customer and makes the sale, but then continues to develop that relationship with regular contact, gains an understanding of that customer and his or her needs, and ultimately makes further sales.

Figure 5.4: Transactional selling versus relationship marketing

Transactional selling	Relationship marketing
Single sale to each	Initially a single sale is made, but over time multiple sales are made
Short timescales involved in attracting customers and making sales	Longer timescales required to develop customer loyalty and build the relationship
Minimal customer contact following the sale	High level of regular two-way customer contact following the initial sale in order to build the relationship
Little or no understanding of the the customers, their circumstances, or their needs	Regular two-way contact enables provider to build an understanding of its customer

All of the things we have looked at so far, particularly relating to the four 'Ps', relate to transactional selling. This is not surprising since their 'roots' were in the marketing of consumer goods where transactional selling is the norm. However, many research studies have indicated that it is far more cost effective to market to and to sell to existing customers than it is to try and attract new ones. This is a particularly important fact in the financial services industry which is becoming increasingly competitive and where product margins are becoming smaller.

The managers of financial services institutions have therefore largely switched from a basis of transactional selling to one of relationship marketing. In order to do this there will need to be some changes to the marketing mix. For example, the product needs to be tailored to suit that customer's needs. If the customer has a two-way dialogue with the organization, allowing the organization to gain an understanding of his or her circumstances and needs, the customer will expect that organization to offer only products which will be suitable and of benefit.

Price becomes much less important, because the customer will buy because of the relationship rather than because it is the cheapest. This said, the price still needs to represent value for money if customer goodwill is to be retained. The method of promotion used will need to be that which suits the customer, e.g. some will prefer to be contacted in writing, some via the telephone or Internet, and others will prefer personal contact.

The one thing that will become extremely important if the organization is to follow a path of relationship marketing is the communications that they have with their customers. The process of retaining customers is an important one in which integrated marketing communications has a vital role to play. It is not simply the frequency of such communications that is important, but the content. If an organization is to make an advocate from a prospect, the communications they have with that person must be very carefully planned.

The customer is unlikely to feel loyal to a company that simply bombards him or her with 'junk mail' for products and services that are not needed. However the customer will see the benefit of useful, targeted information and tailored offers. The tone must be carefully considered in order that each and every communication builds on the relationship and adds value for the customer.

6

How to Organize Market Research

After reading this chapter you should

- Understand the importance of using market research

- Know what aspects of the marketing mix are worthy of research

- Appreciate why companies use customer profiling in order to help their marketing

- Understand how external market data is used

- Know the benefits of keeping up to date with changes on a local as well as national level

- Be aware of the different methods of collecting information

- Know how to interpret and use market research and locally gathered data

- Have an understanding of the Data Protection Act

6.1   Why use market research?

Before we can look at the reasons for using research we need to have a clear understanding of exactly what we mean by the terms *market research* or *marketing research* Probably the most relevant definition is that provided by the Market Research Society, which offers the following:

> *Market research is a means used by those people who supply goods and services to keep themselves in touch with the needs and wants of those that buy and use those goods and services.*

Most financial services companies are large national or international organizations. Even those that started small in a local area are now large organizations, attracting customers from all over the country with varying lifestyles and from a variety of backgrounds and social classes. Although a local branch manager may feel that he or she has a clear view of exactly who the customers are and what they need and want, the size and scale of most organizations means that the marketing manager is unlikely to be able to accurately say the same. This means that in order to ensure that they have the correct marketing strategy, most marketing departments need to have a research function which ensures that the type of information needed about customers is always at hand.

All marketing managers are required to make decisions that carry a great deal of risk if incorrectly made. Such decisions are important, if not crucial, to the company and its business. If the risks of making a mistake are to be reduced, they should be made with a full understanding of all the relevant facts and therefore the best decisions are taken using all the available information. The use of up-to-date, appropriate research can help the marketing function of an organization to reduce the possibility of making the expensive mistakes that could happen if decisions are made on nothing more substantial than people's 'gut feeling'.

Marketing managers are required to make decisions every day regarding all aspects of the marketing mix. For example they need to decide on product features and benefits as well as the price they will charge. All of these decisions benefit from knowledge both of the competitor offerings and prices, as well as information about the organization's customers and what their needs are. Decisions about promotion and distribution also require information about their customer's buying habits and preferences if they are to ensure the best possible outcome for both the customer and the company.

Without information many marketeers would make decisions based on their own experience of the market. However, in financial services the market changes very quickly, and very soon people's experienced view of their consumer becomes out of date. Up-to-date information is therefore essential.

The information itself cannot make a decision. However what it can do is to help the marketing manager to make a more informed decision when planning a marketing strategy or inputting to business plans. In order to provide the maximum help, market research should be seen as an integral part of the marketing function and of any planning process. It must be carefully planed and executed, and the research reports must be studied with an open mind.

Market research becomes more and more important in an area, such as financial services, where there are a great number of suppliers all attempting to attract the same customer. When competition is fierce it is the company whose offering most closely matches the needs of the customer that will be successful. We can therefore see how important it is for a company to remain in touch with its customers and their needs if it is to gain any kind of competitive advantage.

In a competitive environment the company that succeeds is the one that makes what it can sell, rather than one that makes a product and then attempts to find someone to buy it. This strategy of investigating the market, finding where there is a need and designing a product that can satisfy it will be achieved only if adequate research into customers and markets is included as an integral part of the marketing function and the decision-making process.

In the sale of regulated products we know that the adviser must carry out a fact-finding exercise with the customers, investigating their needs before recommending a suitable product for them. Market research should be considered in the same way, as the fact-finding exercise carried out by the marketing department before deciding what products and services are suitable and how they should be promoted and distributed.

6.2   Areas worthy of research

Broadly speaking any activity undertaken by the marketing function can be deemed to be worthy of research. Such activities include product design and development, pricing, promotion and distribution. Let us look at each of the different areas and see what research will be required and how it can be used.

Product research

The marketing function is responsible for the 'invention' of new products, their design and development as well as for the ongoing maintenance of existing products, ensuring that they remain attractive and competitive. It is therefore important that it understands not only the current needs of the consumer, but has sufficient understanding of the market to be able to predict changes and therefore anticipate future product opportunities.

One of the major elements of product research is the examination of competitor products and their features and benefits. A good product manager must always be aware of the nature of the other products with which his offerings are in direct competition. This will involve obtaining details of the comparable products and compiling the data in a format similar to that shown on the opposite page.

Figure 6.1: Product research for term assurance contracts

Product Feature	Comp'y A	Comp'y B	Comp'y C	Comp'y D	Comp'y E	Comp'y F
Min. Age	16	16	18	16	18	16
Max. Age	80	80	79	75	60	80
Min. payment (£)	5	10	20	5	20	5
Premium Guaranteed	Yes	Yes	No	No	No	Yes
Sum Ass. Index linked	Yes	No	Yes	Yes	No	No
Joint Life	Yes	Yes	Yes	No	No	Yes
Waiver of prem. option	Yes	Yes	No	No	No	Yes
Conversion option	No	No	Yes	Yes	No	No
Critical illness benefit	Yes	Yes	Yes	Yes	No	No
Guaranteed increase option	Yes	No	No	Yes	No	No
Large case discount	Yes	No	Yes	No	No	Yes

Part of any product research always includes research into pricing, especially for a product such as term assurance where it is known that price is an important factor in the customer's buying decision. However, we shall look at pricing research separately.

If presented with the kind of information given above the product manager would gain an insight into the competitiveness of his or her product. We can see that company A is offering an extremely flexible and adaptable product because it includes a wide variety of options. It also has a low minimum age and high maximum age, meaning it will be available to most customers, and has a low minimum premium, again making it accessible to most customers.

Company E, on the other hand, has a much simpler product with few additional features. It has a much more restricted age range and a higher minimum premium. However, this does not automatically mean that the product offered by Company A is better than that offered by company E, or that any of the other companies should rush to change their product to match that of company A.

It may be that all of the additional benefits available in company A's product make it expensive, while Company E's simple product can be priced very competitively. It may be that Company A sells to a totally different market and therefore requires different benefits to those required by Company E's customers, and of course it would be useful to know which one is selling in the greatest volume. What is clear is that it is important to find out, not just the details of competitor products, but what benefit those product features are to the customer. Additional features should be added only if they are of benefit to the customer, and of benefit to the provider, i.e. they attract additional business and add to profitability.

Because of the intangible nature of most financial services products, another important aspect of product research involves looking at the packaging. This is particularly important for products that are sold by direct mail or direct response advertising. The packaging, i.e. how the product is presented to the customer, can have an influence on the buying decision if the customer is faced with offers from more than one company. It is therefore prudent for the product manager to ensure he or she understands how the competition are packaging their products and what appeal the packaging has to the customers he is trying to attract.

Pricing research

The product manager needs to make decisions about the pricing of products, and the simplest way to do this is merely to look at the cost of production, promotion and distribution and then add a profit margin. However, the pricing decision is in reality much more complex, and needs to consider other factors, such as the level and the nature of the demand as well as competitor costs. This means that the pricing decision cannot be taken without thorough investigation as the to the charges being applied by competitors for their products.

Once this investigation is carried out and there is an understanding of the competitor costs, the next step could be simply to ensure that the product is price proximate, and hope that this will attract customers. However, we should also consider that the price charged could be viewed by the purchaser to be an indicator of quality, and there may be occasions in which charging more than the competition can be beneficial. Any pricing research should also be studied alongside the product research discussed earlier, because the price charged will also need to reflect the benefits offered within the product.

Once a charge has been proposed, it may well be prudent to carry out some research as to the acceptability of the cost with a selection of people who represent the potential market. If the costs are too high the product will not sell, but pricing too low may arouse suspicions as to the quality of the product or service. Most market research agencies offer help with price testing for marketing managers.

Promotion research

Most financial services companies use a variety of methods to promote their products. Such things as branch displays, seminars, public relations campaigns, and of course television, radio, newspapers and magazines. Choosing which of these methods to use is a difficult and potentially costly decision. Before such decisions are made, the marketing manager needs to conduct research into the various options.

If a company were considering advertising in a newspaper, for example, before committing to purchase advertising space they would want to understand the following:

● How much would the advertising cost?

● How many readers does the paper have, i.e. how many people would see the advertisement?

● Where is the paper distributed, i.e. in which geographical regions will people see the advertisement?

● What is the profile of the readership, i.e. male or female, what age, what socio-ecenomic profile?

● Does this profile match that of the product's potential buyer?

Once this information is known the company can estimate the level of response it will get and decide if that particular method of promotion would be economic. Once the advertisement is placed, all enquiries as a result of the advertisement should be logged so that an on-going evaluation of its success can be carried out. If the promotion is not producing the results expected, it should be stopped and alternative methods of promotion considered.

Customer research

Most financial services organizations carry out a great deal of research into the buying behaviour of their customers. They attempt to find out what influences their purchase decisions, why people prefer certain brands, and how they react to different promotion methods. Companies know that the more they know about their customers and their buying behaviour, the more successful they will be in attempting to cross-sell to those customers and attract more customers like them.

Many organizations have large databases of customers who have bought a product from them. If they are to sell more products to these customers they will want to know as much as possible about them. One way of doing this is to issue them with a customer questionnaire requesting the information. Although not of all these will be returned, those customers who do complete them will be targeted with special offers that apply to their circumstances and are likely to appeal to them. Shown overleaf is an example of a customer questionnaire that could be used for this purpose.

Please give your partner's details	
Please indicate your marital status	Single/ Married/ Widowed/ Divorced
What is your occupation?	
What is your household income?	Under £10,000/ £10,000- £20,000/ £20,000-£30,000/ over£30,000
What is the value of your deposit account?	Under £1,000/ £1,000-£10,000/ £10,000-£25,000/ over £25,000
How much do you save each month?	Nothing/£1-£50/ £51-£100/ £101- £200/ over £200
Which of the following would you consider for saving?	Deposit account/ Unit trust/ Bond/ Personal pension
How would you rate the service you receive from us?	Excellent/ Good/ Average/ Poor
How would you like us to contact you in the future, for example, with special offers?	No contact/ Post/ Telephone/ Internet
Are there any other comments you would like to make?	

6.3   Detailed customer profiling

There are many reasons why the marketing manager may want a detailed profile of the customers that have bought the products or services. For example, he or she

● May wish to see the type of customer who currently buys a particular product in order to specifically target similar customers, thereby increasing the effectiveness of marketing campaigns.

- May wish to see the profiles of the customers who buy the company's product compared to those that buy that product from other companies to see if they are in line with the market, or to attract customers only from particular segments.

- May have had a particular type of customer as a target market for a marketing campaign, and at the end of the campaign, profiling those customers will allow him or her to see how successful this has been.

- May wish to see if there is any difference in the type of customer that is attracted through different media, e.g. local newspaper advertisements vs. national newspaper advertisements. It would also allow the manager to see if there was any difference in the customer profile based on geographical location, e.g. were the customers in the south-east similar to those in Scotland? This knowledge would help to focus more closely on customer needs in future campaigns.

- Could well require a detailed profile of the customers who have bought one product, in order to more successfully cross-sell other products to them. Detailed customer profiling tells the manager what type of customers they are, what lifestyle they have, what their needs are likely to be, and approximately what level of disposable income they are likely to have. This will help by showing the types of product and service they are likely to require and how they may like to deal with the company. This should increase the success rate of any mailing, for example, that the marketing department then carries out.

We can see from these examples that the primary function of detailed customer profiling is simply to gain a better understanding of who the customer actually is and what his or her needs are. The reason for doing this is so that we can more accurately target and focus future marketing activity, and thereby increase success and therefore profit levels.

Now that we know the reasons why detailed customer profiling is required, the next stage is to look at exactly what type of information we may want to know about the customers. Obviously this will focus around the type of information that will be useful for shaping future campaigns, either to these particular people, or to others like them. The information that may prove useful would be such things as:

- *Sex*. Are they predominantly male of female, or is there no bias at all?

- *Class*. What socio-economic group do they belong to? (This in itself will give us large amounts of information about them and their needs, etc.)

- *Age*. Knowing how old they are will give a good indication as to their life stage, and this in itself will give a good guide to their probable needs at any point in time.

- *Income*. The level of their income will allow the marketing manager some insight into their probable lifestyle, and give some indication of their disposable income, i.e. their ability to afford other products that may be offered.

- *Family*. For example, are they single, co-habiting or married? Do they have children who live with them and, if so, how old are they? Are they dependent or have they left home and moved on?

- *Location*. Knowing where they live will give some indication of the best areas for future campaigns to be carried out.

- *Product holding*. It will be useful to know what other products these customers already have as again this will give indications of their needs, buying behaviour and likelihood of further purchases.

- *Lifestyle*. From looking at the details above it will be possible for the analyst to make predictions about their lifestyles and preferences. This will be useful if the marketing manager wants to know such things as the newspapers they are likely to read, the radio stations they are likely to listen to, or the magazines they are likely to buy. It may also give an indication of the amount of time they have to consider financial products and how they like to receive such information.

- *Buying behaviour*. If the product could be bought in several different ways the manager will want to know the preferred method to ensure that this method is used in any further campaigns.

Let us imagine then that a marketing manager has just completed a campaign aimed at attracting customers for a new guaranteed-rate deposit account, with a high minimum deposit. In order to ensure that the next campaign for a similar product is accurately targeted, the manager has requested a detailed customer profile to be produced. The information received will probably look something like this:

Table 6.1: Deposit account investors; June 1999 profile

Sex

	Percentage
Male	63%
Female	37%

Age

	Percentage
Under 20	0%
20 – 39	18%
40 – 49	27%
50 – 59	33%
60+	22%

Income

	Percentage
Less than £15K	12%
£15K - £24,999	14%
£25K - £34,999	29%
£35K - £44,999	31%
over £45K	14%

Financial Mosaic Group

	Percentage
Good paying realists	21%
Capital accumulators	18%
Discerning investors	15%
Adventurous spenders	19%
Farm owners and traders	12%
Burdened borrowers	1%
Hardened cash payers	2%
Equity-holding elders	12%
Just about surviving	0%
Indebted strugglers	0%

Response method

	Percentage
Branch	38%
Telephone	39%
Coupon	21%
Internet	2%

More information could be learned about these customers once things like the financial mosaic groupings are known. For example, the Mosaic Group 'Independent elders' can be subdivided into further categories such as *solo pensioners* or *high-spending greys.*

Once this is known we, the marketing managers, can then make assumptions as to who these people are. The definition of the *high-spending greys* is as follows:

High-spending greys is the type of neighbourhood to which senior civil servants, successful businessmen and the upper echelons of the armed services typically retire. In such areas we find wealthy retired people with large and often indexed pensions who are still in good enough physical and mental health to maintain large detached houses and extensive gardens and drive their own car. Such areas are particularly fruitful for many financial services – high-yield investment accounts, annuities, stocks and shares, for travel and gourmet foods and up-market services. These areas tend to be staunchly conservative and have very high readership of The Daily Telegraph.

The more the manager knows about customers, the more accurately he or she can plan and target future campaigns for similar products, or for cross-sales to these customers. This will have the benefit of increasing response rates and therefore the profitability of the campaigns. It will also ensure that the customer is less likely to receive offers that are not of interest, but will instead receive information that is suitable and well targeted.

Application of external market data

While the marketing manager will have sufficient information about customers to be able to carry out the detailed customer profiling we have just examined, there may be occasions in which additional information is required. We have seen the benefits of knowing as much as possible about our customers, but there are equally valuable benefits of knowing about the people who buy from competitors, or who do not currently buy at all. Market information allows the marketing manager to see:

- Any changes in the marketplace as a whole

- Trends over time

- Potential markets that the company is not currently operating in

- The company's customer profile compared to that of the industry as a whole

- Where potential exists for new products or services

- Customers' changing buying habits, etc.

In order to get this information the manager will need to employ an external agency to provide the information or use other sources of external information. (We will look at the possible sources of external information later in this chapter.) Let us look at an example of how external data may help a campaign manager to improve campaign results.

The manager has run a campaign selling equity ISA investments. He or she has completed the first tranche of the campaign, but is analysing the customers in order to ensure that the second tranche is accurately targeted to obtain the best possible results. The manager organizes detailed customer profiling which reveals that the customers who have bought the product are:

- Predominantly male

- Predominantly over 50

- Mainly retired AB socio-economic groups

- Married with children who are no longer dependent

The marketing manager could decide that this is where the market for this product lies and ensure that the second tranche of advertising is aimed specifically at these people. Alternatively it may simply be that the current products and methods of promotion and delivery appeal more to this category of people, but there are other markets for this product that the company is not currently attracting.

In order to see if this is the case the manager will need to undertake some external research into the market as a whole, and the savings and investment habits and attitudes of the public. This will give the global picture, rather than that of the current market only. The type of thing that will help to find if there are other markets worthy of investigating, and give some guidance on how to go about it, will be such things as:

The profile of the people who currently save at the present time, i.e. what age are they, what sex are they, what socio-economic group do they belong to, etc.

- What type of customer has the highest level of disposable income?

- What type of customer has the greatest wealth?

- How are these people currently saving and investing?

- How much are they saving?

- What are they saving for? (special occasion, retirement, rainy day etc.)

- What do they look for in a savings account or savings plan?

- Which companies do they use?

- Why did they choose those companies?

- How did they choose those companies? Did an adviser suggest them, were they recommended by a friend, did they have a current relationship with the company or did they respond to advertising?

- How did they compare one product to another?

- How many different savings products do they have and from how many providers?

- How old were they when they first started saving?

- Was there any life-stage or event that triggered their desire to start saving?

- How do people actually go about getting information about financial products? Do they read the financial papers, visit branches, request information through the post or search for it on the Internet?

- How do they make the purchase? In person at a branch, through the post, over the telephone or over the Internet?

- Have patterns of saving and investing changed over time?

- How will the market evolve over the next 2, 5, 10 years?

With the answers to these types of questions the marketing manager will have a full picture of the savings and investments market, both now and in the near future. This means that he or she can spot the changes that will occur and take advantage of new and emerging markets. For example, the manager may find that people are starting to save when they are much younger, and that the average age of someone investing in equities has fallen to around 40. This means that he or she may well want to change the look and feel of the advertising and product literature to ensure that it appeals to this type of customer.

The manager may also find that people are increasingly using technology as a way of getting information about financial services products, and therefore decide to introduce an Internet site giving details of the products and services the company offers, and details of how to make an investment.

We can see that while detailed customer profiling is an excellent tool for ensuring that the company fully understands its customers, their needs and how they like to be dealt with, there are occasions where additional information is required. Customer profiling is useful when intending to market additional products to additional customers, but if the company is looking to attract new customers, especially in markets that it is not currently successful in selling to, then external market data is required.

The use of external data about customers in general and the marketplace as a whole will be useful for ensuring that the company is taking advantage of all current opportunities. It will also ensure that the company keeps up to date with changes in the market in order to maintain the level of sales and, therefore, profitability.

6.4 Benefits from keeping up to date with changes in the local community

One of the best sources of external market data is the community in which the company operates. Many financial services organizations have branch networks, and these branches are in an ideal position to gather and record information on behalf of the marketing function.

The staff of these branches see many customers every day and are able to feed back any changes in the type of customer they see, their needs and their buying behaviour. They are also able to pass on a great deal of information about the other products and services that customers have with other providers because they will be in an ideal position to find such information when customers open and close accounts and move them elsewhere. We will look at the benefits of locally gathered information in some detail later in this chapter.

6.5 Methods of gathering information

The method used to gather information depends largely on the nature of the information required. Information can be divided into two basic groups, i.e.:

- *Primary data* – data that is being collected for the first time; or

- *Secondary data* – existing information which may have been gathered for another purpose.

Primary data can be gathered either by observation or by questionnaire. Obtaining information by observing people is an excellent way of gathering accurate information and can be used to check the validity of answers given in surveys and questionnaires. If a company wants information about their customers' buying behaviour, observing customers undergoing the buying process is a good way to collect it. Observation is often used when companies are researching new campaign and promotional ideas. They present groups of customers with the marketing material and both listen to what they have to say about it, as well as observing how they react.

The other and probably most frequently used method of gathering primary research data is by questionnaire. Although sometimes sent by mail these are most often conducted by personal interview. This is probably because the amount of data that can be gathered by observation is fairly limited, whereas the type of information that can be collected by surveying is diverse. The survey must be very carefully planned, compiled and executed if it is to provide accurate results.

The personal interviews should be conducted by well-trained staff and can take place in a branch, in the customer's own home, or can be carried out by simply stopping people in the street. Alternatively they can be carried out over the telephone by calling people at home.

Secondary data can be gathered from both internal and external sources. Quite often the information required is already available in some form within the company. A great deal of information about customers and their transactions is routinely gathered by different departments within an organization, together with information about products, sales and financial matters. Many organizations fail to make the best use of the information they already hold, information that could be extremely valuable from a marketing point of view.

There are many sources of external data, and research companies often have huge amounts of information available for sale or hire. Other information is available from the government, and a booklet entitled *Government Statistics – A Brief Guide to Sources* lists the various departments and the specific data they are responsible for. Other sources of information include the following:

- Census of the population (every 10 years);

- Monthly digest of statistics (information on population, housing and manufactured goods);

- Financial statistics (published monthly);

- Family expenditure survey reports;

- National income and expenditure 'Blue Book';

- Information is also often available from trade associations, professional bodies and newspapers.

6.6 Interpreting and using locally gathered information

One method of conducting research is simply to gather information locally. This is most likely to be an appealing option for those financial services organizations that operate a branch network and therefore have regular access to a large number of people. However there are both advantages and disadvantages to using locally gathered information. The advantages are as follows:

- *Knowledge of the area.* Branch managers and staff who work with the local people every day will have a great deal of knowledge about them and their needs and wants. These staff are able to verify the findings of any locally conducted research or suggest reasons for any discrepancies or unexpected findings.

- *Local variations.* People's needs vary depending on their situations. We have seen that one of the best ways to profile and segment customers is by their geographical location. People living in one geographical location are likely to have fairly similar needs, and these may be distinctly different from those located elsewhere.

  Research conducted on a national basis is essential if the company is planning on designing a product that will be offered nationally, or running a national campaign which will need to appeal to as many people as possible. However, if a promotional campaign is to be conducted at a branch level, it is important that the messages are tailored directly towards the needs of the customers in that area, and therefore it will be necessary to gather information locally.

- *Trust and accuracy.* One of the best ways to gather information locally is for the company to do it themselves. If they do there are the advantages of both trust and accuracy. If the branch is collecting information about its own customers, this information is likely to be very accurate and perhaps more detailed because the customers are used to discussing their situation with the company and will therefore be more comfortable giving them the required information.

- *Cost.* There is often a cost advantage of gathering information locally rather than nationally, especially if the fact that it is being gathered locally means that the research can be carried out 'in-house' rather than having to employ a research agency.

The disadvantages are:

- *Restricted use.* Information that is gathered locally will have a limited value to the company, because there may be major inaccuracies if it is used as a basis for national marketing activities. As we said earlier, people's needs will vary depending on their location, and therefore when making decisions on a national basis, a wider view must be taken and information gathered nationally is required. This said, it would often be of great interest to the marketing manager when conducting national marketing activity to see the differences in the research from different areas of the country.

- *Risk.* Because locally gathered information gives a much more restricted view on which to make decisions, there is an increased risk of making a poor decision. There may be a greater level of subjectivity if the information has been gathered either by employees of the company, or from people who are already familiar with the company or hold its products. This again increases the level of risk attached to decisions made using this kind of information.

Once a company understands both the disadvantages and the advantages of using locally gathered information it will understand that it does have its place in the decision-making process and that if used in the right way, can be of enormous help. Locally gathered information should be used for:

- Inputting ideas for product changes and enhancements

- Providing up-to-date and accurate information on customers' preferences and buying behaviour

- Planning local marketing initiatives

- Helping to plan national initiatives to ensure maximum suitability

- Adapting national marketing campaigns to suit local customers

- Understanding the reasons for success or failure of both local and national sales and marketing initiatives

Data Protection Act

Any company that gathers information on its customers or potential customers and stores that information needs to comply with the Data Protection Act. The Act came into force in 1984 and deals with information stored on computers. As most financial services organizations now store personal information on sophisticated databases, the Data Protection Act is applicable.

The Data Protection Act established a register of all users of personal information. This register shows the names of all organizations using such information, including the following:

- The data user's name and address;
- The type of personal data being held;
- The purpose for which the data is being held;
- The source of the personal information;
- A description of the people to whom the information may be disclosed;
- Names of places to which the data may be transferred.

It is illegal to use data for any purpose other than that stated on the register, and it is an offence to hold unregistered data.

Under the Data Protection Act, the following eight data principles apply:

1. Data should be obtained and processed legally and fairly.

2. Personal data should be kept only for the purposes recorded on the register.

3. Data should not be disclosed for any purpose inconsistent with the register.

4. Data held should be relevant and not excessive for the purposes stated on the register.

5. Personal data should be accurate and kept up to date.

6. Personal data should not be kept for longer than necessary.

7. Individuals should be entitled to reasonable access to the personal data, and have such data corrected if necessary.

8. Appropriate measures should be taken to ensure the security of such data.

There are several implications of the Data Protection Act for people involved in marketing. Firstly, any data collected must be done *fairly and lawfully*. This means that data cannot be collected under the pretence of research if it is to be used for marketing, and therefore data collected during research can be used only for that purpose.

What this has meant for marketing departments is that they cannot use data about their customers for marketing purposes unless the individual is aware when he or she gives that information that it could be used for such a purpose. Obviously this would rule out great sources of information for the marketeers and prevent them from carrying out direct mailings and out-bound telephoning to those customers.

In order to remain on the right side of the law and still gain the revenue that will come from such marketing activities, financial services companies generally obtain the customer's permission to use information given for marketing purposes at the time they collect the information. Most organizations also want to transfer data between the different legal entities that make up the company. For example, a bank may wish to transfer information about its personal banking customers to its life company in order that they can attempt to sell them investment products. In order to be able to do this they need to ensure that the customer is aware this can happen.

Below is an example of the wording that a financial services company may give to a customer at the time he or she are disclosing personal information.

In certain circumstances information may be passed to other insurance companies or professional experts acting on our behalf. Details you provide may be used by our group of companies, your insurance intermediary, or other relevant organizations for marketing purposes. This could include market research and contacting you regarding your insurance and investment needs. If you wish to opt out of our marketing activity, please write to us at the following address. FREEPOST Mailing exclusion, PO Box 220, Sheffield S21 7HF .

7

FEATURES AND BENEFITS OF PERSONAL SERVICES

After reading this chapter you should:

● Understand the difference between a feature and a customer benefit

● Be able to state the features and benefits of

Savings and investments

Credit cards

Cash dispensers

Travel facilities

Home banking

Insurance

Pensions

Trustee services

Unit trusts

7.1   Definition of a feature and a benefit

Before we can go on to look at the different features and benefits of the products and services offered by financial services companies we need to ensure that we fully and clearly understand what the definitions are, i.e. what do we actually mean by the terms 'feature' and 'benefit'.

The dictionary definition of a *feature* is:

A characteristic, or a quality.

A feature of a product or a service is an aspect of that product, i.e. it describes a part of the product, or something that the product offers.

The dictionary definition of a *benefit* is:

Something good to receive, or an advantage.

It describes what good things will actually happen as a direct result of the feature.

What we can gather from these definitions is that the feature is the part of the product or service to which we are referring and describes a part of a product; the benefit then goes on to explain the good things that that particular feature will mean to a customer.

The next question to ask is why we should be concerned with the difference between features and benefits. The answer is fairly easy, although the product manufacturers and people with knowledge of the products will be interested in the 'features', the majority of customers are not. This is especially true in industries where the customer's knowledge is not particularly good, and even more true in relation to products which customers do not find particularly interesting.

We can start to see then that if we are to gain the customer's attention and to interest him or her in the products and services we have to offer, we should talk, not about the product features, but about the benefits of that feature.

Let us look at a few examples of product features and what these mean in terms of benefits. For the purpose of this exercise, we will start by looking at the features and benefits of products outside of our industry.

Example 1

This washing machine has a spin speed of 1600 rpm.

This is a feature of the product, but unless I know a lot about washing machines, my reaction is likely to be

Well, so what?

That is because the salesperson has told the customer about a feature of the product. If he or she is hoping that this will sell the product, he or she needs to go further and turn that feature into a benefit, as follows:

This washing machine has a spin speed of 1600 rpm which means that your washing will be much drier when you take it out, and the drying time will be much shorter.

Now, by turning the feature into a benefit, the customer can see what that feature will actually mean, and the good things that result because of it.

Example 2

This car has power steering.

Again this is a feature of the product. Now if the customer has a good knowledge of cars and knows what he or she are looking for this may be sufficient, but otherwise the customer could well be thinking

Well, so what?

Again, the salesperson should go on to explain to the customer what advantages result because of that particular feature, e.g.:

This car has power steering, which means that the steering is much lighter, and the car is much easier to park.

This statement has turned the product feature into a benefit, and shown the customer what advantage results by having that particular element of the product.

A simple way to check that you have been explaining a product benefit rather than simply stating a feature is to check the following:

If the customer could say:

Well, what does that mean to me?

the chances are that you have simply stated a feature and not gone on to show the benefits to them. If you want to make sure that you always turn features into benefits, then the phrase

Which means that ...

is a very useful one. If you state the feature and then say 'which means that', you will have to go on to explain that feature in terms of the advantages it brings, i.e. you will have stated the benefit.

Let us now look at some of the features and benefits of the products and services offered by financial services organizations.

Home banking

Feature	Benefit
Out-of-hours banking	Home banking means that you can attend to your personal finances at a time that suits you. You can transfer money and conduct other transactions 24 hours a day, rather than being restricted by traditional banking hours.
Conduct business in your own home	This means that there is no need to have to go to a bank branch or even to locate the nearest ATM; you can carry out the transactions from the comfort of your own home.

Travel facilities

Feature	Benefit
Travellers cheques	We can provide you with travellers cheques for your holiday, which means you can take your spending money in a way that is safe against theft and easy to encash.
Foreign currency	We can change your spending money into most foreign currencies over the counter so that you will be sure of having some local money when you arrive, without the hassle of having to plan too far in advance.
Travel insurance	We can arrange your travel insurance for you so that you are covered against cancellation, and against loss and damage of your possessions while you are away on holiday.

Credit cards

Feature	Benefit
Low interest payments	Which means that the interest charged each month will be lower, and you can therefore repay more of the debt with each payment.
Instant credit	Which means that you can buy things when you see them without having to wait and save up, and without having to get a separate agreement each time you want to borrow.
Pre-agreed credit limits	Which means you will know the limit to which you can borrow in advance, and can spend up to that level without needing to contact us and seek authorization.
Low annual fee	Which means the charge made for these facilities is extremely competitive and leaves you more money to spend on the things you want.
Cash facility	Which means that as well as using you card to buy goods, you can use it in any of the cash dispensers and get a cash amount up to your pre-agreed limit if you need to.

| Award points | Which means that every time you use the card to make a purchase you will be credited with a number of reward points, which you can then use to buy other goods and services. |

Cash dispensers

Feature	Benefit
Instant access to cash	Which means that you need never be stuck for money. You can simply go to the nearest cash dispenser and within seconds you will have the cash you need.
Out-of-hours transactions	Which means that you do not have to wait for the bank to open in the morning, or rush there before it closes in an evening. You will have access to the facilities when it suits you, 24 hours a day.
Balance enquiries	Which means that you can always know how much money you have in your account and avoid going accidentally overdrawn.
Printed statement facility	Which means that if you want to know if transactions have been carried out on your account, you can find out by simply using your cash point card in one of the ATMs.
PIN change facility	Which means that while most banks will give you a PIN and expect you to use it, we will allow you to change it yourself to something that's easier for you to remember. This facility will also allow you to quickly and easily change the PIN regularly yourself if you are concerned about security issues.

Life Insurance

Feature	Benefit
Lump sum benefit on death	Which means that if you were to die, a lump sum would be available to repay your mortgage and your personal loans ensuring that your family would not be left in a difficult financial position.

Income on death	This plan means that we would pay a continuing income to replace your income if you were to die. This means that you will have the security of knowing that, should anything happen to you, your family will still have the money they require to pay bills and buy the things they need.
Joint life facility	This plan can be arranged on a joint life basis, which means it will pay the benefits if either one of you were to die, without the need to buy two plans.
Waiver of premium	This feature means that if you are unable to pay your premiums because you are off work sick, the premiums will be paid for you and the life cover will continue.
Critical illness cover	This cover means that the plan's benefits will be paid if you suffer from one of the serious illnesses covered, and thereby provide you with a lump sum of money following an incident such as a heart attack or stroke. This will give you the money you may need for such things as house alterations or a holiday.
Trust facility	This plan can be written in trust, which will ensure that the benefits are paid more quickly should there be a claim, and that you can be sure they will be paid to your intended beneficiary.
Monthly, quarterly or annual premiums	We can collect the premiums at a frequency that suits you and your circumstances.

ISAs and Unit Trusts

Feature	Benefit
Lump sum or monthly savings	Which means that you can invest on a basis that suits you. You can pay in a lump sum if you wish, or if it is more convenient you can pay a set amount to us every month. You can of course have a combination of the two, if this is what would suit you.
Tax-free growth	This means that, unlike the interest that you earn on your building society deposit account, all the growth within this investment is free of tax and therefore you receive the full benefit of the growth you make.
Income	If you wish, you can opt to take an income from your investment, which will ensure that a regular payment is always available to you, paid directly into your bank account.
Encashment	If at any time you want to cash in your investment, you can do so and no additional charges will be made.
Expert fund management	As investing in the stock market can be a daunting prospect for many people, one of the benefits of a unit trust investment is that our expert fund managers will manage your money for you. The fund manager uses his or her knowledge and skill to ensure that you get the best possible growth on your investment.
Low charges	For the services you receive you will be charged, but these charges are low, which means that more of your money is actually being invested and therefore the returns you receive will be that much better.
Pooled investment	The money that you invest will be pooled with the investments of many other people and then invested on your behalf. This allows for a much broader spread of investment than could be achieved if you invested alone, and also allows for economies of scale for such things as charges.

Guaranteed interest rate	This cash ISA offers a guaranteed rate of interest, which means that you can be sure of the return you will receive, regardless of the changes in interest rates.

Pensions

Feature	Benefit
Lump sum at retirement	A lump sum can be taken from your plan at the time you retire, which you can use for any purpose you like, such as buying a new car, going on holiday, or moving house.
Income in retirement	This personal pension will provide you with an income when you retire, which will replace some of the money you are now earning. This means that you will not be dependant purely on the state benefit, and will be therefore much more likely to be able to maintain your present standard of living.
Tax relief on contributions	All of the contributions that you make to this plan will be free of income tax. This means that if you have already paid tax on the money you pay into your plan, the government will repay that amount into the pension, and therefore increase the amount you have invested.
Tax-free growth	Unlike the money that you have saved in the building society, all the growth on the savings you have within your pension fund are free of tax. Paying no tax on them means that you get the full benefit of all the growth you receive.
Premium holiday	If for any reason you find you are unable to save towards your pension for a short time, we will allow you stop making your regular payments, and then restart the savings when your financial situation improves.
Waiver of contribution	This feature means that if you are unable to save because you are off work sick, the pension contributions will be made for you, and therefore you will still receive the pension benefit you had planned for when you retire.

Flexible contributions	The amount that you save in your pension each month can be amended. This means that you can pay us more when you have more money to save, and reduce you payments if you need to. You can also add lump-sum payments to your savings if this suits you.
Transfer options	If for any reason you do not want to save for your retirement with this company any more, you can simply take the savings that you have made and transfer them to a pension plan with another company without charge.
Open market option	Just because you have saved with one company does not mean you have to have that company provide you with your income at the time you come to retire. You have the option to take the lump sum you have saved and 'shop around' to see which company will provide you with the best income in exchange for that lump sum.
Life cover	You can include in your pension plan the facility to have a lump sum paid to your family if you die before reaching retirement. The benefit of including this in your pension plan is that all the premiums you pay for this cover will also receive the tax relief that applies to pension contributions.

Personal loans

Feature	**Benefit**
Fixed repayment term	Which means that you can arrange the loan to match the lifespan of the product you are purchasing. .
Interest rate fixed at outset	This means that you will know in advance what the monthly payments are going to be and will be able to accurately budget for them. You will not suddenly find that payments have increased because interest rates have gone up and will therefore be sure from the outset of being able to afford the repayments.

No penalties for early repayment	If you find that they can afford to repay the loan earlier than the fixed-term expiry date, you can simple make a lump-sum payment of the outstanding amount. You will not be asked to pay any additional fee for this facility, and will therefore be able to repay as soon as you can afford it.
Life cover and redundancy insurance	If you were to die during the term of the loan, the outstanding balance would be repaid by the life cover, which means that your family would not be left with a debt. If redundancy cover is taken, then the loan repayments will be waived should you be made redundant. This means that the financial burden of unemployment will be lessened and payments will not restart until you are employed again.

8

CORPORATE SERVICES

After reading this chapter you should

● Be aware of the features and benefits of services available for corporate customers of financial services companies including:

Corporate financing

Computer-based cash management services

Factoring and discounting

Money transmission (BACS)

Bank loan

Feature	Benefit
Fixed or variable rate of interest	You, as a business customer, can select either fixed or variable rate to suit the needs of your business. With the fixed rate you will know in advance what the payments are going to be and plan around them. This may be useful for a new business which is focused on cashflow in the early years. With variable payments, the business will benefit from any reduction in interest rates throughout the term of the loan.
Money when needed	Will allow you to buy new equipment, for example, at times when you do not have the money yourself, and spread the payments over a number of years.

Bank overdraft

Feature	Benefit
Pre-agreed overdraft limit	Assists with working capital requirements because it allows your company access to a

	pre-agreed amount of money if you need short-term borrowing to help your cashflow.
Good interest rate	The excellent rate of interest means that the charges made are affordable and allow the company to be as profitable as possible.

Equity finance

Feature	Benefit
Money lent in exchange for share capital	This allows a company to start its business even though it is unable to finance it itself. It borrows money from the bank in exchange for share capital or an option for share capital. The loan is repaid and instead of interest the bank takes a share of the profits, again assisting the business with cashflow in the early years.

Foreign services

Feature	Benefit
Expertise in foreign markets	Many companies want to deal with suppliers or retailers in other countries and this involves transmission of payments between the two countries. Most banks have experts in this field who can assist the business in doing this and thereby enable it to trade with other countries.

BACS

This is an electronic fund transfer system service for collection of income by direct debit, and payment of expenditure by automated credit.

Feature	Benefit
Same-day debit and credit	Time saving for the business, which is not waiting for payments to arrive. This also helps with the cashflow of the company.
Payment instructions given to the bank on magnetic tape or disk	Reduced workload for staff who have a simple and clean way of informing their bankers of the payments to be made and collected.
Distribution of payments direct from the company's bank account	Because there is no cheque involved and nothing sent through the post etc. there will

be less chance of anything getting lost or stolen and therefore there is greater security and peace of mind.

Computer-based cash management services

Most major banks have this service available. The corporate customer is given a computer terminal, which allows access to the bank's computer system via the telephone connection.

Feature	Benefit
Out-of-hours access to banking information	Allows the company to conduct its activities at a time to suit itself and its customers rather than being restricted to traditional banking hours.
Immediate access to information about the company's accounts	Allows the customer to make important financial decisions without having to contact the bank for information Also gives up-to-the-minute information to allow the company to produce concise and up-to-the-minute reports on their accounts.

Factoring and discount services

A factoring service is one in which the bank issues the company's invoices and collects the money on its behalf. Discounting is a process whereby the bank pays the amount of the invoice less a discount to the company instantly, rather than it having to wait for the money to be paid.

Feature	Benefit
Administration carried out by the bank	This saves the company time and money because it is involved in less administration.
Bank chases non-payment	Again, the benefit to the company is that it is not involved in this expensive and time-consuming activity because the bank carries it out on its behalf.
Bank pays the money to the company on the due date regardless of whether it has been received or not	This provides great comfort for the company which can be sure it will receive all money owed to it. This gives peace of mind and helps with cashflow.
Discounting allows the company to receive the money owed to them instantly	This helps the company with its cash-flow.

CHAPS

CHAPS stands for Clearing House Automated Payment System. It is a high-speed same-day value system for anyone wanting to make or receive guaranteed funds. For frequent users the bank may allow a direct connection between the company's own computer and those of the bank.

Feature	Benefit
No minimum transfer	The company can make a guaranteed transfer in any situation that it is appropriate, regardless of the amounts involved.
Fund both debited and credited on the same day	No need to wait for the money to clear as it is a guaranteed transfer. This is particularly useful for businesses such as solicitors when dealing with property purchase, as they will wish to have access to the purchase money on the same day as it is deposited by the bank.

Deposit facilities

Feature	Benefit
Instant access	The business can deposit surplus money with the bank, but have access to that money at any time without notice. This is particularly important to corporate clients who may need money instantly to take advantage of an unforeseen business opportunity.
Banded interest rates	Because these are business customers, the amounts of money that are deposited can be considerable. Therefore it is of benefit to them to have an account in which the more they have deposited, the higher the rate of interest they are paid.
Cheque book option	For corporate customers some banks will supply a cheque book with the deposit account, allowing the business to pay for things directly from the account, thereby cutting down on transactions.

9

KNOWLEDGE OF COMPETITORS AND THEIR SALES ACTIVITIES

After reading this chapter you should

- Be aware of what the competition is for each type of financial services organization
- Know which markets are currently under threat
- Understand the features and benefits of competitor services
- Be aware of competitive strengths and weaknesses in key product areas

9.1   Competitors – who are they?

We have already examined the benefits of researching the competition, knowing what they have to offer and understanding the appeal they have to your customer base. However, before we can do this it is essential that we have correctly identified who the competitors are. To do this properly we need to look further afield than simply comparing one High Street bank to the other High Street banks.

High Street banks now find themselves in direct competition for banking services with not only other banks, but building societies, foreign and international banks, finance companies, insurance companies, and supermarkets.

Building societies must now compete for their mortgage business with banks, centralized lenders, insurance companies, estate agents, and direct writers. Insurance companies must now compete for their business with other insurance companies, banks and building societies who either operate as agents or have launched their own life companies, direct writers such as Virgin, and supermarkets such as Tesco and Sainsbury.

What we will do now is to look at each type of financial services organization and examine how they are expanding their product ranges and therefore competing for business that would have traditionally gone elsewhere.

Banks

The High Street bank was always the place that customers would immediately think of if they needed a current account, and they survived by supplying individuals and businesses with the traditional banking facilities. However as customers became more financially sophisticated, the banks realized that they would need to diversify if they were to remain profitable, and therefore started to operate in new markets.

Banks now offer mortgages to the public at rates that enable them to compete with building societies. Throughout the 1980s and the 1990s the position of all financial services retailers has changed; where clear boundaries existed, it is now the case that each organization is attempting to offer a full range of services. Many banks offer estate agency services in order to complement their mortgage offerings. They have extended their investment facilities from simply deposit accounts to include life bonds, unit trusts and ISAs. They have done this either by selling the products of another company in exchange for a commission or by setting up their own investment companies.

It is common to see a bank offering a range of services such as those listed below:

Service

Banking	Current accounts, overdrafts, business banking, etc.
Lending	Personal lending Mortgage lending
Estate agency	House purchase Property sale
Travel services	Travellers cheques Travel insurance Foreign currency
Investments	Deposit accounts TESSAs Bonds Unit Trusts PEPs/ISAs
Insurance	Life assurance Household insurance Pensions
Share dealing	Buying and selling shares

Building societies

Traditionally building societies had operated simply by dealing in mortgage lending and deposits. Throughout the 1970s the building societies continued to grow, attracting a considerable amount of business from the banks. Their growth owed much to the increase in home ownership and therefore the increased need for mortgage finance. The building societies also introduced new technology, including the Automatic Teller Machines (ATMs), which proved very popular with customers and enabled them to operate more cost effectively.

The major breakthrough for building societies came in the form of the Building Societies Act 1986, which allowed them to diversify into areas of financial services from which they had previously been excluded. The act enabled building societies to conduct the type of business shown below:

- Providing unsecured loans up to £10,000

- Establishing estate agency services

- Providing customers with credit cards

- Offering current accounts, including cheque books

- Providing investment business such as unit trusts

- Acting as an insurance broker

- Providing pensions and life assurance

- Providing foreign currency services

Most building societies took advantage of the new rules to increase their customer base and therefore their profits by, for example, establishing estate agency subsidiaries. These agencies not only conducted business in order to make profit, but were also able to introduce mortgage business to the society. An example is Halifax Property Services, a chain of estate agencies operating under a sub-brand of the main organization.

Many societies chose to act as tied agents for insurance and investment companies, with advisers in their branches selling life assurance, pensions and investments on behalf of the insurance companies in exchange for a commission. While this was an excellent first step for these organization to gain experience in these markets, many of the building societies felt that there was more profit to be made by offering these products themselves rather than selling business for another company. This led to many launching their own companies, and a list of the, then, building societies, is shown below together with the companies they launched.

Building society	Life company
Leeds Permanent	Leeds Life
Halifax Building Society	Halifax Life
Woolwich Building Society	Woolwich Life

Soon after the change in the rules, many building societies began offering current accounts and cheque guarantee cards to their customers together with cheque-cashing facilities, therefore operating from a customer's viewpoint much more like a bank. However there are still some restrictions placed on building societies that prevent them from competing equally with the banks. Building societies may not:

- Grant unsecured lending for more than £10,000 to any one customer;

- Allocate more than 15% of their total funds to unsecured lending;

- Devote more than 10% of their secured lending outside of the traditional building society areas.

Meanwhile, as we saw earlier, the banks were starting to compete in the building societies' core markets of mortgages and deposits, and the competition to attract and retain customers was becoming increasingly fierce. Many building societies found that the restrictions outlined above prevented them from competing as they wanted. In order to be able to compete and therefore make the levels of profit they required, many building societies have converted to bank status.

Other building societies have chosen to expand and therefore increase market share by merging. For example, the Halifax and the Leeds merged (although the Halifax has now converted to bank status). Because the building societies often had lower overheads, they are now competing well against the traditional High Street banks.

Life assurance companies

Although their traditional business has always consisted of offering life assurance and pension products to their customers, many insurance companies have also expanded their product ranges in order to attract new customers. They have seen their markets being eroded by the banks and building societies, who are offering life and pensions products instead of referring those customers to an insurance company, and they therefore need to expand their ranges in order to attract the levels of business they need.

Most financial services companies that traditionally dealt with life assurance now also offer investments in such things as unit trusts and ISAs via subsidiary companies. This enables them to use the customer database they have built up from one type of business to market and sell a different type of product, i.e. investments.

Insurance companies have also traditionally sold life products to people who needed to protect their mortgages in the event of death, and savings products to help them to repay mortgages. In an attempt to attract customers who needed such products, some insurance companies started to act as estate agents. They thereby helped customers to both buy and sell residential and commercial property.

Although the decline in the housing market meant that some of these ventures were not as successful as had been hoped, some, such as General Accident Property Services, are still going strong and providing an excellent source of business for their salespeople.

Another new area that some insurance companies have recently diversified into is that of banking business. Some have now formed third-party agreements with banks in order that they can offer their customers the more traditional banking products such as deposit facilities, personal loans and mortgages. Others have taken the further step of actually applying for and being awarded a banking licence in order that they can conduct this type of activity.

Examples of insurance companies now operating in these markets are Prudential, Standard Life and Norwich Union.

The competition among the insurance companies is also leading to a number of mergers and take-overs as companies look to consolidate their position in the market and retain and improve their levels of profit. For example, in recent years we have seen the Prudential purchase Threadneedle Street Investments, and more recently M&G Investments.

Girobank

Girobank was established by the government to cater for the banking needs of the less sophisticated customer. It offered personal accounts whereby customers could pay in and withdraw money at the Post Office. It was acquired by the Alliance and Leicester Building Society in 1981 and now offers a full current-account service. As it is a member of BACS, salaries can be paid directly into Girobank accounts and standing orders and direct debits can be arranged. Other transactions can be arranged by post or over the telephone, and standard stationary, such as pre-paid envelopes, are supplied to customers.

Girobank also allows customers to arrange transfers of money from their accounts to large utility companies, such as the gas and electricity companies, without going into the post offices. It also offers free banking and the use of the Link ATMs for its customers, and through its link with the Alliance and Leicester offers mortgages, personal loans and insurance.

Private banks

All the large banks are public companies, but there are still a small number of private banks, and some that are now owned by public companies (such as Coutts & Co owned by NatWest.) While offering both personal and corporate facilities, the majority of their business involves personal customers. They offer similar facilities to the mainstream banks but differentiate themselves by their level of service. To make their services profitable they often require high minimum deposits and make higher charges for their service than the High Street banks. Their overheads are kept low because they operate very few branches, although they need to employ high-quality staff to ensure that the service levels remain excellent.

The high financial standing of their customers means that they minimize the risk of bad debt, while maximizing the use of the premium services such as investment and portfolio services. These banks pose very little competition to the High Street banks because they are so few in number, and because of their highly targeted customers base.

Finance houses

Finance houses employ large amounts of funds for consumer instalment lending, more commonly known as *hire purchase* or HP. Although they often operate through a branch network, they commonly attract a great deal of business by offering their services through retailers and dealers. For example, if somebody goes to a car dealer and decides to buy a car, the dealer may well offer a finance deal, which will be transacted with a finance house. They also operate in a similar fashion with retailers of such things as furniture and white and brown goods.

Because they are in the right place at the right time they are very successful in attracting customers to take their finance arrangements, and therefore they form a major source of competition for the banks offering personal loans for such purposes. This said, many of the finance houses are in fact owned by the clearing banks as subsidiaries.

Retailers and supermarkets

Retailers made their first move into the world of financial services by offering their customers store cards. These are cards that offer credit to the customer but, unlike other credit cards, can be used only in one particular store or group of stores. There is a minimum monthly repayment and the APR is often higher than with standard credit cards.

These cards were targeted at people who wanted instant credit to buy goods for which they did not have the cash, and people who already had credit cards and wanted to increase their credit facilities. They were also available to people who were purchasing large items and could repay over a term with the flexibility not offered by a personal loan. Thus store cards formed competition to both banks and building societies that offered credit cards, and to those banks and finance companies that offered personal loans.

Another variation on the store cards offered by some retailers are charge cards, where the total balance must be repaid each month, or budget accounts where the customer pays a monthly amount and is in credit or has a credit balance.

Following the success of store cards, many retailers have now gone much further in offering financial services to their customers. Let us take as an example Marks and Spencer. They have for some time offered their customers both store cards and budget accounts, but have more recently being offering those customers personal loans. They were able to offer these loans to their database customers at an attractive rate of interest because they could carefully select those customers who were deemed creditworthy from their previous dealings.

Their next step was to offer their customers savings products, and M&S have been fairly successful in selling personal equity plans by direct mail to their customer database. One of the reasons they have been able to move into an area in which they had no previous experience or track record was because of their strong brand and reputation for value.

M&S have now expanded their financial services offerings further by selling life assurance products and pensions to their customers both over the telephone, and by distributing information in their stores.

Probably the best known example of a retailer moving into the financial services industry is that of Virgin. It began selling PEPs in 1995 and has been extremely successful, becoming one of the top direct sellers of PEPs in the UK. It sells its products via the telephone and through the post, thereby reducing overheads by not operating branches or having salespeople out on the road. It is also now selling life assurance and pension plans in a similar way.

Again the success has been down largely to the brand values and positive image of the company, and has allowed Virgin Direct to become a major competitor for all companies offering investments, life assurance, or pensions direct to the consumer.

The supermarkets have also now joined other retailers in the financial services market. They began by offering loyalty cards to their customers whereby they received points each time they shopped. They could then exchange these points for goods. This enabled them to build up huge databases of their customers and gather large amount of transactional data about them. They then began to offer those customers a card that allowed them credit as well as gathering loyalty points, creating competition for the traditional credit card companies.

Once the supermarkets had gained credibility as providers of financial services they were able to broaden their range of offerings. Both Tesco and Sainsbury now operate banks offering their customers a wide range of banking products, such as deposit facilities and personal loans, in competition with the traditional banks and building societies.

Not content to stop there the supermarkets are now offering their customers such things as personal pensions and travel insurance by advertising the products within the stores, and sending details of the products with their customers' loyalty and credit card statements. These products mean that they are in direct competition with insurance companies.

Other retailers have chosen not to operate in direct competition with insurance companies and banks, but have formed third-party arrangements with such providers whereby the financial services company can then use the retailer's customers database to market to. In exchange they pay a fixed fee or a share of the commission earned.

Solicitors and accountants

Although solicitors and accountants may not immediately spring to mind when considering the competition for financial services, they do in many areas offer services in direct competition to other financial services institutions. Below are some examples of the services offered by these professionals.

Solicitors

- Trustee and executor services, such as drawing up of wills
- Tax and financial planning advice (in competition with other financial services advisers and brokers)
- Legal advice
- Advice on commercial contracts

Accountants

- Corporate finances
- Tax planning

- Small business services

- Information on business finances

- Financial planning for individuals

- Executor and trusteeship services

National Savings

Another competitor for the banks, building societies and insurance companies to concern themselves with in regard to savings is the government, which also competes for customers in the savings market.

They operate through the national network of post offices and sub-post offices throughout the country and the money received by the National Savings Bank and other National Savings schemes is invested in government securities and used to finance the National Debt. They compete for both lump-sum investments and regular savings using such products as those shown below.

- National Savings Certificates

- Index-linked National Savings Certificates

- Income Bonds

- Pensioners Bonds

- Children's Bonus Bonds

Summary

We can see from this brief look at the different types of organization that the financial services companies will need to look much further afield than their traditional competitors if they want to gain a true understanding of the competitive products on offer. They will need also to consider other products that could satisfy the same customer need. For example, if a bank is looking to offer a personal loan facility to its customers it will need to investigate other personal loans and alternative products offered by its competitors, e.g.:

- Personal loans offered by other High Street and personal banks

- Personal loans offered by building societies

- Loans offered by insurance companies with a banking subsidiary

- Loans offered by retailers

- Loans offered by supermarkets

- Loans offered by finance houses

- Credit cards and store cards offered by retailers

Similarly, building societies offering mortgages may now find that the competition comes from sources such as:

- Other building societies
- Banks
- Centralized lenders
- Insurance companies

If a company wishes to be successful in marketing financial services products it must ensure that it stays up to date and knowledgeable about whom the competition is and what it is offering. It will also need to understand the competitive advantages that it has and those of the competitors. It will need to be looking forward and anticipating which of its markets may attract new entrants, and therefore which of its traditional markets are under threat.

9.2 Competitive strengths and weaknesses

We have seen from this overview of the changing market that there are many companies that are entering the market, or expanding their business to attract new customers and deal in areas they were previously not involved in. These new competitors will have strengths that give them a competitive advantage, but also weaknesses that they will need to overcome. Let us look at some examples.

Many of the new entrants to the financial services market have been *shop-assurers* and retailers, such as Marks & Spencer, Tesco, etc. They have the following advantages and disadvantages in the marketplace:

Competitive strengths

- *Retail brand.* These companies have a brand that is well known to the majority of the population as a retail company. They have already established their brand values and many of them fit well with the provision of financial services. Marks & Spencer, for example, has brand values that represent quality, value for money, fairness, etc. and therefore they fit well with the provision of financial services. One of the reasons Virgin has been so successful in this new market is the strength of their brand and what customers believed that brand stands for.

- *Access to customers.* These new competitors have access to very large numbers of customers who use them for the purchase of other goods. This gives the competitors a large database of people from all segments of the community to market to.

- *Distribution.* These retailers have ready-made distribution channels. They have a High Street presence of large numbers of retail outlets and therefore have the capability of reaching large numbers of customers at a very low cost.

- *Knowledge of their customers.* Some of these new entrants also have a huge amount of information about their customers that helps them to segment the database and target those customers more accurately with appropriate offers. Many of the retailers now have reward schemes whereby they issue their customers with cards to use each time they make a purchase.

As well as building customer loyalty, some of these cards are actually *smart cards*. The cards record details of the customers' purchases and allow the retailer to build up a detailed picture of the customers' buying behaviour and lifestyle. Such information is extremely valuable when they are targeting customers for direct offers and other marketing activity.

- *No baggage*. These new entrants do not have the same *baggage* associated with them as the traditional players. For example, they are not associated with the pension mis-selling that occurred in the past, and therefore may find it easier to enter the stakeholder pension market than some traditional pension providers. They will also be able to start afresh with regard to processes and systems, rather than having to work with those that have been in place for many years, and this could well give them a competitive advantage.

Weaknesses

- *Lack of experience*. They have little or no experience of the marketplace and how it differs from that in which they currently operate. Their individual employees may lack the knowledge or experience necessary and they may therefore find themselves having to buy in expertise or enter into joint ventures to enter the market.

- *Customer knowledge*. Although they have access to large numbers of customers, they lack the understanding of the different ways customers behave when buying financial services products. The products such retailers are currently selling are fairly minor purchases for the customer compared to those within the financial services market. Therefore customers' buying behaviour will be totally different. These new entrants must be able to understand the different buying behaviour if they are to fit their sales techniques to match them.

Markets under threat

We have seen in this chapter that there are very few markets that are safe from new entrants. Each and every company must be aware of the other companies expanding their markets and trading in products and services other than their traditional ones. However, there are some areas that are more open to competitors than others.

Competitors are most likely to enter the market selling the products that are simplest to produce and administer, and where the customer is likely to buy without the need for advice. They will firstly attempt to sell simple products that are easy to distribute through their existing outlets or through direct mail etc. to their customer base. They are also likely to enter the market with 'commodity' type products, for which the customer selects on cost rather than wanting an experienced and traditional provider. For example:

- Deposit accounts
- ISAs and other savings plans
- Credit cards
- Motor and household insurance
- Stakeholder pensions when these are launched.

10

PLANNING AND CONDUCTING SALES ACTIVITY

After reading this chapter you should

- Appreciate the benefits of planning

- Understand the planning logic

- Be aware of the templates for sales activity plans

- Understand the interaction of the elements of the plan

- Know how to introduce, control, and monitor the sales plans

- Be aware of the different requirements of selling regulated and non-regulated business

- Be aware of the regulatory and legal issues relating to conducting sales activity

10.1   Benefits of planning

The benefits of planning apply to almost any situation, be it finances, marketing or sales. Put quite simply, in order to achieve what it is you want to achieve, you must plan for that success. Once you have set the objective you want to achieve, planning is the tool that will help you to see how you are going to achieve that objective.

There are some people who would argue that a sales plan should not be created, because they do not understand the true benefits of a thorough planning process. Sales plans can be criticized for not allowing the flexibility to adapt to market changes, but this can be incorporated in a good sales plan that will allow for a re-planning exercise at periodic points throughout the plan.

A good sales planning process allows the sales manager and the individual sellers to assess their objectives and see what they will need to do in order to get there. It will ensure that they have the resources to get the right number as well as the right type of sales. Resources can include such things as:

- Money

- Equipment

- Salespeople

- Prospects (people to sell to)

- Activity levels (marketing, calling, etc.)

Without a solid sales plan the sales manager could embark upon the year and then find part way through that year that there were simply too few salespeople to meet the targets that had been accepted. He or she may find that the activity levels currently being undertaken are simply not producing the levels of business needed or that half-way through the year the sales budget has all been spent. A good sales plan ensures that every detail is considered before the year starts and the manager can see exactly what to do to be successful.

A robust sales plan also allows the sales manager to see which activities have the greatest results, and which ones prove the greatest strain on resource with lesser results. This will allow him or her to prioritize the activities and use resources more carefully.

A good sales plan comes from a manager who has thought through the following questions:

- Where am I now? (understanding of the resources available and current activities)

- Where do I want to be? (the sales targets that have been set)

- How will I get there? (the sales plan)

- How will I know if I am progressing satisfactorily? (the continual measurement)

We can see that once a plan is designed, it will show the salespeople, the sales managers and the senior management team what should be achieved week on week, month on month in order that at the end of the year the objective is met. By being able to see this, they will also be able to measure how well they are progressing towards those targets.

Being able to measure progress has in itself many benefits. It will allow the mangers to:

- See how individual salespeople are performing against their individual plans and therefore take remedial action where necessary, e.g. retraining etc.

- See how the sales force as a whole is progressing towards the plan and take action where required, e.g. increase marketing activity

- Ensure that the resources are adequate and correctly distributed.

A good sales plan is a continuously developing plan that starts with a thorough understanding of the business and its needs. Although sales plans are often for a period of one year, they should take into account the longer-term objectives of the organization. That is, they should consider not only what it wants to achieve in the short term (this year's sales targets), but also what it wants to achieve in the medium and longer term. If this is the case, the sales plan will have the benefit of helping the company to plan for and measure how it will remain competitive and profitable in the future.

10.2 Planning logic

If an organization has not previously had a formalized planning process, implementing one means that they need to manage the behavioural issues and procedural issues that implementation will bring. The first problem to be encountered may well be the lack of acceptance of the planning process itself, especially if the plan is a bottom-up sales plan and the individual sellers are expected to participate fully in the process. Acceptance from senior management is essential if the employees at a lower level are to accept the ideas. (Employees are quick to pick up on which issues are fully supported by the management and which ones are destined to be swallowed up in company politics, never to see the light of day.) Senior management will also need to allocate resource in order to see the planning process through and they will do this only if they are fully supportive of the process.

The organization's commitment to the process, or lack of it, will be instrumental in either implementing the sales planning or sabotaging it before it begins.

Once the agreement and the support are there, the next major task is to start the process. There will in all probability be a number of issues that will need to be taken into account for this to happen.

- The concept of the sales plan must be communicated to all employees, who will be expected to have an input in order that they can understand why it is taking place.

- Some training may be needed so that the people know what to do – at very least they will need some very clear instructions of what to do and how to do it.

- Adequate resources must be put in place to ensure that the planning process can actually occur within the allocated timescale.

- The system must be established so that the ideas and information required can be fed into the planning process once it begins.

- It is probably a good idea to have a 'test run' of the planning process with a small section of the sales force to ensure that any problems are ironed out prior to the main annual sales planning.

- Finally it is important that the sales planning process is tailored to the needs of the organization.

All of the above will take time to put into practice. However, by carefully preparing the introduction of the sales planning process, it is much more likely to have a successful implementation. It should be accepted that it may take two or three years for the organization to perfect the whole process and have it working as they desired.

We have seen the importance of gaining acceptance by senior management to the sales planning process, but the support of the line management is equally important. They will need to provide a great deal of the information required for the plan and will need to encourage their staff to participate fully. Whether their 'buy in' to the process is achieved through training, or by direct involvement and a feeling of participating, failure to achieve their acceptance will severely hamper the success of the plan.

The work involved in preparing a sales plan will involve a great deal of figure work, which many people may find off-putting. This said, financial services salespeople are by their nature highly numerate and are used to their performance being measured against numerical targets. However, in the sales planning process they may need to consider quality as well as quantity, and the company may well need them to consider the long-term benefits for the business as well as short-term gains. The sellers will therefore need very clear instructions as to what the plan is expected to achieve.

Each level within the organization must have a clear understanding of what is expected of it. When the tasks are completed the information will need to be fed upwards. Each level will then have undertaken the planning for its own area with the information being relevant to its own operating environment. Undertaking the sales planning tasks, which will be reasonably time consuming, need not be seen simply as an annual ritual. It should be seen as an on-going task, an integral part of any manager's role.

The planning process for the organization

We saw earlier that the start of any sales planning process had to be the 'Where am I now?' question. It is important that before the actual plans can be designed, the sales manager has a clear understanding of the resources that are available, and the market being competed in. The best way to gain this understanding is to carry out an analysis of the environment in which the plan is to operate.

One of the best ways of achieving this is to carry out a SWOT analysis. We saw in Chapter 4 that as part of the corporate plan and the marketing plan, the senior management will conduct a SWOT analysis in order to decide upon the strategy. Because the sales targets will have been born from the corporate objectives, it will be useful to refer to this. However, the sales manager may well wish to carry out a further analysis concentrating purely on the sales strengths and weaknesses, etc.

Following the analysis stage, the sales manager can then go on to the next stage which is the 'Where do I want to be?' stage. While the obvious answer to this is the achievement of the year's sales targets, there may well be additional things that the organization would like to achieve by the end of the timescale. For example, the sales manager may well state that in addition to the achievement of this year's sales targets, he or she would also want to have a proven capability to sell to a totally new customer segment in preparation for the next year's plans.

Having set clear objectives in addition to the all-important sales targets, the next stage is the 'How do I get there?' question. This is the part that we most commonly know as the sales planning activity because it is the part that shows us how we will achieve what we have set out to do. However, the two previous parts should still be seen as important, as without them the actual planning would be more difficult and less robust.

There are many ways to go about planning the sales activity for a company. The process used will vary enormously depending on the nature of the organization, the type of products sold, the methods of distribution, etc. For example, if the product is sold via direct mail on an execution-only basis, the sales plan is most likely going to be constructed using a 'top down' method of sales planning, i.e. by deciding how much profit is required and working down from there. An example of how this could be done is shown in Figure 10.1.

Figure 10.1: A 'top down' sales planning process

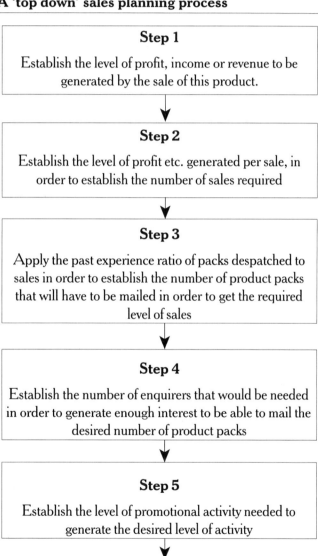

Step 1

Establish the level of profit, income or revenue to be generated by the sale of this product.

Step 2

Establish the level of profit etc. generated per sale, in order to establish the number of sales required

Step 3

Apply the past experience ratio of packs despatched to sales in order to establish the number of product packs that will have to be mailed in order to get the required level of sales

Step 4

Establish the number of enquirers that would be needed in order to generate enough interest to be able to mail the desired number of product packs

Step 5

Establish the level of promotional activity needed to generate the desired level of activity

Step 6

Plan the promotion and sales activity in terms of timing, resources and budgets, etc.

This is probably the simplest possible example of planning sales activity because it relates purely to direct-mail activity and is therefore restrained only by resource such as budget. Where a sales force is involved in the selling process, planning the sales activity will be much more complex because the plans are then restrained not only by such things as budget, but also by capacity issues. The planning process may well therefore need to be more of a 'bottom up' plan considering firstly such things as the number of leads it can generate. The starting point may well therefore be 'how much marketing activity can be undertaken and how much interest will it generate?'

Only when this is known can the salespeople know how many customers they are likely to be asked to see. This will have to be checked against the capacity of the individual salespeople and the sales force as a whole. If there is more interest generated than the sales force can deal with, there are two options:

1. Recruit and train more sellers

2. Reduce the marketing activity

If the planned marketing activity generates less interest than would fully occupy the sales force, again there are options, namely:

1. Increase the level of marketing activity

2. Ask the seller to generate leads for themselves at a branch or individual level

Once the sellers know how many customers they will have the opportunity of selling to, they can start to project their activity and sales. They will be able to project, using past experience, the number of sales they will make from the number of customers they expect to be talking to. If they know the general customer profile they will also be able to project the type of products and services they are likely to sell.

The next stage is to apply the knowledge they have of the customers to estimate the average case size to show how much revenue or income they will generate for the business. If each and every salesperson carries out this activity, each of the individual plans can be collated to show the overall sales plan for the organization.

Figure 10.2: A sales force 'bottom up' sales planning process

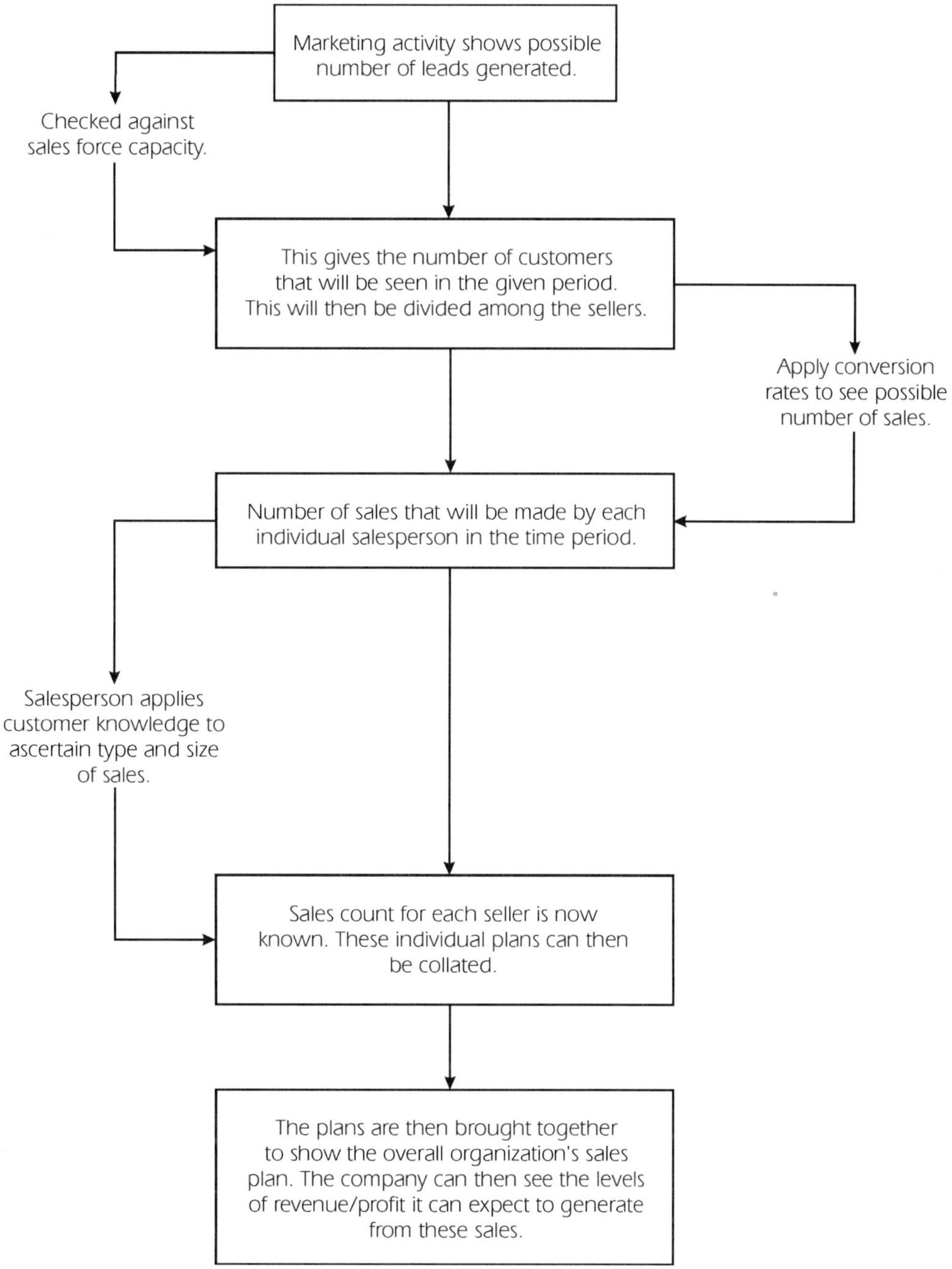

```
                    ┌─────────────────────────────┐
                    │ Marketing activity shows possible │
                    │   number of leads generated.  │
                    └─────────────────────────────┘
   Checked against
   sales force capacity.
                    ┌─────────────────────────────────┐
                    │   This gives the number of customers │
                    │  that will be seen in the given period. │
                    │ This will then be divided among the sellers. │
                    └─────────────────────────────────┘
                                              Apply conversion
                                              rates to see possible
                                              number of sales.
                    ┌──────────────────────────────────┐
                    │ Number of sales that will be made by each │
                    │  individual salesperson in the time period. │
                    └──────────────────────────────────┘
   Salesperson applies
   customer knowledge to
   ascertain type and size
   of sales.
                    ┌──────────────────────────────┐
                    │  Sales count for each seller is now │
                    │  known. These individual plans can then │
                    │          be collated.         │
                    └──────────────────────────────┘
                    ┌──────────────────────────────┐
                    │  The plans are then brought together │
                    │ to show the overall organization's sales │
                    │ plan. The company can then see the levels │
                    │ of revenue/profit it can expect to generate │
                    │          from these sales.    │
                    └──────────────────────────────┘
```

In reality the planning process is likely to be a mixture of 'top down' and 'bottom up' sales planning. There is likely to be some input from each of the individual sellers as to the level of business they expect to produce because this will be needed for the individual branch plan.

Although this can then be taken forward as shown above, there is also likely to be some guidance from the senior management team as to what level of sales is expected. The management will no doubt already have a fairly clear view of the level of profit or activity they want in the coming year, and if the bottom-up plan produces projections that are vastly different this will be unacceptable. There will have to be some reconsideration and some re-forecasting of activity and/or profit in order that the two are compatible.

10.3 Templates for sales plans

When devising a sales plan, rather than starting from scratch each time, and each salesperson finding different ways of planning his or her activity, it may well be easier if the sales manager provides some kind of template for people to complete. The idea of such a template is that it helps individuals to work through the planning process and gives them guidance as to what they should be doing.

Before the template can be constructed, it is essential that the manager has a clear understanding of the current sales process and he or she would therefore benefit from having as much information as possible on such things as:

- Number and value of sales made last year, including the pattern of those sales throughout the year so as to be able to identify trends or seasonal variations.

- Number of sales made per salesperson, including both individual numbers and an average number. He or she may also wish to find similar information regarding competitors' sales forces if possible in order to benchmark the team's performance.

- Number of customers seen by the salespeople in order to achieve the number of sales made last year—again both individual and an average across the sales force. This would probably be most useful if converted to a ratio or percentage—for example, the average salesperson sells to 34% of the customers seen, or our salespeople sell to one in four of the people they talk to.

- The number of calls or interviews that the salespeople have been doing per day. It will also be important to understand the maximum number that it is possible for an individual to carry out so as not to set unrealistic targets.

- The number of products bought by each customer, i.e. do they only buy a mortgage or do they also buy a current account or a credit card, for example? This cross-sell ratio is likely to be of utmost importance for companies that are attempting to move to a relationship marketing environment rather than a transactional basis, and for those whose strategy is one of customer retention and loyalty building.

- Any difference between the number of appointments made and the number of appointments attended. If there is a drop-off rate, i.e. not all customers keep their appointments, then by knowing this the sales manager will be able to plan for an excess of appointments over and above those actually needed.

- If the salespeople get leads or prospects from more than one source, e.g. they could get customers from both marketing activity and from referrals from the branch staff, the manager may want to compare the success rates achieved for leads from different sources.

- The manager will also be interested in the average cost per sale made by salespeople in order to plan the spend that will be needed.

- The average case size will be of interest to the manager, both on an individual basis and as an average for the sales force as a whole. Again if there were more than one source of business for the salespeople, it would be useful to know if there is a difference in this figure for the two sources.

- Number of salespeople, recruitment plans and expected turnover will help the sales manager to plan the number of sales, etc.

- If the salespeople sell over the telephone there will different versions of this information needed, for example the manager would want to know such things as average call time, number of calls taken for each sale made, average amount of a salesperson's time actually spent taking calls, etc.

Once the manager has all the necessary information, he or she can start the process of planning and devising templates. We have already looked at the different planning methods that can be used, i.e. top down or bottom up. For the moment we will concentrate on a top-down process and look at the templates that could be used for this. Before devising the template let us remind ourselves briefly of the process.

Step 1   Establish sales targets for the company as a whole.

Step 2   Divide by number of salespeople to establish individual sales targets.

Step 3   Divide by average income per sale to give number of sales required per consultant for the year.

Step 4   Divide by 43 (number of weeks worked each year) to give number of sales per week required by each salesperson.

Step5   Multiply by the ratio of appointments to sale to show number of appointments the salesperson will need to carry out each week.

Step 6   Increase by the average number of cancellations experienced to show the number of appointments they will need to book each week.

Step 7   Multiply by call success rate to show the number of telephone calls etc. they will need to make in order to book this many appointments.

Figure 10.3: Target template

Month	Jan	Feb	March	April	May
1. No. of weeks worked this month allowing					
2. Annual target (premium income)					
3. Target per month (depending on weeks worked)					
4. Consultant's own average case size (based on past experience and product mix)					
5. No. of sales required (based on monthly target divided by average case size)					
6 Consultant's own conversion rate					
7 Number of appointments needed each month (based on number of sales divided by conversion rate)					
8 Consultant's own lead to sale conversion rate					
9 Number of leads needed (based on appointments divided by conversion rate)					

Figure 10.4: Example of completed template

Month	Jan	Feb	March	April	May
1. No. of weeks worked this month allowing	3	3	4	4	4
2. Annual target (premium income)	◄————		£240,000	————►	
3. Target per month (depending on weeks worked)	£17,000	£17,000	£24,000	£24,000	£24,000
4. Consultant's own average case size (based on past experience and product mix)	◄————		£2,575	————►	
5. No. of sales required (based on monthly target divided by average case size)	7	7	10	10	10
6 Consultant's own conversion rate	◄————		31%	————►	
7 Number of appointments needed each month (based on number of sales divided by conversion rate)	23	23	33	33	33
8 Consultant's own lead to sale conversion rate	◄————		15%	————►	
9 Number of leads needed (based on appointments divided by conversion rate)	154	154	220	220	220

For activity where there is no seller involved or where there is advertising involved at the outset, the marketing or campaign manager will want to plan the activity in order that he or she can be sure that:

- They have sufficient budget available
- The activity is viable
- There are sufficient people in the call centre to answer the queries
- There are sufficient sales people available if the customers require appointments.

Campaign activity can be planned in a similar way—that is both top down or bottom up. The campaign manager could be given a budget and told to attract as much business as possible, or he or she could be given a target amount of business, and the plan would show the level of budget and resource required.

Let us look at the steps involved in creating a campaign plan on the basis that we have been given a target level of business.

Step 1   Establish the campaign target.

Step 2   Divide by average income per sale to give number of sales required throughout the campaign.

Step 3   Estimate a conversion rate from enquiry to appointment.

Step 4   Divide required number of sales by conversion rate to give the required number of appointments.

Step5   Estimate a conversion rate from appointment to sale.

Step 6   Divide required number of appointments by conversion rate to give the required number of enquiries.

Step 7   Estimate the number of responses that will be generated from each media source.

Step 8   Plan media to ensure sufficient number of leads are generated.

The templates used would differ depending on the nature of the campaign and the way in which the business is written, i.e. one stage or two-stage mailing, or with the involvement of a salesperson. There is an example template below. The template is for a mortgage campaign, where the product is advertised in the national and local press, and then the customer is asked to book an appointment with a branch mortgage adviser. The mortgage adviser then sells the mortgage and the associated products such as buildings and contents insurance.

Figure 10.5: Campaign template

Required level of business for the campaign	X
Average case size per sale	X
Therefore number of mortgage sales required	X
Number of cross-sales required	X
Cross-sales ratio	X
Appointment to mortgage sale conversion rate	X
Number of appointments required	X
Enquiry to appointment conversion rate	X
Number of enquiries required	X

Figure 10.6: Example of completed campaign template

Required level of business for the campaign	£50,000,000
Average case size per sale	£37,500
Therefore number of mortgage sales required	1,334
Number of cross-sales required	1,334
Cross-sales ratio	100%
Appointment to mortgage sale conversion rate	25%
Number of appointments required	5,336
Enquiry to appointment conversion rate	12%
Number of enquiries required	44,466

In reality, the plan would be far more complex. The campaign would span a certain amount of time, e.g. ten weeks, and the plan would reflect the activity in each week and would need to allow for the time lag between enquiry and appointment and between appointment and sale.

Once the campaign manager has completed the templates and reached the point where he or she knows how many enquiries are required the activity that will lead to the generation of those enquiries can be planned.

Let us look at a template that could be used for planning a campaign that involved newspaper advertising and radio advertisements.

Figure 10.7: Media template

Press

Publication	Size	Creative	Date	Expected enquiries

Radio

Station	Size	Creative	Date	Expected enquiries

Grand Total

Figure 10.8: Example of completed media template

Press

Publication	Size	Creative	Date	Expected enquiries
The Daily Telegraph	½ page	A in mono	3rd	210
Daily Mail	½ page	A in mono	3rd	180
The Guardian	½ page	A in mono	5th	300
The Times	25 x 4	B in mono	5th	150
The Sunday Times	25 x 4	B in mono	7th	160
Mail on Sunday	¼ page	A in colour	7th	150
The Sunday Telegraph	¼ page	A in mono	7th	130
Daily Mail	25 x 4	B in colour	10th	130
The Times	½ page	B in colour	10th	350
The Sunday Times	½ page	A in colour	14th	330
Mail on Sunday	½ page	B in colour	14th	280

Radio

Station	Size	Creative	Date	Expected enquiries
Classic FM	30 secs	A	7th	75
Broadlands FM	30 secs	A	7th	105
Classic FM	30 secs	A	14th	80
Broadlands FM	30 secs	A	14th	120
Grand Total				2,750

10.4   Interaction of the elements of the plan

Another benefit of ensuring there is a complete and detailed sales plan is that it will allow the individual or the campaign manager to see the interaction between the different elements of the plan. The individual salesperson who plans activity in line with the templates we looked at earlier, can clearly see the way that enquiries lead to appointments and how appointments become sales, etc. This will allow him or her to look at different 'what if' scenarios and see the effect on the overall plan.

For example

'What if I did one extra appointment per week?'

By following the template and reworking the numbers in the plan, the salesperson can clearly see how the extra three or four appointments per month would convert to sales, and how this in turn would convert to premium income towards target.

'*What if my conversion rate increased by 5%?*'

Again, by understanding how the plan is put together and the relationship between the elements, the salesperson would be able to see the increase in the level of premium income generated by increasing the conversion rate. Alternatively he or she could see the reduction in the number of interviews and the number of enquiries to achieve target, if the conversion increased.

Similarly when planning campaigns, the campaign manager needs to understand how the plans are constructed and the interaction of each of the sections in order to manage campaigns and make important decisions about them.

For example

'*What if I sold products with a higher case size?*'

The campaign manager can rework the template and see the effect off having sales of a higher case size and see how fewer cases needed to be sold to meet the target, and how much less lead generation would be needed. He or she can then investigate the type of customer required in order to achieve the higher case size and adjust the media schedule appropriately. The manager can then directly compare the viability of attempting to sell more cases of a lower case size, or fewer cases of a greater case size.

Understanding the elements of the plan and how they interact will also help in the management of the campaign throughout its duration. For example, if part way into the plan it can be seen that the conversion rate from enquiry to sale is better or worse than expected, the manager can act upon this. He or she can use the templates and an understanding of the process to see the effect this difference is going to have on the final result. This will allow reworking of the plan using the new conversion rate and adjustment of the enquiry-generation activity, or adjustment of the projections of the expected levels of business.

10.5   Controlling and monitoring the sales plan

We looked earlier in this chapter at the benefits of a thorough and robust planning process and saw that one of the benefits was the ability to monitor performance on a regular basis and see clearly the progress being made against plan. We have also seen the importance of accurate and up-to-date *management information* (MI) if this is to happen.

If the company is to be able to control the plan it must have the backing of senior management. Their influence will be needed if the salespeople are to report their progress regularly. Some companies have sophisticated technology which may be able to produce information on the number of sales made and such things as the average case size. However, to some greater or lesser degree, there will always be an element of salesperson input into the monitoring and salespeople therefore need to be shown that supplying accurate information is extremely important.

The information will be used on a regular basis in order to make decisions both on an individual and company basis. This means that the information regarding the progress of the plan will need to be supplied regularly. For individual sellers and campaign managers, information supplied weekly will probably be appropriate. The senior management team will probably require information to be presented on a monthly basis.

The first step to monitoring the sales plan is to decide exactly what is to be monitored. We have seen how each element of the plan interacts with the others, for example how a shortage of leads will turn into a shortage of appointments and ultimately a shortage of business. Although ultimately the company is interested in the amount of business sold, because of this interaction it is likely that the managers will want to monitor all the key factors involved in actually reaching the final sale. It is likely that the manager will determine, before the introduction of the plan, what these key indicators are and then monitor those.

For example, if we look at our earlier example template and imagine our sales plan was built around this, the sales manager may well decide that the key indicators are as follows:

- Number of enquiries generated
- Number of appointments carried out
- Number of sales made
- Cost per enquiry
- Cost per appointment
- Cost per sale
- Average case size
- Number of salespeople at or above target

The individual seller will want to monitor his or her own performance. The branch manager will want to monitor the performance of all salespeople against their individual plans. The senior managers will want to measure the performance of the company as a whole against the business plan. Therefore, several different reports may be needed. These will start with the individual reports of the salespeople, and then these will be collated to form a report of the overall progress towards the plan.

Let us look first at how an individual salesperson may monitor a plan. Probably the best way to do this would be to simply measure all the actual numbers against the planned numbers, as shown here:

Figure 10.9: Monthly monitoring

Month	Feb Plan	Actual	YTD plan	YTD actual
Target per month	£17,000	£18,500	£34,000	£33,275
Consultant's own average case size	£2,575	£1680	£2575	£2080
Number of sales required	10	11	17	16
Consultant's own conversion rate from appointment to sale	31%	30%	31%	33%
Number of appointments needed each month	33	37	56	48
Consultant's own lead to sale conversion rate	15%	12%	15%	12%
Number of leads needed	220	308	374	400

As well as the individuals' monitoring, the sales manager and the senior management team will look for a very similar report to be produced for the sales force as a whole. The report will show the company target and progress towards it, average national case size and number of sales made by the organization, etc. This will allow them to see the progress the company is making towards its annual plan and allow them to spot trends and take appropriate action.

For example, they may find that the number of appointments the consultants are doing each week is falling and they can then address this issue by planning and conducting additional lead-generation activity. Alternatively, if the conversion rate from appointment to sale suddenly falls, this could indicate that the product is less attractive than it should be and the managers can investigate this and take the necessary action.

As well as the weekly/monthly figures, the managers also need to see trends, which could be shown in the following format. The graph below shows the trend in the average case size, and something similar could be produced for each of the key elements in the plan, such as number of appointments, number of products sold, etc.

Figure 10.10: Trend in average case size

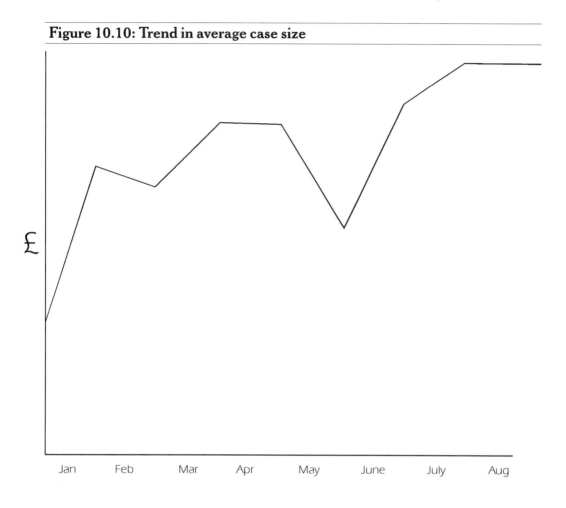

While this shows averages and is useful for spotting trends, we must remember that the entire sales plan cannot be managed on averages, and within these figures there will be some consultants whose case size is above plan and some whose case size is well below plan. There may well be local factors that explain the differences, and this is why it is important that the individual salespeople are monitored and managed closely by their own branch managers.

There are also other factors that the senior managers need to be aware of to ensure that the overall sales plan is achieved. For example, the sales plan may be reliant on having a desired number of salespeople within the branches or a certain number of counter staff selling the products. If so the managers also need to ensure that this is the case, and therefore among the regular updates they receive should be information regarding the number of branch advisers or counter staff who are trained to sell the products. For example:

Figure 10.11: Number of counter staff trained to sell cash ISAs

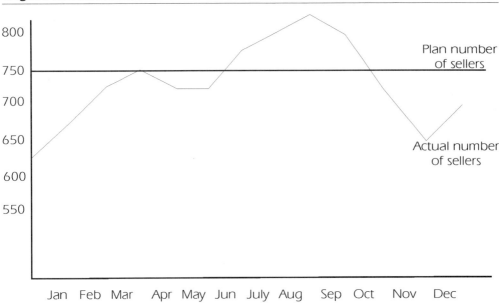

The results of individual campaigns also need to be controlled and monitored in a similar way. Again the best way to do this is to ensure that there is regular and accurate management information regarding the key elements of the plan. Let us look at the plan we put together for our advertising campaign and see how we could monitor the results and therefore measure the performance against plan.

The campaign was intended to attract mortgage business and involved press advertising. The customer was then invited to the branch, where the branch mortgage adviser would complete the sale.

As the campaign was planned to last for only ten weeks, the campaign manager would require information on a weekly basis to monitor progress and judge the eventual outcome. The information could be presented as follows:

Figure 10.12: Monitoring the mortgage campaign (week 2 example)

	Week 2	To date	Campaign Plan
Mortgage business written	£3,287,060	£11,248,412	£50,000,000
Average case size per sale	£46,958	£51,836	£37,500
Therefore number of mortgage sales	70	217	1,334
Number of cross-sales	67	212	1,334
Cross-sales ratio	96%	98%	100%
Appointment to mortgage sale conversion rate	15%	19%	25%
Number of appointments	465	1,143	5,336
Enquiry to appointment conversion rate	10%	13%	12%
Number of enquiries	4649	8792	44,466

10.6   Sale of regulated products

Most financial services providers deal with a mix of both regulated and non-regulated business. By this we mean that they sell products regulated by the Financial Services Authority or by the Investment Managers Regulatory Authority, as well as those that are not. Regulated products include such things as pension plans, some life assurance policies, unit trusts, and ISAs. There are rules and regulations that apply to the advertising of any product, but these regulated products have additional rules surrounding the way in which they can be advertised and sold.

These requirements cover such things as:

● The wording that can be used in advertisements.

● The comparisons that can be made with other products.

● The amount of product information that must be given in an advertisement.

● The way in which the benefits of the product are presented in the sales literature, including the way in which the key features of the product are explained to the customer.

● The amount and detail of the information that must be given to a customer before he or she can buy the product off the page.

● The information that must be given by the salesperson before he or she can sell the product, including such things as disclosing commission or the cost of advice.

- The way in which the salesperson explains the need for the product, i.e. the reasons why he or she is recommending the customer buy.

- The amount and type of information that a customer should receive following a purchase.

- The customer's right to have a change of mind within a short time of having made the purchase.

These are just a few examples of the things that must be carefully considered if the company is selling regulated products but do not necessarily apply to the sale of non-regulated products. It means that a campaign manager or sales manger planning for this type of activity would need to be fully aware of all the rules and regulations, and ensure that all of the advertising, sales literature and processes complied with the rules.

Because the requirements are onerous and the penalties for getting it wrong severe, most companies have strict procedures for ensuring that the rules are adhered to. All companies selling regulated products have a compliance department whose role is to understand and keep up to date with all of the regulator's requirements. They then interpret the rules and ensure that they are applied to all the activity undertaken by the company's marketing and sales functions.

The compliance department is probably sub-divided, and has a team of people who comment specifically on advertising and campaign material. This means that campaign managers dealing with regulated products need to ensure that, throughout the planning stage of the campaign, they are continually consulting the compliance department to ensure that everything they are planning falls within the rules. They will need the compliance department to agree all the advertising material, as well as the product literature, the sales material and the processes. This may well mean that for regulated products the planning stage of the campaign is more detailed and more time consuming.

11

Campaign Selling

After reading this chapter you should

- Be aware of the constituents for success in campaign selling
- Understand the process and benefits of postal selling
- Understand the process and benefits of telephone selling
- Be able to compare and contrast local and national campaign selling
- Know how to write a campaign brief
- Be able to identify target audiences for campaign selling
- Understand how different approaches are required for different target audiences
- Know how to measure the success of a campaign

11.1   Campaign success

When a marketing manager is planning a campaign it goes without saying that he or she will want to ensure the campaign is a success. If this is to be the case, there are several things that must be considered well in advance of the start of the campaign.

Objectives

The first thing to consider is the objective of the campaign. The marketing manager can measure if the campaign was a success only if there is an objective against which to measure the results. The campaign will be carried out to support one of the marketing objectives and therefore the objectives of the specific campaigns follow on from the marketing objectives.

For example, one of the marketing objectives could have been

> To attract 10,000 new credit-card holders from socio-economic groups A and B by the end of the year.

In order to do this the marketing manager is likely to have a range of activity planned, one of which may well be a postal campaign or series of postal campaigns. As the campaign falls

147

directly from the marketing objective, the campaign objective will follow it closely. For example

To attract 2,000 new credit-card holders from socio-economic groups A and B at an acquisition cost of less than £30 per customer.

It is useful to remember at this point that any objective set should meet the following criteria. It should be precise, so that there can be no arguments later about exactly what the objectives were. It should be realistic and achievable. There is little point in setting an objective that will never be achieved. While objectives should be stretching and challenging, there should also some realism about them, otherwise the campaign is destined to fail and this is de-motivating for everybody concerned. Any objective set must be measurable. The reason for setting an objective is so that when the campaign is over, the manager can assess the success. For this to happen there must be clear measurements that can be compared and contrasted.

The objectives then need to be clearly communicated to everybody who is working on the campaign so that they are known and understood. Only if everybody concerned knows what is expected of him or her will the campaign have a real chance of achieving what is required.

Of course the objective does not always need to be one of sales. There are several other reasons why a marketing manager may initiate a campaign. It could be to raise awareness of a service, to build customer loyalty, or to increase brand awareness and build brand values, for example.

Marketing mix

Once a clear objective has been set, the next step is to ensure that the marketing mix is properly planned for the campaign. For the campaign to be a success the managers must have considered all of the elements, i.e:

- Product
- Price
- Promotion
- Place
- People
- Process

They firstly need to consider the product or service that they are to offer. Let us take as an example our campaign to attract new credit-card customers. The precise nature of the product being offered needs to be that which is most suitable to those customers or prospects being targeted. We know we want to attract customers from socio-economic groups A and B. This includes people with good jobs, high incomes and who are fairly sophisticated in terms of financial services matters. Research may well prove that these people are frequent users of credit cards, but use them for convenience rather than for the actual credit.

The campaign manager may well decide to offer a gold card to these people and offer a relatively high credit limit. As these are likely to be people who already have at least one credit card, the product offering will need to be sufficiently attractive to persuade them to move away from their current provider.

One way of encouraging them to do this would be through the pricing. If the campaign is to be success them it is essential that whatever is being offered is being offered at the right price. As far as credit cards are concerned the price relates to the annual fee and the interest rates charged. The group of customers we are targeting here will be well aware of the prices charged and will compare what they are being offered with what they have already.

Of course we are not implying that for a campaign to be a success the price must always be the lowest. It should be deemed to be good value for what is being offered. Customers are often willing to pay more for what they consider to be a better product or service. However the price must always be considered in relation to the product being offered, the customer being targeted and the price of the competitor's product if the customers are likely to shop around.

Having made sure we are going to offer the right product at the right price, we now need to ensure that the correct methods of promotion and distribution are selected. Again these should be selected on the basis of the product being sold and the customers being targeted.

Let us look first at the method of promotion. Our credit cards could be promoted via displays in the branches and branch windows, in newspaper advertisements, by direct mail or on the Internet, to name just a few. Each option needs to be assessed against the target market to decide on its chances of success. For example, the branch may be discounted as a method of promotion if it were discovered that the majority of the target market prefers not to visit a branch, but currently uses telephone or home banking services. Newspapers could be used, but the marketing manager would need to carefully select the newspapers whose readership most closely matched the profile of the required customers.

Again the distribution method selected will depend on the product and the target market's preference for dealing with the organization. If the product is simple then it can probably be sold over the telephone, or by the customer filling in forms that are sent through the post. If the product is very complex it may need to be sold by salespeople in the branches who will be able to offer explanations and answer questions. If this is the case, another element of the mix comes into play. The people selected to sell the product must be selected with both the nature of the product and the customer in mind.

Again the essential thing to remember if the campaign is to be a success is that the methods of promotion and distribution selected must be those that complement the product and the target market.

Finally, to ensure that the campaign has the best possible chance of success, the marketing manager should make sure that all the processes for launching the campaign and handling the responses are in place and working smoothly before the launch.

Campaign management

A successful campaign needs good campaign management. A good campaign manager ensures that all of the elements of the marketing mix are correct as discussed above. He or she will manage everything necessary for the launch of the campaign, oversee it throughout, monitor responses once the campaign is underway and make changes to any of the above factors throughout the term of the campaign if necessary. A good campaign manager will have excellent marketing skills, a sound knowledge of the industry and the products, an understanding of the customers and their needs, a good eye for detail, and a working knowledge of the organization and its processes.

Management information

Another essential item is good management information. This will ensure that the campaign manager has the information required to judge whether or not the campaign was a success. It will also help in planning future campaigns if the manager can look back and see the results from previous campaigns and see what worked and what did not. Good management information can also be used to make amendments to the campaign as it progresses.

The detail of the information required depends on the ways in which the campaign manager wishes to use the information. For our credit-card campaign, we obviously want to know the number of card applications received in order that we can judge the campaign to be successful. However let us say that the campaign was conducted with a mix of newspaper advertisements and targeted direct mail. We may well also want to have accurate up-to-the-minute information on the following:

- *Response rates per advertisement.* This enables the campaign manager to see which papers and which size advertisements are the most successful and adjust the media schedule accordingly.

- *Cost per response.* This gives some early indication as to whether the cost per sale objective is going to be met.

- *Response rates to certain direct mailings.* Again this helps the campaign manager to judge the success of mailing to different target groups and adjust the remaining plans if necessary.

- *Conversion rates from response to purchase.* Early indicators of this conversion rate help the manager to predict the number of sales that can be expected throughout the campaign. It also indicates the likely cost per sale.

The campaign manger needs to decide during the planning stage what information he or she needs and ensure that everything is in place to provide it.

11.2 Postal selling

Most financial services organizations use the post as a distribution method in one form or another and a great number of campaigns are conducted through the post every year. In fact most campaign use the post as a part of their activity.

Most people are used to receiving offers and information through their letterboxes from companies that they deal with, and some that they do not. A marketing manager calls this activity direct mail; all too often the recipient calls it junk mail. The challenge for the marketeer is to ensure the item sent through the post does not get classed as such.

People consider things to be 'junk mail' if they contain an offer or information that not only have they not requested, but that is of no interest to them. For example, the individual who lives in a basement flat but receives some mail with an offer about conservatories will just throw it straight in the bin and begrudge the time spent opening it. The way to avoid the same happening to our mailing is to ensure one thing:

Very careful targeting is essential.

If you want customers to take the time and effort to open and read the information you have sent them, and then respond to that information, the mailing campaign must be very carefully targeted. People will only read something they have been sent if it is of interest to them. They will only respond to that mailing if it is relevant to them. For example, a campaign manager who is undertaking a postal campaign in order to attempt to sell personal pensions would need to ensure that the mailing was not sent to customers who were already in occupational pension schemes. This is because these people would already have their retirement planning in place and would therefore be totally uninterested in the contents of the letter.

Obviously the more targeted the recipients are, the greater the chances of the postal campaign being a success. The pension campaign could be further targeted by including only people within a certain age band, who had a certain level of salary, who had a set level of disposable income and who had ideally shown some previous interest in planning their retirement. While it may not be possible to get all of the above information we need to bear in mind that the more targeted the mailing is, the less chance there is that it will be considered to be junk mail and immediately thrown away.

There are several ways in which the post can be used in a marketing campaign. Let us look at a few.

- *To impart information.* If the campaign manager's objective was to raise awareness of a product or service, or to raise brand awareness, then telling people about the brand or the product via a letter to their homes may well be a method of achieving the objective.

- *To sell a product or service.* Sometimes the campaign manager will mail everything the customer needs to receive in order that he or she can actually go ahead and buy something. The information sent will contain the details of the product as well as an application form and method of payment. This one-stage approach may work well for the less complex products such as current accounts, credit cards, personal loans, etc.

- *To raise the customer's interest.* The mailing must interest them sufficiently to prompt them to request further information about a product or service. This further information will then be sent and will contain the information and items needed for the customer to be able to make a purchase. This two-stage approach is most often used for more complex products for which the information needed to make a purchase is more lengthy and therefore may be off-putting if received totally unprompted.

- *To encourage a customer to visit the branch* to see a member of staff to discuss the company's services. Many customers never actually visit a branch of their bank or building society, and therefore any branch campaign informing people about products and services will not be seen by them. The campaign manager may wish to use direct mail to try and reach these people and encourage them to have a discussion with one of the organization's salespeople.

- *To encourage people to make a telephone call to the company.* If the organization is selling motor insurance, for example, it may decide to mail people to encourage them to telephone the company for a quotation the next time their motor insurance is up for renewal.

- *To seek further information.* The campaign could be to gather further information about customers' finances and preferences. Many companies are keen to enhance the information that they store on their databases in order that future campaigns can be more accurately targeted.

These are just a few examples of the many uses that campaign managers will find for the post. Often they are not used in isolation but form a part of an overall contact strategy that may well include telephone, branch-based displays and advertisements, etc.

11.3   Telephone selling

Another method a campaign manager may choose to communicate with his target audience is by using the telephone. When contacting prospective or existing customers by telephone it is just as important to ensure that they are accurately targeted as it is with the postal method. The telephone can be used in a variety of ways.

- To *cold call* customers in an attempt to make an appointment for the customer with one of the company's sellers.

- To find out further information about a prospect, prior to sending out information in the post.

- To sell the customer a product or service over the telephone. There are some products where this is a viable method of sale, but for regulated products there are restrictions as to the way in which business must be conducted if the contact was initiated by the company over the telephone.

- To follow up the issue of a one-stage or two-stage mailing. If a prospective customer has been sent some information in the post, the campaign manager may wish to have people telephone those customers and encourage them to read and complete the information. This is a tactic often used by marketing managers because it has a positive effect on the number of people who do respond.

There are several advantages and disadvantages to including telephone contacts as part of a marketing campaign. The advantages are:

- It can prove to be a very cost-effective method of contact. Often the cost of a call is less than the cost of a letter or mail pack.

- The response is instant, whereas with the postal approach there are much greater timescales for the letter to be prepared, distributed, read and responded to by the customer. For this reason it can be extremely useful where timescales are tight.

- If used in conjunction with mailings it can greatly improve the response rates.

The disadvantages are:

- The database may not hold telephone numbers for all customers, and if trying to source telephone numbers, many customers may be ex-directory, making them unreachable.

- It means employing people to work outside of the traditional office hours. Many of the prospects work during the day and ware therefore reachable only in the evenings.

- Many people screen out calls by using their answer machines, and therefore the actual number of people you can contact may well only be as high as about 50% of those you initially targeted.

- Many people find unsolicited telephone calls intrusive, especially when called in their homes in the evenings. Again the way to reduce this is to ensure that what you are offering them is relevant and of interest. Otherwise they will consider it only as a slightly more intrusive version of junk mail.

The telephone can prove an excellent method of communicating with new and existing customers provided that it is used with the type of customers who is happy to deal over the telephone, and that the offer is of interest.

11.4 Local and national campaigns

A marketing campaign can be carried out on either a national or a local basis. There are benefits as well as drawbacks to both. We will now take a brief look at each including the circumstances in which they may be used and the way the campaigns would differ from each other.

National campaigns

- Would be used to support a national marketing objective or corporate objective.

- Would be used for large-scale campaigns where the organization wished to attract a large number of respondents with no geographical preference.

- Would be suitable for such things as a brand awareness campaign.

- Has the benefit of consistency, as people would see the same message being communicated wherever they are.

- Could use a wide variety of media for communicating with the target audience, such as national television or radio advertising, national newspaper advertisements, a national branch campaign, direct mail, poster campaign, inserts, etc., to name just a few.

- A national campaign would benefit from economies of scale.

Local campaigns

- Would be used to support branch objectives and to assist in the achievement of branch or individual objectives.

- Would be used where the company wished to attract customers in a particular location, either because of their profile, or because they have specific needs that can be met by the benefits of the product or service being offered.

- Local campaigns can be used to test the effectiveness of a particular campaign before it is carried out on a national basis.

- Running a campaign on a local basis will allow it to be tailored to the precise needs of the potential customers in that particular area.

- A locally-run campaign may need to use different methods of communication. National television, newspaper and radio advertising would not be suitable. However the campaign could include such things as boards and flyers in the local branches, mailings to specific postcode areas, leaflet drops, and advertising in local papers.

- Running a campaign on a purely local basis will allow the area manager to conduct the activity at a time that fits best with the other activities in his or her particular branches, rather than having to accept the timings decided by the marketing manager at head office.

11.5   Writing a campaign brief

Having decided to undertake a campaign in order to promote and sell a product or service, it is usual for the marketing manager to employ the services of a specialist marketing agency. The company may have one agency that it uses to regularly produce all of its campaign material, or it may select a different agency for each piece of work it undertakes.

The first step in the campaign planning is therefore to write a campaign brief for the agency. The purpose of the campaign brief is to explain to the agency exactly what the company is trying to achieve, and how it wishes to go about achieving those results. It also outlines exactly the role that the agency is expected to play.

If the company selects a different agency for each campaign that it runs, it may well decide to give the campaign brief to more than one agency, and then invite each of them to 'pitch' for the business by presenting their campaign ideas. The brief provided may vary depending on the nature and size of the campaign, but would always follow roughly the outline given below.

Introduction

The brief is likely to start with a short introduction explaining what the document is and its purpose. The introduction may also contain a contents list of what is contained throughout the brief.

About the company

If the agency has not previously worked for the company it is useful to give it an overview of the company, the markets in which it operates, the products it sells and the type of campaigns and promotional work it has previously undertaken. This will give the agency some background information on which to base its ideas, although it will probably undertake some research of its own. This section also needs to give information about such things as the company's brand values as these will need to be supported by any advertising. It should also contain details of any corporate guidelines that need to be adhered to.

Marketing objective

The reason for the campaign will stem from one of the objectives stated within the marketing plan, and it therefore follows that the briefing should start by outlining what that objective is. For example, the marketing objective may be something like:

To double our market share of personal pension business over the next two years.

The campaign objective will be born from this marketing objective.

The campaign objective

The brief will then go on to explain what the objective of the campaign is, i.e. the criteria against which it will be measured in order to determine if it has been a success or not. This objective could be an amount of business, it could be a certain number of contacts, or it could simply be to build awareness of a product or service and enhance the brand. For example:

> *The campaign must*
>
> ● *Create impact, and raise awareness of the bank as a personal pension provider.*
>
> ● *Promote the benefits of the pension product.*
>
> ● *Educate the customers as to the benefits of retirement provision.*
>
> ● *Provide 4,000 leads for sales consultants to contact regarding this product.*
>
> ● *Result in 1,500 personal pension sales.*

Target audience

The brief will then explain the type of customer that the campaign should be aimed at. This will enable the agency to ensure that the communications are targeted at the correct level and that the methods of communication they select are appropriate. For example:

> *The customers we should be targeting are both male and female, aged ideally between 30 and 55 (although the product is available to a wider range of ages). They should have an income of at least £15,000 and not currently belong to a company pension scheme. They are likely to be professional singles, couples with no children, or couples whose children are older.*

The product

The next stage in writing the campaign brief is to ensure that the agency is aware of the product, what it is, what it can do, and what the customer benefits are. It will also need to be aware of any restrictions the product has. Probably the easiest way to do this is to give a summary of the product in the brief and to attach a copy of all of the product literature, such as terms and conditions, as an appendix.

Distribution

The next step is to explain the methods of distribution. The campaign will most likely attempt to contact potential customers and communicate a chosen message to them. However it is important that before the campaign is designed, the agency understands how the customer can purchase the product, as this will influence both the message and the designs. The distribution could be via a branch network, through third-party brokers, or directly from the provider via the telephone, for example. Whatever the distribution method is, it must be clearly stated in the brief in order that the campaign is geared towards getting the customer to take the required action.

The competition

The next step is to outline who the competition is, i.e. other organizations who will be attempting to reach the same people to offer similar products to those being promoted by the campaign. This will give the campaign designer a feel of what is currently being promoted, and what is successfully attracting customers. Although it would be usual to include in a brief a list of competitors, the agency and campaign designer are likely to conduct their own research into the marketplace and the competition.

USP

If the product or service has a unique selling point, i.e. it offers the customer something that is not available from any of the competitor products, then this must obviously be pointed out in the campaign brief. Any USP will be an excellent message to convey to customers and ensure that this advertising stands out from that of the competition. However, the financial services industry is highly competitive and the level of regulation imposed means that there is little opportunity for providers to establish a true USP. Any product or service differentiation achieved is often only temporary, as other companies will always be quick to follow suit. Therefore if the company does feel that it has something unique to offer the customer it is essential that it is highlighted and that the campaign design promotes this point strongly.

Key messages

The brief should also contain some guidance as to what the marketing manager considers to be the key messages he or she wishes the campaign to communicate to customers. These messages will depend on the product or service being provided, the nature of the need they are designed to satisfy and the profile of the customer who is expected to receive the message. They will also need to fit with the overall brand values of the company and the corporate objectives outlined in the corporate plan. An example of key messages is given below.

Key messages

- *The product is very keenly priced.*
- *It is easy to buy.*
- *It is a product that most of our customers need but many have not yet bought.*

Overall the offering should be positioned as being a sensible, straightforward quality product giving financial security in later life, all offered by a name you can trust.

Deliverables

The next stage in writing the creative brief is to highlight to the agency exactly what is expected of it, i.e. what it needs to deliver. It may be that the agency is expected to recommend the best way of conveying the message to the potential customer, or it may be that the marketing team has a very clear view of how it expects the campaign to be executed and can therefore list exactly what is needed. Either way, whatever is expected needs to very clearly specified. For example

> *We require a promotional campaign which is to include branch advertising, newspaper advertising, direct mail and PR. You are expected to deliver the following:*
>
> ● *A strong consumer message.*
>
> ● *A series of three posters for use in branch displays.*
>
> ● *An A5 flyer for use in branch display areas.*
>
> ● *Two newspaper advertisements for use in the national press.*
>
> ● *A fulfilment pack consisting of a product brochure, terms and conditions, and an application form.*
>
> ● *A mailing pack consisting of brochure, terms and conditions, and application form for mailing to existing customers of the company.*
>
> ● *Recommendations for PR activity.*

Timing

The agency must then be given timescales, showing it when it is expected to have this material available, together with any key milestones.

Budget

The brief should also contain details of the budget available. This will show not only how much the agency can expect to be paid for the work that it does, but also how much money is available for such things as press and direct mail. The amount of money available will dictate many things about the campaign, for example the size of the advertisements and therefore how much information they can contain and whether they can be colour or black and white.

This is a just a guide to writing a campaign brief. Each company and probably each marketing manager will have their own style and their own approach. How much information it contains will depend on the nature of the promotion and the knowledge of the person who is to use the brief.

Identifying target audiences

If the marketing manager is to undertake a campaign and ensure it is a success, then one of the most vital elements of the planning is selecting the right people to target. We have touched on this briefly when looking at the constituents for success, but now will examine this matter in a little more detail.

The target audience obviously needs to be selected largely on the basis of the product or service being offered. By examining the nature of the product and the need it fulfils we can make a judgement about the type of customers who are most likely to purchase it and target those. If the product is one that the company has not previously sold it may need to conduct research in order to ensure that it has correctly assessed the prospective market. If the product is one that has previously been sold by the company, then it may decide to profile the customers who are currently buying the product and target similar customers in the campaign.

When profiling existing customers the campaign manager will be able to build up a customer profile. This will tell him or her what to look for in potential new customers. For example, it will say if the existing customers are predominantly male or female, what socio-economic grouping they belong to, what age they are, and what buying behaviour they display. The manager will be able to see the income range of the existing customers and their level of disposable income.

Another piece of information, which may be useful when selecting a target audience, is to find out if there has been any link between product holdings. For example, it may be found that existing current-account holders have been shown to be more likely to apply for a credit card from you than have existing mortgage holders. It may be that there is some direct link between the number of existing products held and the customer's propensity to reply to a further product offering.

Once the manager has built a profile of the target market, he or she can then profile the database to look for customer segments that have the same characteristics as the target market. Of course there have to be enough people in that target group to make the campaign worthwhile. If not the manager may need to select other segments to target.

He or she may wish to do this anyway, because the profile of the existing customers may be in part determined by the promotion and distribution methods that have previously been used to attract them. If different methods of promoting and selling are being used, the customers being targeted will need to take account of this. If the campaign is not aimed at existing customers but at new prospects, the profiling is just as valid because it will help the campaign manager to select such things as media and promotion methods that will appeal to the target market.

Another important factor to consider when selecting the type of customers to target is their affinity with the brand. Different brands with different brand values appeal to different segments of the market. A company that has a reputation for selling mass-market products in bulk at low prices may well feel that it would like to target high-net-worth individuals. However, as their brand values may well be seen as 'cheap and cheerful' by the public, it is unlikely that any offering they make will appeal to the top end of the market.

Another factor that needs to be considered when selecting a target audience is the likely profit that will be made from recruiting that particular type of customer. For example, customer type A may be more likely to respond to the campaign than customer type B. However, if customer type A is never likely to buy another product from the organization, the marketing manager may well need to consider the wisdom of targeting that customer. He or she may decide that while customer type B will be a little more difficult to attract and therefore mean a higher cost per sale, if these customers go on to buy a further two or three products they will have proved to be a wiser choice of target audience.

Summary

When selecting a target audience for a marketing campaign it is important to remember the following:

- They must have needs that can be satisfied by the product being offered.

- The segment of potential customers being targeted should have shown some propensity to buy.

- They must fit with the company brand and brand values.

- The segment should be large enough to make the campaign viable.

- They must be customers who will prove to be valuable for the company, i.e. they may well purchase other products and will remain a customer for a reasonable length of time.

- Their buying behaviour must fit well with the promotion and distribution methods available to the company.

Different services require different approaches

Financial services organizations offer a wide range of products and services, most of which are the subject of a marketing campaign at some time or other. However, because of the diverse nature of the offerings, a single approach simply would not work. The nature of the product and the potential customer mean that different services require different approaches regarding the nature of campaigns. Let us look at some examples.

Campaign objective	Campaign characteristics
New Mortgages	• Highly targeted to attract those people who are likely to be moving house.
	• Likely to be time sensitive (people are more likely to move house in the spring than in the winter).
	• Price-driven market, so the communication will need to be price focused.
	• Advertising is likely to encourage the customer to visit a branch to discuss an application, although it could be two-stage mailing with an application form being sent with the information.

Credit cards	● Simple product will lend itself to a one-stage mailing campaign, or branch/press advertising campaign followed up by one-stage fulfilment.
	● Wider audience because applications for a credit card is not an event-driven purchase
	● May be some seasonality (around Christmas and holiday season) but not significant.
	● Price-based creative that will be used for a single campaign, but can be reused if successful.
	● Campaign must produce a low cost per lead because product margins are thin.
Brand awareness	● National campaign using a wide variety of media.
	● Some targeting, however wide audience due to media selected (e.g. national television).
	● No response mechanism required because the purpose of the campaign is not to generate action.
	● Particularly strong message required that has longevity, i.e. can be used for some time to come.
	● Campaign success measured by testing levels of consumer awareness, and looking for uplift across all products and services.
Retirement planning service	● Campaign could be either local or national; this would dictate the communication method selected.
	● Careful customer selection required.
	● Campaign should drive respondents to agree to a consultation with one of the organization's salespeople.
	● Proposition is not price-driven, therefore the message communicated will need to be one of service, need and brand.
	● Success will be measured in terms of response, appointments booked, and pension products sold.

Student accounts	• Very targeted campaign, probably conducted nationally. Method of communication selected will need to be tailored to the target audience, e.g. adverts in student and youth magazines, leaflet drops at universities, television advertising during youth programmes.
	• Message communicated will need to focus on the benefits for students, e.g. low-cost overdraft facilities, cash point cards, etc.
	• Campaign response would probably be uplifted by the offer of a free gift to all applicants, e.g. record vouchers, takeaway meal vouchers, free book bag.
	• Creatives used will need to be modern and fun if they are to appeal.
	• Distribution would need to involve convenience for the student, i.e. through branches situated on university campuses, or applications through the post. (Freepost of course!)
	• Campaign success measured in terms of new applications received. Long term in terms of the length of the customer relationship and the cross-sales made.
Share-dealing service	• Again tightly focused campaign aimed at those customers with sufficient income and investments to need such facilities.
	• Creatives will need to reflect the values of the target market.
	• Message will need to be based around the benefits of the service compared to those of the competition, i.e. charges and convenience.
	• Media selected could be direct mail sent to customers from the database, profiled in line with target market.
	• Response likely to be driven via telephone/postal dealing as well as branch visits.
	• Success measured in terms of increased usage of share dealing service. Unlikely to be an instant response. Customers will use the service as and when they need it rather that immediately they receive the information.

11.6   Cross-selling

Often campaign selling will be used to cross-sell, that is to attempt to sell existing customers further products or services. We have seen throughout this text that providers are increasingly looking to move to relationship selling rather than transactional business. They have recognized that it is far more cost effective to sell to someone who is already a customer than it is to try and find a totally new prospect. There are several reasons for this.

● The organization already holds some information about that customer and his or her personal circumstances. This will enable it to make more focused offers, tailored to the customer's needs. This will lead to a higher response rate.

● These customers have already shown that they are comfortable with the company and its brand values. This is one thing fewer that needs to be put across by the campaign.

● Customers are more likely to open and read a mailing that is sent from an organization with which they already do business, therefore again, higher response rates can be expected.

● Research has shown that the more products and services a customer holds with the organization, the longer that relationship will last, i.e. the less likely they are to take their business elsewhere.

● It can be considerably cheaper to mail to existing customers than to new prospects, because the information can be included in other items that are already being sent, thereby greatly reducing the costs.

Many banks and building societies are so keen to achieve good rates of cross-sell that they are willing to offer special rates or special deals to existing customers who go on to purchase a further product. This is a worthwhile strategy because it will uplift the responses to any campaign activity, and will also ensure that the customer feels he or she is getting better treatment and therefore builds customer loyalty.

Let us look at how a bank could carry out a campaign to increase the cross-sales, i.e. the number of product holdings per customer.

Research has shown that the customers who are most receptive to cross-selling are those who hold one of the bank's primary products, i.e. a mortgage or a current account, plus those people who hold shares in the bank. The bank would like to cross-sell these products and a number of other offerings. The campaign manager feels that the best way to achieve this is by the development of a customer loyalty programme, whereby the customer receives discounts and special offers depending on his or her current product holdings.

The campaign manager decides to mail all current account holders, mortgage holders and shareholders with the offer. To keep the costs down he or she decides to 'piggy back' mail the current account holders in their next monthly statement and again in six months time, the mortgage holders in their annual statement, and the shareholders in their next half-yearly divided announcement.

The mailing consists of a letter outlining the programme and explaining how valuable their custom is. It contains a pre-paid reply card whereby customers can tick to show which additional products they would like information about. It also contains a glossy sheet showing customers at a glance the special offers they can receive.

11.7 Customer loyalty programme

Table 11.1: Customer loyalty programme

Product held	Mortgage	Current	Shareholder	Two or more of; Current account Mortgage Share holder
Product being purchased				
Current account	Free £100 overdraft facility	N/A	Free £100 overdraft facility	Free £100 overdraft facility
Financial advice	Free financial healthcheck	Free financial healthcheck	Free financial healthcheck	Free financial healthcheck
Mortgage	N/A	Free valuation	Free valuation	Free valuation and ¼% rate reduction
Personal loan	½% rate reduction	½% rate reduction	½% rate reduction	¾% rate reduction
Travel insurance	£5 reduction	£5 reduction	£5 reduction	£10 reduction
Share dealing	£5 fee reduction	£5 fee reduction	£5 fee reduction	£10 fee reduction
Home and contents insurance	10% reduction	10% reduction	10% reduction	20% reduction
Credit card	Free payment protector	Free payment protector	Free payment protector	Free payment protector and 50% reduction in annual fee

Measures for success

Once the campaign has been carried out, the campaign manager will obviously want to know if it was a success. Measuring how well the campaign went will involve measuring results against objectives, and this is the point at which we can see how important it is to set clear, precise, measurable objectives. It will also only be possible to measure the success of the campaign if the collection of management information in line with the objectives has taken place. We can now see why, when we looked at the criteria for success, we said that forward planning regarding MI was essential.

Obviously the measures against which the campaign is judged to be a success or failure will be those measures outlined in the objectives. Here are just a few examples of the type of criteria that could be used to measure the success or failure of a campaign.

- Did the campaign attract the expected level of response?
- Were the responses achieved within the pre-determined cost per lead?
- Did the required number of people visit the branch as a result of the campaign?
- Were the required number of sales received?
- Did the campaign attract customers that matched the desired customer profile?
- Were the desired number of cross-sales achieved?
- Did those sales meet the desired case size and therefore profitability?
- Was sufficient data collected for the enhancement of the database?
- Has there been the desired uplift in product/service/brand awareness?

There are some fundamental questions that should be asked at the end of every campaign to assess it success, for example:

- Did the campaign run within the set budget?
- Was the campaign sufficiently well planned? i.e. were the right people targeted? were the creatives suitable? were the right processes in place?
- Was it well executed? i.e. were the correct number of people mailed? were the branch display boards delivered in time? was there sufficient literature produced?
- Was the campaign well managed once in progress, i.e. was the progress monitored and the right corrective actions taken?

All of these answers will be yes if the campaign was a success, and therefore these types of questions are likely to provide important pointers if the campaign failed to meet its objectives.

11.8   Regulatory issues

Telephone selling

The British Direct Marketing Association, conscious of the problems involved in marketing by telephone, produced telephone-marketing guidelines, which are binding on its own members. The Office of Fair Trading has also issued guidelines for firms making unsolicited calls to approach consumers. A company that makes outbound calls to attempt to attract financial services business needs to bear the following in mind:

- Callers need to check with the customer that the call is at a convenient time, and if the customer says it is not, they should to offer to call again at a more convenient time.

- Unsolicited calls should not be made after 9 o'clock in the evening.

- The caller should ensure that from the start of the call the individual is made aware of the purpose of that call. Calls should not be made under the guise of market research.

- The caller may not mislead the individual, nor can he or she exaggerate the truth or use half-truths.

- The caller must always recognize the right of the individual to terminate the call at any time.

- The individual must have the opportunity to refuse the appointment or any offer made.

- If the caller makes an appointment for a salesperson to visit the individual's home, he or she must give a contact point so that the individual may cancel the appointment.

The Advertising Standards Authority

The ASA is an independent body founded by the advertising industry. It investigates complaints from members of the public about advertising and ensures that any advertisements that are misleading or breach the Code of Advertising Practice are withdrawn. Each month the ASA publishes its findings in a report, and it is the threat of this bad publicity that forms the major deterrent against poor advertising. It also publishes details of cases that it considered but ruled in favour of the advertiser, giving reasons why.

As well as investigating complaints made by the public, the ASA also monitor advertisements that appear in the press and other media. It examines a selection of the advertisements that appear in all daily and weekend national papers, local papers and consumer magazines to ensure that the advertisements comply with the code of practice.

The ASA is also responsible for ensuring that the Code of Advertising Practice is kept up to date and that the self-regulation is working sufficiently. A copy of the ASA Code of Advertising Practice is shown as Appendix 1 at the end of the book.

Regulation of the selling of financial services

The main legislation covering the financial services sector is the Financial Services Act 1982. This Act provides a framework for investor protection and stipulates that all people involved in the promotion and sale of regulated products must either be authorized or exempt.

The rules concerning advertising categorize advertisements into three groupings, A, B, and C.

Category C advertisement are those that make a specific offer to the consumer or invite the public to make an offer. All direct response advertising would be considered as category C advertisements.

Category B advertisements are those that deal with a particular investment or product, but are not making or inviting offers.

Category A advertisements are any other form of advertising.

In addition to this there are separate rules relating to any advertising through which the customer can buy the product as a direct result of the advertising. These rules ensure that the customer receives all the information he or she needs to make an informed decision.

In 1997 the government announced that there was to be a new structure of financial services regulation in the United Kingdom. If the UK was to maintain a competitive advantage in the financial services sector then the regulations should be seen to be effective and up to date. It also wanted a regulatory regime that was seen as fair, coherent, open and cost effective.

In October 1997 the new regulator was launched under the title of the Financial Services Authority (FSA). Most insurance companies and financial services professionals are regulated by the Financial Services Authority, which ensures that they adhere to the regulations set out in the Act.

The FSA has three areas of operation, each managed by an appointed managing director. The three areas are Operations, Financial supervision and Authorization, enforcement and consumer relations.

Much consultation took part with the industry before the formation of this new regulator in order that it would meet the needs of both the industry and the consumer. The FSA is also responsible for banking supervision, although the Board of Banking Supervision continues in an advisory role.

The FSA has a consistent set of powers across the financial services industry and will build a legal and practical framework which is comprehensive, easily understood and are seen to be sensible in its approach.

The FSA is keen to be seen to facilitate innovation in the industry and not simply to be regarded as a 'policeman'. It operates a single compensatory scheme with a common point of entry for consumers.

12

THE SALES INTERVIEW

After reading this chapter you should

- Understand the buying process
- Know how to prepare for a sales interview
- Be aware of the need to set objectives for a sales interview
- Know the structure, content and style of a sales interview
- Be able to identify customer needs and match those needs with product benefits
- Know how to overcome customer objections
- Be aware of the different ways to close the sale
- Understand the importance of follow-up activity after a sales interview

Understanding the buying process

In order to know how to sell to a customer, we first need to emake sure that we understand how and why people buy. Understanding the process that a customer goes through when he or she makes a purchase will enable the seller to match his or her actions to those of the customer and therefore have a successful sales interview.

The understanding of buying process relates to the acts of anybody who purchases goods or services, either in a branch environment or in an interview at home, and to ensure that we make the best use possible of this information we must bear in mind the following:

- The desires, needs and opinions of the customer are of paramount importance and a seller will ignore these at his or her peril.

- With the proper research we can gain a reasonable understanding of customers and how they behave in the buying process.

- Our sales activity should then use this knowledge and this understanding of customers' behaviour in order to influence what they buy.

By their nature the products of financial services companies are one-off major purchases, and they therefore involve the consumer in a fairly high degree of decision making and selection. This decision is of much greater significance than that needed when purchasing things such as food or toiletries, for example, and therefore the process they go through during the purchase also differs.

The following flowchart illustrates the stages that a customer goes through and the behaviour displayed when making a purchase that involves a large amount of money or with significant impact. We shall in turn look at each of these in more detail and try to determine what influence, if any, we can have on the customer's behaviour and decision making.

Figure 12.1: The buying process

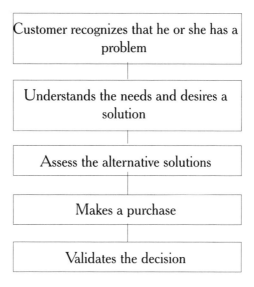

Customer recognizes that he or she has a problem

Understands the needs and desires a solution

Assess the alternative solutions

Makes a purchase

Validates the decision

Recognizing the problem

The first stage of any major purchase must be the customer's recognition of the fact that there is currently a problem. The problem is usually one of a gap between what customers have at the present time, and what they would like to have or need to have. This recognition can often be triggered by a change in circumstances which highlights that the present situation is inadequate.

Marketing efforts can play a part in helping the customer to recognize that there is a problem and many companies have used advertising to attempt to do this. However the only really successful way for this stage to be influenced by the organization is via personal contact with the customer, i.e. with branch staff or salespeople spending time with customers and examining their current situation.

Understanding the problem and desiring a solution

Once customers reached the point of being dissatisfied with the gap in their circumstances they have recognized, they begin to think about the consequences of that gap. Depending on the effects they see they may well decide that they need to take some action, and improve the situation.

Assessing the alternative solutions

During this stage of customers' behaviour they are looking at all the alternatives that are available for satisfying the need that they have. This involves them looking at the different products that would be suitable and comparing their benefits.

Having decided which product best suits their needs, they may then look at the offerings of different providers and compare their features and prices.

It is during this stage that the salesperson can have most influence on the customer's behaviour, and where the marketing activity he or she undertakes can be of most success in influencing and indeed changing the behaviour. All elements of the marketing mix can help to influence the decision. Advertising the product and its features or its price may be central in persuading the customer to make a purchase. Alternatively it could be the method of promotion or being in the right place—somewhere that is convenient for the customer may be the factor that gets the business

Making the purchase

Having decided which product or service best satisfies the need they have the customers will go ahead and make the purchase.

They are likely to ask questions and raise queries about the product or service that they are buying during this stage of the process.

Validating the decision

When customers makes a purchase which is large in terms of financial commitment and the effect that it has, they are likely to require some sort of reassurance that they have done the right thing. This will be apparent in the fact that they may ask questions following their decision to buy regarding the product and its benefits. It is important that the company does not lose any of the sales it has made and therefore the after-sales service it offers, and any mailing it does to the new customers must offer them reassurance that they have made a good decision.

Influences on the buying process

There are a number of factors that influence the consumer's buying process and it is worth looking at these to see how they may effect the marketing and sales of the organization's products.

The family unit

This is an important factor in customers' buying behaviour, as it affects both the volume and type of products they consume and influences their attitudes and desires. It is also important for the seller to consider how the consumer behaves as part of a family unit because they account for such a large proportion of the population. The needs of the family and the way it chooses to satisfy those needs depends on whether they have children and if so how old they are, whether there are two parents or one, and whether both work, etc.

The social background

The customer's background is likely to have an influence on his or her buying behaviour. This explains why segmenting customers into socio-economic classes is such common practice. Their social class will influence their tastes and preferences and so must be considered when selling.

Culture

A person's behaviour will be influenced by geographical location, nationality, ethnic background or religion or educational background. It is important to remember these cultural differences and the way in which they affect the customer's buying behaviour if we are to avoid making embarrassing and expensive blunders.

Applying the knowledge of buyer behaviour

Once we have an understanding of how our customers and prospective customers may behave, we need to use this knowledge to ensure that our marketing and sales activities are directed to the areas and the behaviour where the organization believes it can be most effective in influencing that behaviour. For example, in an industry where the customer is likely to want the product rather than actually need it, the marketing manager may feel that there is little point spending time, money and effort attempting to help customers with the 'recognizing the need' stage of the behaviour pattern. Instead the manager may feel that the customer will recognize the need himself or herself and therefore the organization would be well advised to concentrate its efforts on the 'assessing the alternatives' stage. If this is the case, the promotional activity will be focused on highlighting the product benefits and making comparisons with other offerings in the market.

Another benefit of understanding the stages in a customer's buying process is that when a salesperson is attempting to make the sale, he or she can match behaviour to that of the customer. The diagram over the page shows how the different stages of the buying process and the sales process can be matched.

Figure 12.2: Matching the sales process to the buying process

Outer circle – buying process

Inner circle – selling process

Let us now have a look at the sales process in more detail.

Identifying the customer's needs

Once the customer has agreed to have a sales interview or discuss the situation with a member of the branch staff, the salesperson needs to help the customer to see exactly what his or her needs are. The depth of this discussion depends largely on the nature of the financial product being sold. For example, if the salesperson is selling car insurance, the discussion will simply involve such thing as the make and value of the vehicle, who will be driving, and what type of cover is required, etc. However, in certain parts of the industry, such as the sale of life assurance, the salesperson has a duty to know the customer before he or she makes recommendations and will therefore try to gain a full and clear understanding of the customer's financial situation. This means that this part of the process can be fairly lengthy.

Throughout the discussion the salesperson will be gaining a clear picture of the customer's needs and deciding which, if any, of the products available will fit the needs the customer has.

During this stage, customers who were unaware of their financial needs will be made aware of the needs they have. Helping customers to recognize their needs is an important part of the sales process and requires a great deal of skill from the salesperson, but is vital if the sale is to progress any further.

Selling the solution in terms of features and benefits

Once both the customer and the salesperson clearly understand the customer's needs, the salesperson will present the solution to those needs. Because the products are largely intangible, the salesperson will have very little that can actually be shown to the customer; therefore this stage of the process requires a degree of skill. He or she should to describe the features and benefits of the product, always relating these back to the needs that the customer expressed.

Dealing with queries (handling objections)

Very few people make a decision to buy without asking questions about the product, and this is particularly true of financial services products with which the customer is often less knowledgeable, and which may well involve large amounts of money or fairly lengthy commitments. The salesperson will be involved in answering those questions and may even modify the solutions recommended following the queries. Many sellers refer to these queries as 'objections' and assume that this means that the customer does not want to buy. However, queries at this stage of the process are quite normal. A salesperson needs to be able to view these positively, and deal with them efficiently if the process is to continue,

In order to maintain an on-going relationship with the customer and create some customer loyalty, it is important that the salesperson sees this stage as part of the selling process, even if the queries arise after the sale is completed.

Closing the sale

Once the queries have been successfully dealt with the seller needs to close the sale– that is, the seller needs to move the customer to the stage in the process where he or she actually goes ahead and makes the purchase. We shall look at this stage in more detail later in this chapter.

Follow-up and on-going service

The customer may well require service throughout the life of the product. This may be given directly by the salesperson, or by other members of staff. However it is important that this is viewed as part of the sales process because it offers the ideal situation for seeing when customers' situations are changing and therefore their needs may have changed.

12.1 Preparing for the sales interview

When salespeople have customers coming for an interview, they know that they must do the best job they can because they are representing their company and providing a service on its behalf. In order that the interview gets off to a good start, the seller must take a few minutes before the customer arrives in the branch to prepare for the forthcoming interview.

Each and every interview requires that certain items are readily available to the adviser to enable the proceedings to run smoothly and effectively. It is also good business practice to be familiar with any information that the company already holds about that customer. If the group includes a number of companies, such as a life and pensions company as well as a bank, the customer would expect the interviewer to be aware of all dealings with the group and therefore checking the customer's details needs to done across the group.

Understanding the customer's existing dealings with the company ensures that the interviewer looks professional and capable in front of the customer, and also saves the customer from answering lots of questions about information the company already has. If no records can be found and it therefore appears that the customer has not dealt with the company before, then the seller should check with the customer that this is the case at the start of the interview.

Ideally the seller would benefit from knowing details of the customer's account before the interview as this will help to get a clearer picture of the customer's circumstances and help in the provision of 'best advice'. It would therefore seem sensible to research such details before the customer arrives. However it must be remembered that to comply with the Code of Banking Practice, the customer must consent to the release of such information. This could normally be achieved by the person who booked the sales interview, requesting such information when the interview is booked. If the customer does not grant this permission, details of accounts cannot be researched as part of the interview preparation and will need to be done during the interview itself.

As well as obtaining all the relevant information about the customer and any current dealings with the company, there are other basic preparation checks that the seller should do to ensure that the interview runs smoothly.

Hardware

- Ensure that you have access to a PC or laptop computer if the type of interview being conducted requires it. It is likely that such equipment will be needed for such things as recording information, producing quotations, etc.

- Make sure that the equipment is working and that all the correct leads/plugs etc. are available.

- If a printer is needed, ensure that this is available, in working order and has sufficient paper loaded.

- Check that any other equipment, such as a calculator, is at hand.

Literature

- The seller should have a business card available to give to the customer so that he or she can remember whom they dealt with and keep the name and telephone number in case there are any queries after the interview.

- If the salesperson is involved in the sale of regulated products, he or she needs to give the customer a *terms of business letter* explaining the salesperson's status and the extent of the advice he or she can offer. This should be at hand before the customer arrives.

- Any other information that the salesperson is likely to need should be sought out before the customer arrives, e.g. tax tables, etc.

- The seller should also have on hand all relevant details of the company's products that may be needed for the customer, e.g. product brochures, application forms, details of interest rates etc.

Interview area

- The seller must have booked a suitable interview area for the appropriate time and ensure that it is available for the full length of the interview.

- The seller should make sure that reception is aware of the arrangements and is ready to greet the customer, knowing where to direct him or her on arrival.

- The seller should ensure that they will not be interrupted during the interview and will therefore need to divert the telephone or make sure that no calls are put through.

- The seller should ensure that there are sufficient chairs if the customers are a couple and may both come along, and the whole interview area, especially the desk, should be free from clutter.

Home visits

Of course not all sales interviews are held in the branch; some salespeople travel to people's homes and carry out the sales interview there. Generally the principles for preparation are very much the same, although they are probably more important. If the seller is conducting a sales interview in a customer's home and forgets some piece of literature for example, he or she cannot simply nip out of the office to the store cupboard to get it. With the exception of the interview area preparation, home visit preparation should be carried out as above, with a few additions.

- Any existing customer records or details of dealing the seller has previously had with the customer should be loaded onto a floppy disk if they are to be used on a laptop computer in the customer's home.

- The seller needs to ensure that the laptop computer is fully charged and take a mains adapter to the interview.

- The seller needs to carry any copies of literature etc. that may be needed.

- The seller needs to know exactly where the customer lives and allow sufficient time for the journey in order to arrive on time.

Setting objectives

One of the most important elements of preparing for a sales interview is for the salesperson to set some objectives for that interview. There are several reason why it is important for this to be done:

- It allows the salesperson to judge whether the interview was a success or not, i.e. were the objectives achieved.

- Setting objectives allows the salesperson to create a structure for the interview that will lead to achieving the objective set.

- It will often form an introduction to the interview for the seller to use with the customer. For example the seller could start the interview by saying 'What I'd like to do today is to find out all the details of you requirements and then show you the most suitable mortgage product to meet your needs'.

While initially we may think that the objective for any sales interview is obviously to make a sale, this is not always the case. Some sales calls take place face-to-face but others take place over the telephone, some in branches, others in customer's homes or place of business. Some sales are simple and are completed in one interview, other more complex products may well require several interviews before the sale is agreed. Some salespeople make pre-sales calls as well as conducting an interview, and these should also have objectives set.

Because of the diverse nature of sales interviews, and indeed the different ways in which salespeople work, the objectives set for any one interview could be very different from those set for another. Here are a few examples of the objectives a salesperson may set before meeting or speaking to a potential customer:

- To explain the service that the company offers, and gain an interest from the customer.

- To gain the customer's agreement to a full sales interview.

- To establish a rapport with the customer and therefore begin the process of relationship building.

- To gain enough information about the customer to be able to accurately assesses his or her needs.

- To present to the customer the details of the products and services you believe would meet those needs, and to gain some commitment from the customer to address them.

- To make a sale.

- To make a number of sales.

- To investigate wether the customer is happy with the products and services previously bought from you, and to thereby maintain and build upon the customer relationship.

- To review the products the customer has previously bought, and make a further sale.

- To gain a thorough understanding of the customer's business in order to understand how the organization can be of help.

Of course there is nothing to stop the salesperson from setting more than one objective for each sales interview, in fact it would be prudent to do so in many cases. These could either be two objectives that could both be achieved, or a secondary objective, i.e. a fallback position if the primary objective is not fulfilled. For example

Interview objectives could be:

1. To make a sale of an investment product

   and

2. To gain the customer's agreement to have the adviser review any retirement plans and offer advice on retirement planning.

Alternatively the objective of a call could be:

1. To gain the customer's agreement to a sales interview to discuss business banking arrangements

   Or failing this

2. To gain the customer's agreement to have the bank call again in six months to see if this would be appropriate at that time.

Whatever the nature of the financial services products being sold, and whatever type of distribution method used, the salesperson should always set an objective for every contact with the customer. This will ensure that the sellers are highly organized. They will the make the most of every opportunity, for even though every interview will not end in a sale, every interview should produce some benefit to both the customer and the organization.

Structure, content and style of a sales interview

The structure of a sales interview and what is contained within it depend largely on the nature of the product being sold, as well as the customer and his or her current relationship with the organization. This said, most sales interviews follow the buying process to some greater or lesser degree, and therefore most follow a similar basic structure.

Figure 12.3: Basic sales interview structure

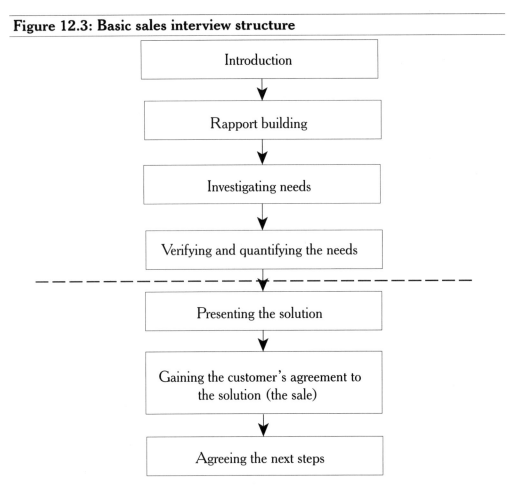

Introduction

Here the seller introduces himself or herself and gives the customer details about what will happen in the interview. This should cover such things as the time the interview is going to take and the purpose of the meeting, relating this back to the original reason for making the appointment. If the salesperson is selling regulated products he or she will also cover the compliance elements during the introductions including such things as company and individual's status. The introduction is important because it sets the tone for the whole interview and gives the seller an opportunity to put the customer at ease.

Rapport building

At the beginning of the interview the seller may feel that a brief informal chat with the customer will be a good start. It is a good idea to build rapport with the customer, especially if he or she is to feel comfortable divulging detailed information about financial status. This said, the seller should not chat just for the sake of it with old clichés about parking or holidays, but should use this rapport building to obtain more information about the customer.

Finding information about the customer's likes and dislikes, about preferences and tastes will help the seller to tailor the interview style and presentation style to suit that individual. The most successful salespeople are those who can speak to a customer in the way in which he or she wants to be dealt with. The seller should use the information gained here to discover such things as the customer's current level of understanding of financial services and pitch the interview accordingly.

Investigating needs

The next stage of the interview is to establish what needs the customer has. This can vary from a simple question and listening to the customer explain the needs, to the more complex investigation of needs that is required for selling regulated products. Again this section differs greatly depending on the nature of the product being sold and the actual customer being interviewed.

Verifying and quantifying needs

The next stage is for the seller and the customer to ensure that they are in agreement as to exactly what the needs are. Some customers may have come to the interview with an idea of their needs, and simply need to clarify them and quantify them; others will have been unaware of all their needs and will have them explained by the seller. It is important to gain the customer's agreement to the needs before progressing any further with the interview.

Presenting the solution

After agreeing the needs the salesperson presents the customer with the product or service that satisfies those needs. The seller will be much more successful if this is done using benefit statements rather than simply explaining the product features. During this section of the interview the seller will also be dealing with any queries the customer has and handling any objections that arise.

The sale

The next stage is to gain the customer's agreement to the solution, the sale itself. The salesperson needs to ask the customer for the business, and we will look at ways of doing this later in this chapter. Once the customer has agreed to go ahead with the sale, there will be applications to complete, etc.

Agree next steps

The final stage is to agree the next steps. The salesperson should explain to the customer what will happen to the application, what he or she should expect to receive, and anything else that has to be done. The seller should also agree the date of the next interview or telephone contact, if this is appropriate. Most companies are now moving away from transactional selling to a basis of relationship marketing and therefore this is an ideal opportunity to explain to the customer the future contacts that can be expected.

Of course not all interviews are the same, and when selling some of the more complex and regulated products, there may need to be more than one interview to complete the sale. Where this is the case, the structure would be the same, but the dotted line on the chart shows where the cut-off between first and second interviews would be. Of course if this is the case the seller should end the first interview by explaining what will happen next and making a second appointment. The seller will need to open the second appointment with a brief introduction and a recap of the first, but the basic structure will remain the same.

Sometimes the nature of the customer or the circumstances of the interview mean that the structure needs to be amended, and that parts are omitted or the order amended slightly. This will be down to the skills of the salesperson to judge when this is appropriate and tailor the interview to suit.

Interview style

Each salesperson has his or her own individual style, and using a personal style should be encouraged. However we need to remember a few points:

- The style should be adapted to suit the individual customer.
- The best sellers are those whose style allows the customer to feel relaxed and able to talk.
- The style adopted should ensure that the seller meets the objectives, i.e. makes the sale without putting the customer under pressure.

Let us look briefly at the way in which a salesperson could adapt the style to suit the customer. During the rapport building at the start of the interview, the salesperson will have been listening carefully to the things the customer says, and should try to adapt style to match. For example, some customers love detail and will require every bit of information available, whereas others need much less detail in order to reach a decision, and the salesperson needs to pitch the presentation to suit, otherwise the customer will simply switch off.

The seller should also try to talk the same language as the customer. For example, some customers talk in terms of visuals, e.g. 'Let me see' or ' show me'. These customers will like figures and charts and will want to be shown examples.

Other customers talk in terms of hearing, e.g. 'I've heard that' or 'tell me', while others talk in terms of feelings, e.g. I 'feel that,' or 'the way I feel about it is'.

The salesperson needs to match like for like, visual for visual, feeling for feeling if he or she is to gain an understanding with the customer.

Example of mixed styles:

Customer   *Tell me about your latest..............*

Salesperson   *Certainly, let me show you.............*

Example of matched styles:

Customer   *Show me the details of the plan.......*

Salesperson   *Certainly, here you can see the ....*

What we can see is that while the seller must have a personal style and one with which he or she is comfortable, it is essential to be able to adapt this style to suit the individual interview, while remaining professional.

Identifying and validating needs with benefits

Once the customer's needs have been identified, the salesperson needs to match these with the benefits of the product being recommended. Obviously the customer's needs will dictate which product or service is suitable, and the seller can then use the needs to explain why he or she is recommending the selected product.

We saw in Chapters 7 and 8 how to turn product features into benefits and why it was important to do so. In the sales interview we need to go one step further and turn them, not only into benefits, but also into benefits relating specifically to that customer and his or her particular needs. Let us look at some examples of how this can be done.

Figure 12.4: Needs to benefits, to customer benefits

Customer need identified	Product feature, turned into a benefit and related to the customer
24-hour access to money	"Our card cash facility will enable you to withdraw money at any time of the day or night from any of our cash dispensers. This will give you the access you need to your money even though you find it difficult to visit the branch."
Small overdraft facility with little or no charge	"Our buffer zone facility allows you to go £50 overdrawn without charge, so this will cover you for those little emergencies or oversights you were concerned about."
Replacement car if the customer is involved in an accident and needs garaging	"Our motor insurance will provide you with a hire car for the period of the repairs, and you can therefore be confident that you will still be able to get to work and back, even though your own car is off the road."
Income if off work sick	"Our Income replacement policy will provide you with 75% of your income if you are unable to work because of long term-illness. This means you will not have to worry about paying your mortgage or bills if you are ill."
Income in retirement	"Our pension plan will provide you with the income you require in retirement and therefore enable you to travel and go on holiday as you have planned."

| Flexible mortgage payments | "Our mortgage allows you to pay extra in some months and take payment holidays, which will be ideal for someone whose income fluctuates as your does." |

12.2 Handling objections

We said earlier that few customers would purchase something as major as a financial services product without asking questions and raising queries. These need to be dealt with as a routine part of the sales interview and should be viewed as a positive sign. If the customer is not asking questions, he or she is probably not moving through the sales process and will not therefore make a purchase.

However, while queries are a positive part of the buying process, the customer may also raise objections, either in question or statement format. For example:

- I don't think I can afford this at the moment

- I'm not sure that this is the best one for me

- I'll need to go away and think about it before I decide

- I think I can get a better deal elsewhere; I'll need to shop around

If the customer raises these types of objections, it means that there has been a problem with some stage of the sales process. The customer will only raise objections if the seller moved through the stages of the sales process faster than the customer was ready to move through the buying process. For example, the objection "I don't think I really need this at the moment" shows that the seller had moved on to explain the features and benefits of a product before the customer had fully recognized the need. If the customer feels that he or she could get a more suitable product elsewhere, this probably means that the seller has not sufficiently explained the features in terms of benefits to the customer, etc.

From this we can see that the best way to avoid objections is to ensure that the sales process is perfectly matched with the buying process, and therefore objections will not occur. In other words – prevention is better than cure.

This said, all but the most experienced seller will have situations in which they face objections from their customers. Let us now look at some of the different ways a salesperson or member of the branch staff can overcome such objections.

All objection-handling techniques have one thing in common – they require careful listening. Listening to the objection and the way in which it is expressed helps the seller to diagnose the real cause of the objection. Experience and training provide the seller with a 'toolbox' of techniques for handling objections. They can then select the appropriate approach, depending on the specific situation and the nature of the objection.

Understanding the real objection

The first stage in handling objections is to be sure that the seller fully understands the objection, and the best way to do this is to ask back. This will enable the seller to clarify exactly what the real problem is and judge if this will stop the customer from buying the product. Only when the seller fully understands the problem can it be dealt with. One of the ways to clarify the objection is to question it. Let us look at an example:

Customer	I find your organization very bureaucratic and therefore difficult to deal with.
Seller	I'm very sorry to hear that. Can I ask specifically what problems you have encountered?
Customer	Well there are so many forms to fill in and they are all so long and detailed.

Now the seller understand the real problem is that the customer does not like to complete forms and can therefore deal with the problem by offering some help with them. If the seller had simply accepted the objection as it was first presented he or she may well have lost the business.

Provide an answer

Some objections simply require an answer. They may be due to a misunderstanding or the fact that the customer needs more information, and these objections can be handled fairly simply provided that the seller is well prepared and knowledgeable about the products and the company, etc. Once answered the seller can move on to close the business. Other objections may be raised because the seller has done a poor job of moving the customer through the buying process.

Returning to the buying process

One of the best ways to overcome objections is simply to identify the stage of the buying process which the customer has not clearly moved through, and return to the corresponding sales activity. For example, if it is obvious that the customer has not yet seen the need for such a service, the salesperson would return to the questioning techniques used in identifying customer needs. For example, 'what would happen if you didn't have unemployment cover and were unfortunate enough to lose your job? How would you maintain your payments? How would you manage? Does this concern you?'

Cost objections

One of the most common objections raised by the customer is that of price; the customer may say that he or she cannot afford it or that the price is too high. A salesperson should know the customer's circumstances sufficiently to know if this is a real objection, or if the customer can afford it and has just not appreciated the real benefits. Usually an objection to price means that the customer feels the price is too high for the benefits that will accrue – there is a direct relationship between the price people are willing to pay and how much they feel they want or need something.

Figure 12.5: The relationship between cost and perceived benefit

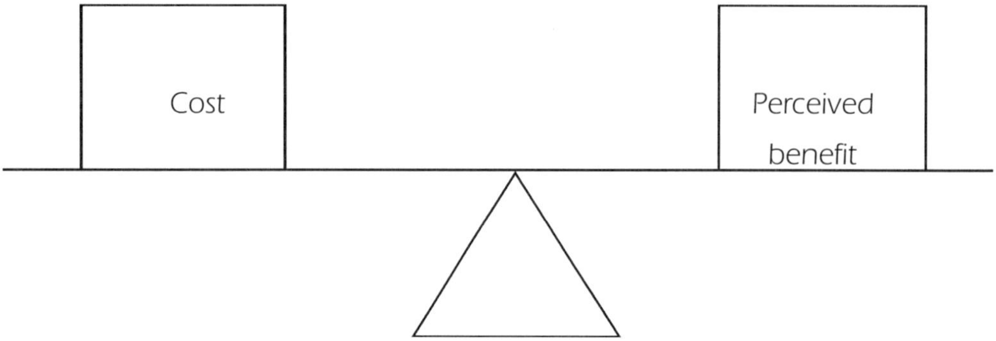

If the cost appears to the customer to outweigh the benefits he or she will not want to make a purchase. Customers decide to buy only when they feel that the benefits outweigh the costs. Within the financial services industry, most sellers are unable to influence the cost of the product. This means that the only way to tip the 'see-saw' in their favour is to add to the benefits side, i.e. to go back to the customer's needs and explain what the product can do for the customer to satisfy those needs. As the customer sees more and more benefit from the purchase, the cost becomes less and less of an objection, and then the customer becomes willing to buy.

This technique of outweighing the objection with benefits can be used in most scenarios where the customer objects to something that the seller cannot change.

Put-off

Putting off handling an objection is valid if the seller feels that it is better handled later, perhaps after the features and benefits have been discussed, for example. While this is a good way of dealing with objections if the seller can be certain to deal with it at some later point, it may be worth checking that the point has been satisfactorily dealt with before moving on to try and close the sale.

Deny

If the seller denies the objection raised by the customer, it needs to be done tactfully so as not to upset the customer. However in some circumstances, this method is really the only one suitable. It should be used where the customer is claiming something that is definitely untrue, for example 'your bank's interest rates are always higher than anyone else's.' In such circumstances a polite denial would be the best way of dealing with it.

Convert

Turning the customers objection into a selling feature is one of the most powerful techniques in handling objections. Here the seller listens to what the customer is saying and uses this to highlight a benefit of the product. Let us look at an example.

Customer	I certainly like the idea of moving my money from the deposit account to something where I could have the possibility of more growth, but the risk of losing my capital would worry me too much.
Seller	That's what we found many of our customers felt, and it is exactly the reason that we designed our capital protected bond. It means you can have the growth potential you're looking for without having to have sleepless nights worrying about your capital sum.

Summary

It is important to understand that the better the selling process and the seller, the fewer objections that will arise. This said, there will always be occasions when the customer will raise an objection and being able to handle it competently is an essential part of the selling role.

Closing the sale

In any book about selling there is a section about 'how to close the sale' and many sellers make the mistake of thinking that if they learn some great closing techniques they will become great salespeople. The fact is that the close is simply the conclusion of the selling process and that all other elements of the process must be done well if the customer is to buy.

The other common mistake made by many salespeople is that the close must always come at the end of the sale when all other elements are complete. While this is often the case, the customer may well give out buying signals much earlier in the process and these must not be ignored. Commitment to buy can be gained at any point throughout the sale, not just at the end.

The fact is that the whole sales interview is aimed at getting the customer to commit to buying something. Therefore closing the sale should be something that is carried out throughout the whole process and not some magical technique that is suddenly brought in at the end of the interview. This said, the seller does need the customer to make a decision to buy the product or service on offer, and that means that in some form or another, the seller has to ask the customer to take that action. This is the close.

There are many closing techniques being taught to and used successfully by salespeople in the financial services industry. The best way to ensure a successful order is to study the different methods, try them out, and find one that you feel comfortable and natural using. The table below gives some of the most commonly used techniques and an example of how each could work.

Closing technique	Example
Simply ask for the business (sounds simple but many salespeople forget to).	So, can we go ahead with the application?
The alternative close, the either or option.	Would you prefer an appointment in the morning or the afternoon?
Assumptive close (the belief that you will get the order).	As you obviously see the benefits of this service, I'll get you an application form.
Concession close (using an incentive to help the customer over the decision-making hurdle).	If you apply now the discounted rate will apply, which of course it won't if you delay for a month.

Summary

Although a lot of emphasis is put on 'closing techniques' by some training books and selling skills training, it is important to remember that a good close will not on its own win the business. The close is an important part of the selling process and should be considered all the way through the interview, not just at the end. The better the seller and the more skilled he or she is in matching sales behaviour to the customer's buying behaviour, then the easier the close will be. When all is said and done, a close is simply a way to ask the customer to buy the product. The most important thing is that this is done, rather than the way in which it is done. Each salesperson should find a way of asking for the business that he or she feels comfortable with, and make it work.

12.3　Follow-up

We have seen in earlier chapters the importance of customer retention. We know that the competitive nature of the financial services industry means that once an organization has found a customer it should always attempt to have an ongoing relationship in order that he or she remains a customer. This means that the job of the salesperson is not just to make one sale, a quick win and then move on to the next customer.

The marketing activity that has gone into attracting the customer and getting to the point where he or she is in front of one of the company's salespeople is a long and expensive process. Such an outlay will be recovered only if the customer is retained and goes on to purchase further products and services from the company.

Even if the individual does not go ahead and make a purchase, it is important that the seller remains in touch with such customers. When their situation changes and they need financial services products in the future, the on-going contact will mean that the seller is in an ideal situation to discuss those needs and make a sale.

We can see from these points that it is important that the salesperson does not see that the acquisition of a new account, for example, is the end of the sales process, but instead views it as the start of the seller/customer relationship.

Following the sales interview in which the seller has explained the features and benefits of the company's product or service, the customer will have expectations as to the service etc. that he or she is going to receive. In order to retain the customer's goodwill the seller needs to keep in contact with the customer and ensure that expectations are being met.

We saw earlier when examining the buying process that the making the purchase is not the end of the process and that customers are likely to have queries once they have made the purchase. They will expect the seller to be helpful with any queries and to deal with them efficiently and effectively. The seller should view these as part of the selling process.

We also saw that the next step in the buying process is that, over time, the customer's situation may change and therefore they may have needs for other services. If the seller has maintained a relationship and built up a rapport with the customer, such customers are likely to turn for advice once they recognize their need.

It is important that the time spent on follow-up activity is not wasted or unproductive sales time, and therefore throughout the follow-up activity the seller must be keeping up to date with the customer's situation and spotting new sales opportunities. Following-up on sales is an investment that will improve the prospect of winning future business. Loyal customers are a very valuable asset to any company and any salesperson.

There are a number of steps that can be taken to ensure a positive follow-up. Thanking the customer for the business seems an obvious thing to do, but can easily be forgotten. This makes the customer feel appreciated and therefore starts to develop customer loyalty. The simple act of thanking people makes them feel that their custom is important to you and therefore makes them think twice before taking it elsewhere.

If the contact with the customer has resulted, not in business, but in the chance to provide a quotation or some product information, then the follow-up activity is vital. The salesperson should ensure that he or she follows up the contact to establish that the right information was issued, and see if any further help can be given. This follow-up activity will then give the seller the ideal opportunity to ask for the business.

If the sale involved a long-term commitment from the customer, such as a pension plan, for example, then the salesperson needs to maintain regular contact with the customer throughout the product's life. This will enable the seller to give on-going advice to that customer both about that particular product and any others that would be suitable.

Summary

Staying in contact with a customer following a sale can have a number of direct benefits. These are:

- It can lead directly to increased business.

- It provides the basis for a long-term relationship which will again eventually lead to more business.

- It represents a pro-active approach to ensuring customer satisfaction, and will therefore lead to far fewer customer complaints.

- It gives the salesperson the ideal opportunity to ask for referrals, i.e. introductions to other people who may be interested in the same product or service.

Every salesperson should remember that, the easiest and most cost-effective sales always come from satisfied customers.

13

CREATING A SALES TEAM

After reading this chapter you should

- Understand the requirements of a sales team
- Be aware of individuals' different personal motivations for effective selling
- Understand the role played by sales targets
- Be aware of the different methods of rewarding salespeople
- Know the benefits and drawbacks of using incentives with a sales team
- Know how to monitor, review and enhance sales performance

13.1   Recruitment and training

The first stage of creating a sales team is to recruit the sellers. Recruiting suitable salespeople is very important for the following reasons:

- A successful salesperson improves branch efficiency, customer relations and ultimately creates greater profit for the organization.
- Employing the right person for the job reduces staff turnover and the time and expense involved in the recruitment and training of a replacement.

Within most organizations the first stage of the recruitment and selection process is carried out by the personnel department. They advertise, either internally or externally, with or without the help of an external recruitment agency. There are several agencies that specialize in the recruitment of salespeople for the financial services industry and they screen candidates and carry out first interviews if required.

Having identified the characteristics that should be present in a good salesperson, the personnel department has to test the applicants to ensure that these qualities are present, i.e. that they have the right level of education, intelligence, numerical ability, and mental diligence.

As well as these easily measurable criteria, we know that a successful salesperson also needs to display certain character traits. They should have drive, enthusiasm, self-discipline, patience and empathy. It is the presence of these characteristics that is likely to make the difference between success and failure. We can see that an ability to detect them in a recruitment process is vital.

Many companies use personality questionnaires to assist in the detection of such characteristics, although these are not guaranteed to be accurate. It therefore usually falls to the sales manager to spend some time with the individuals, getting to know as much as they can about them and how they would work. They then need to use their knowledge of the job, and their experience of both good and bad sellers, to make a valued judgement as to whether that person has the necessary attributes to be able to sell.

Figure 13.1: The recruitment process

Advertisement is placed explaining the sales vacancy and highlighting the experience and attributes that are required in the successful candidate.

↓

Personnel department sifts through the applications, rejecting those that do not meet the base criteria.

↓

There may be an initial screening of these applicants by telephone, particularly if the role requires the seller to use the telephone to contact customers.

↓

Those who pass the initial screening will be invited to take verbal and numerical tests as well as to complete a personality questionnaire. The results of these are then used as a basis of questioning in the interview.

↓

Those candidates who demonstrate the required levels of numeracy etc. then attend an interview with the sales manager. If the company is looking to recruit experienced sellers, they may also be asked to carry out a role-play of a sales situation in order that the manager can gain a better understanding of their skills levels.

↓

An offer will be made to those candidates who successfully complete all areas of the recruitment process. IF the candidate accepts the offer, then references will be sought.

Sales training

After recruiting the right individual, the next stage is to ensure that he or she receives the right type and level of training. Such people will have been recruited because the sales manager believes that they have the right skills and attributes to become good salespeople. However they still require a great deal of training if they are to realize their potential in their new role. This applies equally to those people who will be selling full time and those who will have both a selling job and other duties to perform.

For regulated products the training is governed by the rules set out by the regulatory bodies, and each company must document its training and competency procedures. All training must be carried out in accordance with the T&C guidelines, and documented as a record that this has taken place. However, whether or not the training is regulated, it generally needs to consist of the following elements.

Technical knowledge

Salespeople need to be able to display a level of technical knowledge relating to the part of the financial services industry in which they operate. The amount of training depends on the type of selling role that they will be performing as well as the current knowledge and past experience of the individual. In some areas of the industry the salesperson is expected to pass examinations set by external bodies such as the CII (The Chartered Insurance Institute) and the CIB (The Chartered Institute of Bankers) in order to demonstrate this knowledge. If this is the case, most companies offer training and support in order to help them to pass.

Product knowledge

As well as technical and industry knowledge, individuals need to be given training on the products that are offered by the company. They will need to be well equipped to describe these products to customers, explain how they meet the customer's needs and be able to answer any questions relating to the products and their features. While they will not be selling other company's products they may well want to have a general understanding of the other types of products that are available to customers elsewhere.

Application of knowledge

This is a vital area of any salesperson's training and must be included in any training programme. Often technical details and product features can be taught using distance learning or computer-based training. However it is important that the seller can take that knowledge and apply it to a customer's situation in a selling environment. It is this application of the knowledge that may well require the most time and assistance from trainers and experienced salespeople.

Skills training

Once the sellers have gained all the necessary technical and product knowledge and understand how to apply it to a sales situation, the next step is to teach them the skills they will need to become a successful seller. Often this skills element to training gets overlooked or receives less attention than is really necessary. Most sales skills take a great deal of time and practice before they become a natural part of the individual's behaviour. The skills training therefore needs to be given a high level of emphasis in the initial training, and continued by the sales manager once the training is finished and the individual is back in the branch doing the job. If this is not done, then whereas the individual will be technically competent, he or she is likely to regularly under-perform in relation to sales targets. Such under-performance leads to a drop in the drive and motivation of the seller and could eventually lead to staff turnover.

On-job training

Not all of the sale training needed for a new salesperson can be carried out in a classroom environment. Once the basic level of knowledge and skill has been acquired, the new recruit is allowed back into the branch to do the job. This should not however mark the end of the training. The training, particularly the skills training, needs to continue once the individual is up and selling. The on-job training will ensure that knowledge and skill continues to grow, and remains up-to-date with changes in the industry or the company's product offerings.

Figure 13.2: Example outline training plan for new salesperson

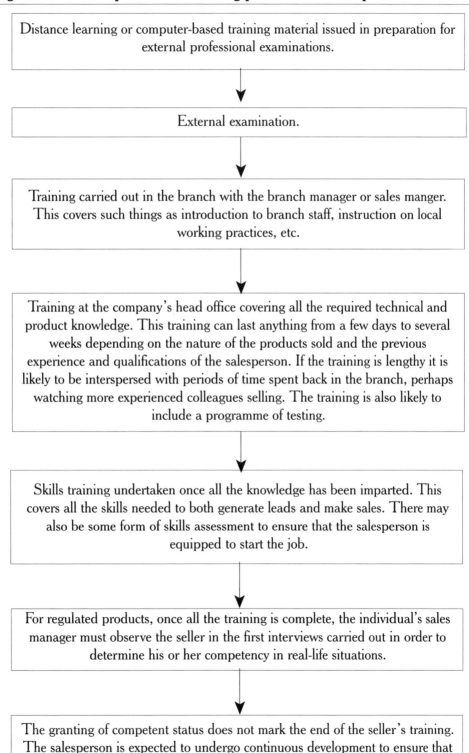

Distance learning or computer-based training material issued in preparation for external professional examinations.

External examination.

Training carried out in the branch with the branch manager or sales manger. This covers such things as introduction to branch staff, instruction on local working practices, etc.

Training at the company's head office covering all the required technical and product knowledge. This training can last anything from a few days to several weeks depending on the nature of the products sold and the previous experience and qualifications of the salesperson. If the training is lengthy it is likely to be interspersed with periods of time spent back in the branch, perhaps watching more experienced colleagues selling. The training is also likely to include a programme of testing.

Skills training undertaken once all the knowledge has been imparted. This covers all the skills needed to both generate leads and make sales. There may also be some form of skills assessment to ensure that the salesperson is equipped to start the job.

For regulated products, once all the training is complete, the individual's sales manager must observe the seller in the first interviews carried out in order to determine his or her competency in real-life situations.

The granting of competent status does not mark the end of the seller's training. The salesperson is expected to undergo continuous development to ensure that that skills and knowledge remain up to date.

Personal motivation for effective selling

The word 'motivation' comes from the Latin word meaning 'to move to action'. Therefore to motivate yourself or someone else is to provide a reason for doing something. A good sales manager understands the importance of motivation and is able to use an individual's personal motivations to stimulate interest and therefore help him or her to carry out certain tasks and achieve the desired results.

Obviously this is a much simpler task if the individual is naturally self-motivated and wants to achieve success, and therefore the recruitment process is extremely important when employing people for sales roles. A well-motivated salesperson shows an evident and definite desire to do well and has energy, determination, drive and strength of purpose. The role of the sales manager is to recognize this motivation, deepen and develop it and then show the salesperson how to use motivation in order to become effective at the job of selling.

There are some tasks that have to be performed by a salespeople that they do not enjoy or find repetitive or boring. The very nature of a salespeople means that they are likely to find paperwork boring and time-consuming. However in a regulated industry this paperwork is essential. Sellers in both branch and non-branch environments may need to make cold calls to customers to tell them about the services they have to offer, and many staff do not enjoy this activity. The manager is responsible for ensuring that the individuals are sufficiently motivated to carry out these tasks

Let us have a look at the ways in which a manager can help to motivate a sales team to become or remain effective sellers.

- *Always be motivated oneself.* Set an example to the staff by always showing a real enthusiasm for success.

- *Create a positive feeling about the job in all members of the team.* Make sure that all the people in a selling role are proud of the job that they do and the service they offer. In other words the sellers must be made to feel good about what they do and helped to see that the job they do is of benefit to the company, and most importantly, is of great value to the customers.

- *Set challenging but realistic targets for each of the salespeople.* For example, if a salesperson hates telephoning to make appointments, the manager could set a daily or weekly target. The target must be challenging enough to give the salesperson a real sense of achievement when completed, but must be realistic and achievable in order to avoid the demotivation that would come from constant failure.

- *Giving regular feedback to all salespeople about their performance shows individuals that they are important and that a real interest is being shown in their successes.* Regular discussions motivate because the seller sees the manager taking time to talk regularly, and gives the manger a chance to inspire the seller.

- *A good manger knows that motivating a salesperson to achieve good results means treating each person as an individual.* The thing that motivates one person may be totally different to the thing that motivates another. Motivating factors can be in the form of either the 'carrot' or the 'stick', and different people react differently to each.

For those people who are motivated by potential reward rather than be the threat of punishment, the reward can take many forms and is not always monetary. Although money is often seen as being the only motivator for salespeople, many studies have shown this to be untrue. Being rewarded sufficiently for the job that you perform is important for anybody, not just those who sell. Believing that you are not correctly remunerated can be very de-motivating. However, provided that the level of pay is fair for the tasks performed, additional money is often shown to be less motivating than other factors. Although many salespeople are rewarded with additional money for extra performance, it is often the fact that this shows their efforts are being recognized that provides motivation, more than just the money itself.

Other motivators can include the following:

● A sense of achievement.

● Recognition by management or by their peer group that they are successful.

● An advancement in status, i.e. a promotion.

● The granting of additional responsibility once they have achieved a certain level or completed certain tasks.

● Additional incentives, such as trips.

Motivation is a very personal thing, and entirely dependant on the individual's needs and desires. A sales manger should to be able to recognize those individual motivations and use them to ensure the person becomes an effective seller.

13.2 The role of sales targets and the criteria for ownership

Any person whose role is that of selling within the financial services industry needs to have a sales target. This is true of salespeople who are full-time sellers, or whose role is only partly to sell. It applies equally to branch-based salespeople and to those who are 'out on the road' or sell over the telephone in a call centre environment.

The very nature of salespeople means that they tend to be people who like to be able to see their results measured and to have other people see their results. Everybody who works for an organization is likely to have objectives set for them, that is, their manager will state clearly what he or she expects that employee to achieve for the company. Salespeople are no different, they need to know exactly what is expected of them, and this is done by the setting of a sales target.

There are many reasons for an organization to set sales targets, some of which are as follows:

● Sales targets give the individual sellers something to aim for, a goal to be achieved day by day and week by week. It allows the seller to see how well he or she is doing in a chosen role.

- It allows the managers to see how well an individual salesperson is performing and allows the manager to make easy comparisons between different sellers in terms of progress towards target.

- It is an excellent way of motivating salespeople. Providing the sales target is challenging but still achievable, it will motivate the seller who will try to work that little bit harder to reach or exceed the target. It will also provide a sense of real achievement for the salespeople when they see that they have reached their sales target or surpassed it.

- When each individual seller has been set a realistic sales target, the targets can then all be added together to show the overall company sales target and give the senior managers a view on the level of business that is expected to be written in that year. This is essential for planning purposes. However in many instances, the process may happen the other way round, i.e. the company planning process shows how much business needs to be written and this will then be divided by the sellers to give them an individual sales target.

- Having a sales target allows the individual sellers, branch managers and senior managers to judge how the business is progressing throughout the year in relation to the business plan. This provides an early warning system if things are not progressing as expected and allows the company to take remedial action or carry out re-forecasts and re-targetting if necessary.

- Sales targets give part-time sellers the necessary focus for this particular part of their role and ensure that they give sufficient time and attention to it.

When we consider sales targets we need to ensure that we include all the different types of targets that a seller can be set. The most obvious sales targets are those that refer to the amount of business written, but the best sales planning involves targeting the salespeople for a number and a variety of things in order to ensure that the overall business plans are met. Examples of the types of targets a seller can be set are shown below.

- The seller could be expected to achieve a certain number of sales in a given period, e.g. 5 product sales per week or 200 product sales per year.

- Alternatively the seller could be targeted with a value of sales rather than a number, for example a target could be to write investment business of £500,000 in the next twelve months, or attract deposits of £50,000 per week, etc.

- As well as these final sales targets, the majority of organizations are aware that the right level of activity needs to be carried out if sales targets are to be met, and they are therefore likely to target other activity in addition to actual business written. For example, a target could be something like 'to carry out 10 customer interviews each week' or 'to conduct 1 sales seminar each month'.

- Salespeople who work in call centres are also targeted on such things as talk time, i.e. how much of their working day they actually spend on the telephone to customers and how many calls they take.

- Another important area for salespeople to be targeted is on the amount of business they lose. The organization want its sellers to write large amounts of business, but because of the costs involved in this, it wants to ensure that the business they write will stay with the company for some time. They therefore target their salespeople to achieve as low a level of cancellations as possible.

- They may also want to target their sellers on the level of service that they provide to ensure as well as achieving the sales, they do so in a way that enhances the company's reputation and builds on their brand values. This is particularly the case if the individual is selling regulated products, where all of the advice is likely to be checked by a supervisor who may set targets concerning the maximum number of errors/ommissions that are permitted.

- Although the level of business written is going to be the ultimate target for any salesperson, the other targets regarding activity levels especially need to form part of the overall targets for the individual. These help to guide the individual's activities to ensuring that the overall targets are met, and allow the sale manager to see if volume/case count targets are likely to be achieved, and if not, why not.

Once the sales targets have been set it is important that people take ownership of these targets, and feel a level of responsibility for ensuring that they are achieved. We saw earlier in the chapter on planning sales activity that the sales targets can be set in one of two ways:

1. *Top down* – The senior management decide on the overall sales required by the business to achieve the growth/profit/shareholder value that is required by the corporate plan. This is then divided between the areas of the business, and then by region, area, individual branch and individual seller to give a salesperson his or her sales target.

2. *Bottom up* – The individual salespeople look at their own circumstances and customer base etc. and plan their activity for the coming year. They then set their own sales targets based on what they think they can achieve. These are then collated at branch, at region and finally at business level to show the amount of business that can be reasonably expected that year.

In reality what may well happen is a combination of the two. Whereas option 1 is the better way of ensuring that the sales plans match the corporate plans, option 2 is the better for achieving ownership of the plans among the sales force. If option 2 is to be adopted as a planning method, there need to be some measures imposed to ensure that the total of the individual's plans eventually match those targets set out in the corporate plan.

This said, an individual seller is more likely to feel ownership of sales targets if he or she has had some input into setting them. There are many benefits to having a seller feel ownership for sales plan, for example:

- The seller starts the year feeling that the plan is achievable, rather than feeling he or she has been allocated an impossible task. This may well be the case, even if the self-set target ends up the same as would have been set by the management. Because the seller has been involved in the process of planning the activity he or she will be able to see how a challenging target could be achieved.

- Salespeople will be much more committed to a target they feel they have set themselves and that they truly own, and therefore be much more willing to put in that extra effort that may be needed to achieve it. This is because if they do not achieve it they will feel that they are letting themselves down as well as their managers and the organization.

- Some salespeople set themselves higher, more demanding targets than would have been set for them by their managers because they base the targets on their own skills and abilities rather than those of the sales force in general.

But of course the individual seller is not the only person who needs to feel ownership of the sales targets. If the business is to be successful, then it must achieve the targets it sets for itself in the corporate plan and every person involved in the selling process in any way must accept some responsibility for, and feel ownership of, part of those sales plans and those sales targets. This will include:

- The individual sellers who must own their own individual sales targets and take responsibility for achieving them.

- The branch managers who must take ownership of the collective branch plan, i.e. the sum of the individual sales targets, and ensure that as a branch they meet the targets they have been set.

- Area and regional managers who should own the sales targets for their total areas and regions and ensure that everything that is needed to be done to achieve them, is done.

- The national sales manager should take ownership of the total sales targets, and assume responsibility for the sales plan as a whole.

- All senior managers need to feel that they too have some ownership of the sales plan, and some responsibility for their part in ensuring that targets are met. For example, the marketing manager is responsible for ensuring that there is enough advertising carried out, and that there are sufficient leads provided for the salespeople to allow them to meet their targets. He is also responsible for ensuring that the products are sufficiently competitive and tailored to the customers' needs to enable the salespeople to sell them.

What we can see from this brief look at the role of sales targets and their ownership is that properly set, realistic yet stretching sales targets have many benefits for both the individual and the company as a whole. However if the maximum benefit is to be gained from setting sales targets, everybody involved in achieving them needs to have some ownership of them and feel some level of responsibility for that achievement.

13.3   Reward

There are two basic ways of rewarding salespeople for the job they perform. They can either be paid a salary regardless of what they sell and in what volumes, or they can be paid in commission, i.e. they only receive reward related exactly to what they have sold. There are financial services companies rewarding their salespeople in either one of these ways because there are advantages and disadvantages to each.

Salaried sales force

A salaried sales force has the following advantages over a commission-only sales force:

- The stability of a regular salary is likely to attract more people to the job, because they will be sure of an income to cover their commitments.

- They may gain an image advantage with the public; i.e. an individual may trust the salesperson's recommendations more if it is known that the seller is not being paid for each individual sale.

- The company may feel more secure in the knowledge that the salesperson will not be tempted to oversell and therefore cause compliance problems and customer complaints for the company.

The disadvantages of this method of rewarding them are as follows:

- The company pays the sellers whether they sell or not and therefore the salespeople may lack the motivation to do well. Salespeople are often allowed to manage their own time, and if unmotivated may well not make the maximum effort.

- If all sellers are being paid the same, there is the possibility that the very successful ones may feel they are not being fairly rewarded for their efforts and leave to join a company that pays on results, leaving a sales force of poor sellers.

Commission-only sales force

The arguments for this method of reward work pretty much in reverse to those set out above. The advantages are:

- Because they be paid only for what they actually achieve, the salespeople are motivated to work hard and achieve high volumes of sales.

- The company does not lose large amounts of money paying people who are not suited to a role as a salesperson.

- The company may be able to attract proven successful salespeople from other companies, who are confident that they can achieve high levels of sales and therefore earn large amounts of money.

The disadvantages are as follows:

- They may struggle to recruit large numbers of people, especially if they are completely new to the role.

- They may need to think very carefully as to how they position such a package with the public, particularly such things as life and pension sales where there is a duty to disclose the level of commission paid to the saleperson for the sale.

- They may be open to the possibility of overselling on the part of the salesperson if they are rewarded purely on sales volume, and therefore close monitoring will be vital.

Combined salary and commission

Because there are advantages and disadvantages to each of the methods or remuneration, many financial services salespeople are rewarded by a combination of salary and commission. They are paid a low basic salary and then a reduced level of commission on the sales they make, or are paid commission only when they have reached a certain level of sales. The aim of this is to try to achieve the best of both worlds, i.e. attract the right people, but reward the best performers and motivate everybody to do well.

Many companies use other methods, apart from pure pay, to reward their sales staff. These additional rewards can be such things as gift vouchers, merchandise or travel, and are used as incentives for the high achievers and as recognition for extra performance. We shall look at the use of incentives in more detail later in this chapter.

13.4   Recognition

As well as being paid for the job that they perform, many salespeople are motivated by receiving recognition both from their managers and their peers as to the fact that they have done a particularly good job. Most companies and most sales managers understand the importance of recognizing when an individual has put in a particularly good performance or made special effort and use this to improve or maintain sales levels. Some examples of the way that managers can give recognition are as follows.

Use of league tables showing the company's star performers, for example, top 10 mortgage advisers, top branch manager, top 3 investment consultants. These can be issued monthly and sent to all relevant employees, so that the top performers know that everybody is being informed of their outstanding efforts.

A letter from the sales manager is a good way of showing that good sales performance has been recognized. Many sales managers write either on a regular or ad hoc basis to the individuals who have done especially well or whose performance has improved dramatically.

A call from a senior business manager thanking the individual for their contribution to the success of the company and achieving of the business or marketing plan also works well in showing people that their efforts are appreciated.

13.5   Using incentives

Giving salespeople incentives to achieve targets and in fact exceed them, is common practice in the financial services industry. The more extensive use of incentives and the more lavish incentives were probably more commonplace in the insurance companies that operated direct sales forces. However with the banks and building societies moving into new markets and their existing markets becoming increasingly competitive, these organizations are also incentivizing their staff for sales and service excellence.

Let us first look at the reasons for doing this before we go on to see what type of staff this may be applicable to and what form these incentives may take.

The role of incentives

There are two main reasons for offering an incentive to a salesperson. Firstly it is a great motivator for a lot of people. We saw earlier in this chapter the importance of having a motivated and enthusiastic sales team if the targets are to be achieved. Although they are already being paid to do a job, many of the sellers find the promise of some additional reward extremely inviting. This then pushes them to do that little bit extra and work that little bit harder. Also many incentive schemes' benefits are awarded to the top x number of sellers or the top x% of the sales force. This creates competition among the sellers who are all keen to do better than their colleagues. Therefore the better each seller performs, the better the others want to perform in order to be more successful. An element of friendly rivalry can often be useful in helping to boost sales performance.

The other reason for offering incentives is that it enables a manger or company to reward certain types of activity at certain times. Most sellers are paid on the level of business produced and this always remains the best measure of performance. However the manager may wish to reward other elements of the role from time to time without the complications of amending the salary package. For example, the manager may offer an incentive for the highest number of referrals made in one week, or the largest number of telephone calls answered in one month. This is a good tool for the manager who is managing sales activity and wishes the sellers to put in extra effort to one particular activity for a period of time.

Who to incentivize

The obvious people to incentivize in order to improve sales performance is the sales force, and the majority of incentive schemes are run for the benefit of the sellers. However these are not the only people whose work influences the sales results. Let us take as an example the bank that also operates an investment company selling unit trusts and ISAs. If the bank wishes to ensure that their ISA sales targets are met they could well decide to offer an incentive to the people who sold the most, or achieved the highest number of sales against plan. What they should also remember is that the majority of customers who have discussions with, and buy products from, their investment advisers have been referred to them by the counter staff.

The counter staff recognize customers who may potentially benefit from these products and sell the benefits of the investment adviser service to them. If these people did not do their job, and do it well, then the ISA sales targets would no doubt be missed. Because of this dependency, the company may decide to offer an incentive to all staff who make such referrals. They may also offer a further incentive to the individual who proved to be the most successful at making such referrals.

The staff in customer services departments are also vital to the organization, because customers who are unhappy with the service they receive are unlikely to buy again. For this reason the company may decide to offer an incentive to the best customer service staff in recognition of their efforts.

Type of incentive

The type of incentive can vary enormously and depends largely on the staff to whom it applies and the nature of the task they are expected to perform in order to receive it. At the bottom end of the scale the incentive could be something like a bottle of wine or a £5 gift voucher. These types of incentives are likely to be awarded to support staff or customer service staff.

Other more exciting incentives such as weekends away, activity days such as off-road driving, or trips to sporting events are more likely to be offered to salespeople who undertake the selling role either full time, or as a large part of their role. They could be awarded for such things as most successful salesperson for the month or the quarter. Other companies may prefer to offer such things as electrical goods if they feel this will be more effective.

At the top end of the scale, some companies offer their most successful salespeople lavish incentives such as holidays abroad for them and their partners. Obviously in order to be awarded an incentive such as this the company would expect to see exceptional performance over a long period of time. Such an incentive is therefore likely to be awarded, for example, to the top salesperson of the year.

Summary

The need to have a well-motivated sales force and to be able to encourage certain behaviours at certain times have meant that the use of incentives in the financial services industry is widespread. They can be extremely useful in shaping behaviour and increasing motivation. The important thing to remember is that they must be used correctly if they are to achieve the desired result. They must be properly targeted at the people whose actions can really make a difference, and they must be appropriate. There needs to be a great deal of though to ensure that the correct balance is reached, i.e. the incentive needs to be enough to encourage people to change or enhance their behaviour, but the timescales need to be considered also. Sometimes a lesser incentive received almost immediately can be as motivating as a large incentive that requires a full year's work.

The manager also needs to ensure that the incentive motivates everybody, and therefore offer something that everybody has an equal chance of getting. If not, then those people who do not have an equal opportunity to receive the incentive will be de-motivated, rather than encouraged.

Monitoring, reviewing and enhancing sales performance

So far in this chapter we have examined the ways in which a sales team is recruited and trained, the ways in which sellers can be rewarded, and how to set their sales targets. Once all this is done, the team members are then set to go and do their job, i.e. to speak to the customers and sell the company's products.

When they are doing this it is essential for the manager to know how well, or indeed how badly, they are doing their job, and he therefore needs to constantly monitor and review their sales performance. He needs to do this for a number of reasons:

● To see how well salespeople are progressing towards their sales targets.

● To ensure that any shortfall in sales is addressed as soon as possible.

● To spot any knowledge or sales skills defficiencies and rectify them as soon as possible.

● Sales need to be monitored if sellers are paid and/or incentivized by the level of sales they make.

We can start to see how important it is to have accurate and up-to-date management information. Both the individual salesperson, his or her manager, and all the senior managers need a clear picture of how sales are progressing if they are to properly manage their business. The individual wants to know how he or she is progressing towards the sales targets. The manager wants to know the same for each seller in order to judge how well the branch or area is progressing towards its sales targets. Senior managers need an overall picture of the sales results in order that they can judge how the business as a whole is moving towards its goals.

All of this means that all of the sales activity needs to be monitored and reviewed regularly. Although this type of information could be collected from the individual sellers in the form of manual statistics (they could each report their activity each week, for example), many companies have recognized the importance of having accurate and up-to-the-minute MI and use computer-based systems. If all sales activity is recorded on a computer, it will be easy for individuals and managers to request and examine such information, knowing it is accurate and timely.

What we need to consider next is the type of information that has to be recorded in order to monitor and review a salesperson's performance. In the same way as we considered setting sales targets, the most important measure for any seller is of course the number and value of products sold and therefore this always needs to be recorded. However we also said that we would need to target other activity that was essential for the seller to be successful, and if it is targeted, it needs to be monitored and reviewed.

For the rest of this chapter we use an example seller to look at the ways in which we should monitor and review performance. Our example seller is a full-time salesperson who works for a High Street bank. He or she works in the branch selling the bank's mortgage products to new and existing customers. As well as selling mortgages the salesperson is targeted to sell additional products, such as buildings and contents insurance, and other banking products, such as current accounts. Each branch has a similar mortgage adviser, with a total of two hundred throughout the company.

Obviously the individual seller wants to know exactly how he or she is doing against each of the targets that have been set, therefore the monitoring of sales performance may need to look something like this.

Figure 13.3: Monthly sales performance statistics

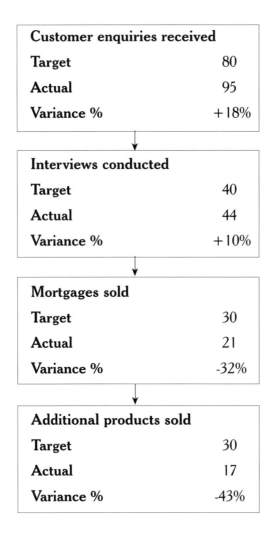

Customer enquiries received	
Target	80
Actual	95
Variance %	+18%

Interviews conducted	
Target	40
Actual	44
Variance %	+10%

Mortgages sold	
Target	30
Actual	21
Variance %	-32%

Additional products sold	
Target	30
Actual	17
Variance %	-43%

Both the individual seller and the manager will be interested in the information shown above. Each of the statistics should be examined carefully in order to assess the seller's performance. For example, what we can see from the set of information presented above is that the national or branch advertising campaign, which is being used to generate enquiries, seems to be successful because the salesperson is receiving more than the planned number of enquirers.

We can also see that the individual is successfully turning those enquirers into appointments, as has conducted more than the required number of interviews for the month in question. Where he or she does seem to have a problem is in converting those interviews into business. Although the seller has carried out the required number of interviews he (let us assume the seller is a man) he has written much less business than expected.

His targets show that he is expected to sell a mortgage to 75% of the people who go to see him, and yet we can see from the statistics that he is selling only to approx. 50% of the people he sees. Also his sale of additional products is well below target. He is targeted to sell on average one additional product to each person to whom he sells a mortgage, i.e. 30 a month. Although it could be argued that his cross-sales are down because his mortgage sales are down, we can see that he has still sold another product to only 85% of the customers who bought a mortgage product.

With this information at hand the manager can start to make judgements about the individual's performance and what is needed in order to get back on target. The manager first needs to investigate the reasons for the shortfall in performance and this may well mean spending some time with the seller and watching him in his role, as there could be several reasons why he is not meeting sales targets.

In the case of our example mortgage adviser, it could be that the quality of the enquiries is low, i.e. there are a lot of people coming in to have an interview who are not actually ready to make a purchase. It could be the products that the salesperson has to sell are uncompetitive and therefore people are rejecting them. Alternatively it could be the individual is lacking in some of the skills needed to turn enquiries into sales and is therefore losing business.

It is the role of the individual salesperson's manager to monitor and review the seller's performance on a regular basis. They should meet at least on a monthly basis and look at the activity that has taken place and how the seller is progressing towards sales targets. They will then need to agree between them the remedial action needed if there is a shortfall in performance. The type of action required depends on the reason for the shortfall and we will examine this in more detail later in this chapter.

13.6   National sales performance

Whereas the individual seller and the manager will closely monitor and review an individual salesperson's performance, the senior management of the financial services organization needs to monitor and review sales performance on a national basis. Although they will need to be aware of individual's performances, they will be primarily concerned with how the company is performing as a whole against the sales targets set out in the business plan. Because of this they are likely to gather information on a national level. This said, they will still be interested in all of the same statistics as the individual sellers, i.e. number of enquiries generated, number of interviews carried out and the level and value of sales made. This information could be presented to the senior management team as follows.

The senior management team will want to monitor this type of information and review it regularly. They may well request such information on a national basis in order to see how the company is performing as a whole. However they may also wish to see the information shown by region or area, or even by individual branch if they feel this will enhance their understanding of the figures. They may also want to see figures on the market as a whole in order that they can review their company's performance against that of the market, and allow for any market trends and fluctuations.

By getting together and going through the figures they will be able to discuss such things as:

- The effectiveness of the marketing activity being carried out both nationally and locally in order to generate interest in the products and services. They will be able to judge whether it is sufficient or if more activity needs to be carried out. The statistics, together with feedback from the sellers and their managers, will also indicate whether the marketing activity is attracting the right type of customer as well as the right quantity.

- The ability of the sales staff to turn those enquiries into appointments with mortgage advisers. They will see on a national basis how many customer discussions are taking place, and will be able to predict the number of mortgage advisers that are necessary for the organization to meet its targets.

- They will see the number of sales being made and will be able to discuss the sales ability of their staff. They can see if there are individual problems or if there is a general reason why sales are not as high, or are indeed higher, than they had predicted.

- They will be able to spot problems in the marketing mix, for example, they may see that there is some problem with the pricing of the product if a large number of customers attend meetings and then reject the product offering when they have discussed it and seen the terms.

- They will be able to spot sales management issues, such as problems with certain branches or areas that are not meeting target and deal with them at an early stage before targets are missed.

- They will be able to spot trends in the figures and act upon them, for example, they may see a dramatic increase in enquiries and therefore they will be able to ensure that more advisers are recruited and trained in order to deal with them.

- They will be able to use these figures to see how the company is performing against the targets set for the year, and if necessary they will be able to carry out re-forcasts of business levels, either higher or lower than was initially planned. They can then see the effect that these business levels have on the company's profits and either accept them or make the necessary actions to remedy the sales figures and bring the results back in line with the corporate plans.

Summary

What we can see from this brief look at monitoring sales performance is that the sales a company makes are of vital importance in the meeting of the corporate objectives and in the profitability of the organization. Because of this, the sales performance is not something that can be neglected throughout the year and considered simply at the end of the year as part of the company's results. The sales performance needs to be constantly monitored to ensure that the targets are being met and that the sales volumes and value are progressing as desired towards the organization's targets. As well as monitoring the sales performance on a national basis, it also needs to be monitored and regularly reviewed on an individual basis to ensure that every salesperson within the organization is achieving what he or she needs to achieve to ensure the business is a success. Monitoring and reviewing individual performances will enable the managers to spot weakness and shortfalls as they arise and rectify them quickly. After all, if each individual meets personal sales targets, the organization as a whole will meet its sales targets.

We can also see how important it is to have accurate Management Information if the senior managers are to be able to use such information to make accurate and well-informed decisions about the marketing mix and the future plans of the company.

13.7 Enhancing sales performance

If the monitoring and reviewing of the sales performance highlights a shortfall in the sales results, the manager needs to take action to rectify the problem. This said it then becomes obvious that the first step in enhancing sales performance is to:

Identify the problem

This sounds simple, but is actually much more difficult than it seems. It is fairly easy to look at the management information and to spot that one of the mortgage advisers is considerably below target with sales figures. However, accurately diagnosing exactly what the problem is can be extremely tricky. There could be a number of reasons for poor sales performance, for example:

1. Not enough customer enquiries, i.e. the adviser simply does not have enough people to sell to.

2. The quality of the leads could be poor, i.e. the enquirers could be customers who do not fit within the organization's lending criteria and therefore the adviser cannot sell them anything.

3. The products that the adviser is attempting to sell could be uncompetitively priced or unsuitable for the target market and are therefore being rejected by the customers. If this

was the problem it is likely that it would effect the sales results of all sellers not just the odd one.

4. It could be that the problem lies with the individual salesperson. It could be that he or she is simply not working hard enough, i.e. not putting in enough hours, or not carrying out enough calls, for example. Alternatively it could be that the seller does not have the necessary knowledge or skills to make the sales and that he or she is therefore losing business that should have been written.

It is the job of the salesperson's manager to spot the problem and identify the cause. In some cases the seller volunteers the information, and may well be only too eager to explain that there are not enough customer enquiries, for example. However, in other cases, particularly where the problem lies with the individual, he or she will be much less forthcoming with an explanation.

Salespeople are reluctant to tell their managers if they have a knowledge or skills defecit that is causing them problems. In some cases they may well not even be aware themselves that this is the problem. It is therefore up to the manager to spend time and effort with that individual to fully understand the cause of the problem before rectifying it in order to enhance the performance.

Having accurately diagnosed the problem, the next step is of course to:

Take action to enhance sales performance

The action taken depends totally on the nature of the problem. Once the manager has accurately seen the reason for the shortfall in sales, he or she can take the necessary steps to ensure that performance is increased. This could well involve one, or a combination of, the following:

- Increasing marketing activity, either on a national level if need be, or on a local branch level if this is where the enquiries are required.

- Amending the type of marketing carried out, or re-focusing the message to attract a different target audience.

- Improving the sales skills of the staff who deal with the enquiries to ensure that they get the maximum number of customers to take their enquiry further.

- Improving the knowledge of the adviser, by retraining to ensure that he or she can deal with all customer's questions and accurately represent the benefits of the company's products and services.

- Improve the sales skills of the individual by training them or by allowing them to observe other sellers in their role. The skills defecit could be in any area of the sales process, for example, identifying customers needs, selling the benefits, handling objections or closing the sale. The manager should ensure that the salesperson understands where the problem lies and ensure that sufficient help is given along with the opportunity to practise and improve those skills.

- The problem could be one of morale and motivation. The manager needs to use management skills and knowledge of that individual to find a way to improve morale and to give the additional motivation required to increase sales performance.

- There may be a problem with the product and therefore some enhancements to the products or some changes to the pricing could be needed in order to bring about an up-turn in the company's sales performance.

- It could be that there simply are not enough people doing the selling to bring about the number of sales required, and therefore employing more people in the selling role may enhance the company's sales performance.

- There could be changes in the sales procedure that would result in an improvement in sales. For example, an improvement in the underwriting procedures giving a quicker mortgage decision may well mean that more sales are made and figures improve dramatically.

- The systems and paperwork needed to allow a sale to be made could be improved if improved sales performance is required. For example, it may be that changes can be made that will make it easier for the salesperson to make multi-sales, i.e. sell more than one product per customer.

What we can see from the above is that in one way or another, any improvement in sales performance can be linked to the elements of the marketing mix. Therefore if an individual salesperson or an organization wishes to enhance sales performance, it should look to the different elements of the mix and see what changes can be made and what results those changes would bring about.

Of course an individual or an organization should not restrict the enhancement of sales performance to those times when the results show that there is a shortfall against the business plan. Looking to improve sales performance should be a constant objective for any seller as well as for the manager and senior management team.

Even if the sales figures are well above the level planned there is always room for improvement, and everybody employed by the organization should constantly be looking for ways in which the sales performance can be enhanced.

14

UNDERSTANDING INDIVIDUAL CUSTOMER EXPECTATIONS

After reading this chapter you should

- Understand the importance of creating, maintaining and developing, customer relationships

- Be aware of the customer's current service needs and possible future service needs

- Know how customer satisfaction surveys can be carried out and what use they can be to the organization

- Understand how services are charged for

- Be aware of codes of conduct and the levels of professionalism customers can expect to receive from financial services providers

14.1　Building and maintaining customer relationships

Why adopt relationship marketing?

Often the marketing carried out by many companies is designed to target a specific customer. We saw in previous chapters the methods that marketeers use to segment their customers and the population as a whole into groups of like-minded people, and then select certain groupings to try to sell to. They do this because they are trying to select the type of people that it will be profitable to do business with.

To carry out such segmentation and to design promotions and distribution methods to suit these target customers is costly. As markets become more competitive the cost of finding new customers increases, particularly in maturing markets where there are a limited number of new customers to sell to and the organizations find themselves increasingly competing to attract the same consumers.

Wherever this is the case, as it is in the financial services industry, providers find there is a benefit to be gained from ensuring that they keep the customers they already have. It is far easier and less costly to keep the customers they already have than to try to keep attracting customers from their competitors. The way to do this is by building long-term profitable relationships with their customers, and hence the move from transactional selling to relationship marketing.

Relationship marketing can be defined as follows:

The art of creating and maintaining over time a strong and value-driven relationship with customers.

In today's environment financial services companies cannot take their customers for granted. Gone are the days when the loss of a customer can be shrugged off, and the business quickly and easily replaced by the acquisition of another customer. Today organizations need to view their marketing and sales activity in terms of the 'net' gain they have made, i.e. the number of new customers they have acquired less the number of existing customers they have lost.

The smartest of providers pay close attention to the rate of customer loss and take steps to reduce it. They need to spend time and resources looking closely at the reasons for customer loss and take steps to eliminate it. They must ensure that they understand the reasons that customers may take their business elsewhere. This could be because of a number of things, such as poor products, unsatisfactory service, or an uncompetitive price. It must be seen to be equally important to get all elements of the marketing mix right for existing customers as it is for new customers.

To show the benefit of doing this, companies should calculate the lost revenue they will suffer when customers leave the organization and go to a competitor. To do this they need to work out the customer's lifetime benefit to the organization, i.e. how much revenue would the customer have brought to the company if he or she had stayed a customer and carried on transacting business with them?

The company will find that if they assess the value of a life-long customer and therefore the loss they will suffer by not retaining that customer, this will by far outweigh the costs that are involved in taking steps to retain that business. Add to this the comparative cost of acquiring a new customer to the costs involved in keeping an existing one, often five times as much, and we can see the benefits of building strong customer relationships.

Although many marketeers focus their activity and product mix issues on attracting new customers and making new sales, the most successful put equal effort into retention of those they have previously worked so hard to obtain. Simply looking at ways of attracting new customers is a short-term strategy; companies must take the long-term view and see the lifetime benefit of the people who do business with them.

The best way of retaining customers is to deliver a level of high customer satisfaction through product, price and promotion, etc. This will result in strong customer loyalty and make those customers far more open to buying further products and services, as well as far less likely to be attracted by offers from other financial services companies.

How to build customer relationships

If a company is to move from transactional selling to relationship marketing, the organization needs a suitable structure. Those financial services companies that are themselves segmented, with different sales forces selling different products from their range, find it more difficult to build successful relationships because they have a number of salespeople dealing with the same customer at different times. Effective relationship building requires the active cooperation of all departments within the company.

It also requires the managers to recognize that keeping the customer requires more than just good products and an active sales force. It needs to be a coordinated activity across the entire company if they are to create a value-laden relationship. Relationship marketing is based on the theory that in order to feel valued by their provider customers need focused, tailored and continuous attention.

This attention can come from the salesperson who first introduced them to the company and sold them their product, or from a central source within the company such as the marketing department, and the decision as to which is most effective is dictated by the customers' preferences.

The most effective and successful salespeople are not only good sellers, good objection handlers and good closers. They have excellent interpersonal skills and are good problem solvers and relationship builders. The best salespeople have customers who have dealt with them for years, for all their financial needs, and who see them as friends as well as business acquaintances.

These salespeople do not only call on their customers when they feel there may be an opportunity for more business, they remain in constant contact with them, problem solving and showing an interest in their needs and requirements. This approach, building a business relationship, will improve the chances that the customer will carry our further business with them when the need arises and will reduce the chance of that customer being attracted by approaches by other financial services sellers.

Selecting which customers to build relationships with

Relationship marketing is the art of attracting and keeping the customers that are, or will prove to be, the most profitable for the company. Not all customers bring profit to an organization. Some purchase only products with low margins and demand high levels of servicing; therefore they do not make money for the company. Of those that do bring profit to the organization, some bring more than others.

Financial services companies have huge numbers of customers—some of them have many millions of people on their databases. They cannot possibly successfully build relationships with every one of those people. The role of the marketing manager is to recognize which of those people should have more time and effort spent on them.

The way to do this is to categorize the customers in terms of the lifetime value they could bring to the company, i.e. the amount by which the revenue they could generate throughout their life-long relationship with the company will exceed the cost of their acquisition and servicing. The company should only attempt to build relationships with those customers that have the potential to bring profit to the company.

Shown below is one way the company could categorize customers. They are ranked as A, B or C depending on the worth and potential profit. The customer worth is determined by how much they earn, i.e. how much net disposable income they have and can therefore afford to spend with the company. The profit is judged by the profit levels in the products they have bought or are most likely to buy. We can see that the best customers are those with a high level of disposable income who have bought products with high profit margins.

Figure 14.1: Customer relationship categories 1

		Customer value		
		High	Medium	Low
	High Margin	A	B	B
Product profit	Medium	A	B	C
	Low	B	B	C

Because the company cannot build relationships with each and every customer it puts the bulk of its resource into the customers categorized as A, followed by those considered to be Bs. They spend less time and effort on those considered to be Cs. If the groupings of A, B, and C are likely to be confused with socio-economic groupings, the company could decide to call them Gold, Silver and Bronze customers, for example. The diagram over the page shows another, slightly different method of categorizing customers.

Figure 14.2: Customer relationship categories 2

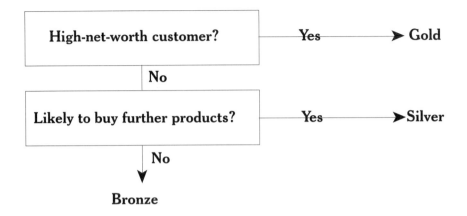

There are different levels of service and communication that an organization can offer to its customers. It could offer the very basic sales service, it could offer a level of customer service on a reactive basis, or it could choose to be pro-active in its service provision.

Basic   Sells the customer a product but offers no follow-up activity.

Reactive   Sells the product and then encourages the customer to contact the salesperson or customer services department whenever there is a problem or a further need.

Pro-active   Sells the product and then contacts the customer on a regular basis with suggestions of other suitable products and services, and helps with problem solving.

If the company wants to develop relationships with its customers it will need to offer the reactive approach as its very minimum, and the pro-active approach with its best customers.

We said earlier that in order to build a relationship with the customer and build customer loyalty the company would need to have frequent and focused contact with those customers. We also saw that it would be necessary to focus the resource on the Gold customers. Therefore the company needs to develop a contact strategy for each type of customer, involving the type of contact that builds loyalty and adds value to the relationship.

The table on the next page shows how one company is planning to add value for its customers by issuing useful and timely communications to each of its product holders. The communications it sends depend on the perceived lifetime value of the customer.

Figure 14.3: Communications plan for relationship marketing

Customer category	Gold (pro-active)	Silver (pro-active)	Bronze (basic)
Communications	Regulatory requirement	Regulatory requirement	Regulatory requirement only
	Three-monthly telephone call from adviser	Six-monthly telephone call from adviser	
	Half-yearly customer newsletter	Quarterly special offers for other products	
	Quarterly special offers for other products		

In the table above we can see that the plan is to send the most value customers special offers, i.e. a discount off other products. This is just one of the ways that the company can build loyalty. Let us look at the range of methods it could use to do this.

Financial benefits

Offering financial benefits is certainly a popular way of rewarding customers for their loyalty and for repeat purchases. This is most common in other industries where such things as frequent-flyer programmes are common, as are discounts for frequent users of hotels, and supermarkets who reward their customers with money-off vouchers dependent on the level of their spending.

With this type of customer benefit, it is usually the company that does it first that gains the most publicity and makes the greatest gain in customer loyalty. This type of offer is fairly easy to copy and in most cases competitors will be quick to follow in a defensive move, to ensure that they retain their own customers and do not see them tempted away by the first company's offer.

Social benefits

By this we mean the building of a relationship between the customer and the staff of the company, be this an individual salesperson or the staff at a particular branch. In an attempt to do this many companies encourage their staff to call the customers by their names and to chat with them while serving them. If they see the customers regularly and can remember information about them and their preferences, this helps to build this social relationship and encourage customer loyalty. After all, people often buy off people they like, even if they do not offer the most competitive product.

Structural ties

Another way of encouraging customer loyalty is to offer the customer help that he or she will find it difficult to do without. For example, a company that is selling group pensions to a business may, as part of the offer, include help with the payroll. This kind of structural tie will make the business think more carefully about moving to another provider.

Value-added communications

One way of adding value to the relationship is to give the customer a benefit from having that relationship, which does not necessarily need to be financial – it could be educational, for example. The company could send their customers regular information aimed at improving their knowledge and helping them to understand better their future purchases.

Financial services

As we saw, more and more financial services companies are trying to move to relationship marketing and introducing benefits for their customers in an attempt to build customer loyalty and add value to the relationship for the customer. In an attempt to do this they have designed programmes with a variety of different approaches.

We have seen companies advertising the benefits of their advisers' personal and friendly services (social benefit) and other companies who have rewarded their customers for multi-purchases with a financial benefit. A good example of this is Legal & General which advertised a 'buy one get one free' type advertisement for their PEP product. If a customer bought a Personal Equity Plan from them two years running and held those plans for a certain length of time, the company would refund all the charges on one of the products.

Others have adopted the 'Club' approach whereby buying a product from the company automatically entitles the customer to be a member of the club and receive certain benefits. These benefits are both financial and added-value benefits. For example, a club for people who have bought household insurance could include such things as the following:

- A newsletter containing information relating to the home, such as decorating tips, gardening items, and helpful advice on home security.

- Special deals on buildings insurance for people with contents-only insurance, and vice versa.

- Special offers for related products such as household goods or home security systems, arranged through other providers.

If done well such customer loyalty programmes can help to bond the customer to the company and create strong and lasting business relationships.

Another example that shows evidence of financial services companies' desire to build relationships with their customers and retain those customers for life, is the level of activity that banks are undertaking to attract students to their organizations. Many of the banks are offering incentives for students to open current accounts– such things as restaurant vouchers, record vouchers, etc.– as well as offering them special rates on overdrafts and student loans.

The reason they are so keen to attract students is that the bank has calculated the lifetime benefit of those customers. They see them as being the potentially wealthy customers of the future and see enormous future potential in them. They feel that if they can attract them when they are young and build relationships with them through excellent services and value-added service offerings, they will continue to be a customer throughout their future working life.

14.2   Customer expectations of present and future service requirements

When customers enter into a relationship with a financial services organization by buying a product or service, they have expectations of the service they should be given. These expectations are shaped by their previous dealings with other financial services providers and retailers in general. Their expectations are also shaped by the type of product they have purchased, the price they have paid, as well as such factors as the company's brand and advertising messages.

If the company is to successfully build on the relationship it has with the customer it needs to understand the customer's expectations in order that it can meet them, or indeed surpass them if at all possible. While individual customers have different expectations of the service, the company should expect that it probably will not be able to meet absolutely all of them. There will, however, be many that are common to most customers and these must be met if the company is to retain these people and enjoy repeat business from them.

The customers will have expectations that relate to the branches and offices they visit, the staff that deal with them, and of the business as a whole. Let us look at the type of service standards the customer may rightly expect to receive.

Branch   Customers may expect:

- A good location which is near to the town centre and with parking facilities, for example.

- The interior to be smart and clean with sufficient room for people to move about and queue if necessary.

- Staff to be smart in appearance, probably in a uniform.

- For there to be interview rooms where they can discuss their financial affairs in private if they need to.

- Opening hours to suit their needs, and out-of-hours facilities such as ATMs, etc.

Staff   Customers may expect the staff to be:

- Honest, both in their dealings with them personally, and in general.

- Helpful and friendly, always appearing to enjoy helping the customer.

- Knowledgeable about the company and their products and services.

- Competent in their dealings with them.

Business   The customer may expect the company to:

- React quickly to any requests made by them.

- Ensure that all their personal details remain confidential.

- Get it right first time, and correct their error quickly if they do not.

- Have procedures and technology that is customer focused.

- Treat them as an individual.

Of course the customer's needs will change over time and therefore so will their expectation of service standards. In recent years customers have become far more demanding of the service they expect to be provided with, and financial services providers have managed to keep pace with those expectations. However if they are to keep up with the consumer's ever-changing demands they will need to ensure that they have some method of assessing exactly what those requirements are and measuring their performance against them.

14.3   Customer satisfaction surveys

As the service provider the company may feel that the service they are offering is exactly meeting the requirements that their customers have. They could well believe that they have got everything right regarding their dealings with customers. They may well have conducted research before launching their services to try to ensure they know what customers want, and may have tested this service with potential customers. If these service standards are then implemented, the company could well think that this ensures their customers will be entirely satisfied.

However they cannot be confident that the people who now experience the service are entirely satisfied with it. There are many reasons why the actual level of customer satisfaction may be below that which the company is expecting, for example:

- There could be a difference between the level of service that the provider thinks the customer expects and what those customers actually expect.

- The staff of the company may not be applying the service standards as laid down by the provider. There could be several reasons for this: it could be that they are unaware of the service standards they are supposed to be adhering to, it could be because they are under pressure because of heavy workloads, or it could be because they are dealing with changed processes etc.

- As time goes by, customers expectations of the service they should get will change, and if the company does not regularly monitor and modify its service standards it will soon become out of date.

There is obviously a need for the service manager to know how customers feel about the service they receive, and the best way of doing this is to ask them– hence the customer satisfaction survey.

These surveys can be as simple or as complex the company wants to make them. The type of questions asked and the methodology used depend on the objectives of the survey. Companies often send short written questionnaires through the post to customers who have recently experienced a particular element of the service offered by the company. They are asked to rate different aspects of the service they received, and comment on anything they feel particularly strongly about.

A company could do this as a single exercise that it repeats every few months, or it could mail a selection of customers on a continuous basis. Whichever way they choose it will be able to monitor the results, correct any common problems and see any trends that are developing.

Below is an example of the sort of questionnaire that could be used for this purpose.

Figure 14.4: Survey form

Customer satisfaction survey

Co. Logo

Thank you for your custom. To help us to improve our customer care and ensure that the service we offer meets the expectations of our customers, we would be grateful if you could answer a few questions about the service you received from us.

What prompted you to contact us in the first place?

Existing customer ☐

Recommended by friend/family ☐

Recommended by financial adviser ☐

Saw the name in the papers ☐

Other ☐

If other please state details

When you rang us was your call answered quickly and courteously?

Yes ☐   No ☐

If no, please tell us why that was

If no, please tell us why that was

Did the person who answered your call deal with your query to your satisfaction?

Yes ☐   No ☐

If no, please tell us why that was

If we needed to call you back, did we do so promptly?

Yes ☐   No ☐

Overall, how would you rate the service you received from us?

Excellent ☐

Good ☐

Average ☐

Poor ☐

Very Poor ☐

What did you think was particularly good/poor about the service we provided?

If there was one thing we could improve, what do you think that should be?

An alternative method of using the customer survey idea to test service standards is to conduct a larger, more in-depth survey among a large number of customers as a one-off exercise. This will act as a 'spot check' of how well the company is meeting its customers' expectations.

The benefit of this approach is that it will be a much more detailed study and therefore provide a greater amount of information for the company. This type of survey could be conducted using a written questionnaire posted to customers, or could be conducted over the telephone, and there are advantages and disadvantages to each. In order to get up-to-date information the survey should be conducted among customers who have experienced the service within the last six months, for example.

Such a survey could be used to measure such things as:

- How satisfied the customers felt after the service encounter.

- Which aspects of the service they feel are particularly important.

- Whether the service experience had left them with a more positive or more negative feeling towards the company.

- If the service the customer received would make them more likely to buy again from the provider, or less likely.

- Which areas of the service could be improved

- What the customers' expectations of service may be in the future.

- How the company can improve the service it offers.

- What the priorities should be if there is more than one thing that needs changing.

Although the more in-depth surveys are useful because of the amount of information they provide, they are often expensive and time-consuming to design, carry out and analyse. The short questionnaires are easier to administer and provide on-going information, allowing the manager to see the changes in customers' expectations as they develop. However these shorter questionnaires obviously provide far less detail. If the service manager is to get a clear picture of the customers' expectations of service and how well the company is currently performing against these expectations, he or she needs to find a balance between these two extremes.

Mystery shopper

One of the best ways to test how the service standards appear to customers is for a person from the company to put himself or herself in the position of the customer, and try out the service. Ideally it needs to be sombody who is not known to the staff, so receiving exactly the same level of service as is given to anybody else.

The person posing as the customer calls into the branch and makes enquiries about products and services. He or she asks a list of questions and records both the information given, and the way in which it was given.

If the company has specific service standards in place the 'mystery shopper' can comment on whether those standards are being delivered. This method can be used to test a small part of the overall service delivery such as:

- How long it takes the customer services operators to answer the telephone.

- How quickly literature requested over the telephone is delivered.

- How well the branch staff can answer questions about specific products

These are just a few of the things the mystery shopper could check. Alternatively such an exercise could be used to test an entire service proposition. For example, it could be used to test the investment advisory service. The mystery shopper could book an appointment and have an interview with the adviser, thereafter commenting on every aspect of the service.

Most companies use the mystery shopping technique to test their service standards or benchmark aspects of the service they are providing. However the company's managers and staff are not the only people who do this. Some financial services providers carry out mystery shopper exercises with their competitors, that is they will call into the branches of their competitors posing as customers to check out the level of service they are offering.

Any other interested party can also mystery shop and check out the company's service standards. For example, the *Financial Adviser* is a weekly industry paper that is read by many professionals from the industry, both financial services providers and intermediaries. It carries out a mystery shopper exercise each week and publishes the results in the paper. An example of the kind of thing they check out and the type of comments they publish is shown on the next page.

	Protection Office	Protection Office	IFA	IFA
Speed of response	Time of call: 11.15 Thursday. An adviser answered the call after four rings. **Score: 5/5**	Time of call: 11.40 Thursday. Having obtained the London number from directory enquiries, the shopper was passed around in an attempt to find the local office. It took nearly 10 minutes to get through to the right office. **Score: 0/5**	Time of call: 12.10 Thursday. An adviser answered the phone after three rings. **Score: 5/5**	Time of call: 12.20 Thursday. The adviser picked up the call after five rings. **Score: 4/5**
Telephone manner	The adviser was helpful and friendly without being pushy. He was prepared to give his time. **Score: 5/5**	The original telephonist had no idea which department the shopper needed. When the shopper was finally given the number of the nearest branch in Watford, the adviser was particularly unhelpful. **Score: 0/5**	The adviser was friendly, willing to talk to the shopper and knowledgeable about critical illness cover. **Score: 5/5**	The adviser was happy to have a chat over the telephone. **Score: 5/5**

	Protection Office	Protection Office	IFA	IFA
Guidance given	The adviser said he could give basic details. He said BUPA offered three basic options – the price varying depending on age, level of cover given, occupation, and family history. The minimum contribution was £10 a month, which did not offer much cover. **Score: 4/5**	The shopper was given very little guidance. The adviser was initially fairly friendly and asked for a few details, but quickly lost interest when the shopper said she did not want to give her address or phone number. **Score: 1/5**	The adviser explained critical illness was a complex type of cover because it paid out a lump sum on diagnosis, rather than on death. He said a lengthy underwriting process or a premium penalty could be involved depending on the hereditary family illnesses. **Score: 4/5**	The adviser said critical illness could be a good form of financial security. He said the death benefit part was questionable, as the shopper had no dependants. He said it would be straightforward to send out a quotation. **Score: 4/5**
Knowledge	The adviser made it clear he could offer only BUPA products. He gave the shopper an overview of critical illness plans and explained the different types of medical underwriting needed for different levels of cover. **Score: 4/5**	Although the adviser asked about family history and the shopper's basic requirements, he would not go into any detail about their critical illness plan. He was only prepared to send information in the post. **Score: 2/5**	The adviser said most of the leading insurers had agreed on a basic number of illnesses covered under a basic critical illness policy so it was possible to compare companies. He seemed to know the market well and explained it clearly. **Score: 5/5**	The adviser ascertained personal details and was clear on what constituted a critical illness plan. The shopper was disappointed that he did not ask about family history, but he was up-front about remuneration. **Score: 4/5**

	Protection Office	Protection Office	IFA	IFA
Verdict	The shopper felt comfortable with the adviser and would have been happy to meet him. He was knowledgeable without bombarding the shopper with unnecessary information.	The shopper felt she was being given the brush off when she declined to give out her work and home phone numbers. The adviser became increasingly rude and ended the conversation abruptly.	★★★★★ **SHOPPER'S CHOICE** The adviser was thorough and devoted a significant amount of time to the shopper. It was good that he explained the impact of family illness on premium levels. ★★★★★	The shopper felt comfortable talking to the IFA and would have felt happy making an appointment.
TOTAL SCORE	18/20	3/20	19/20	17/20

14.3 Charges for service

Historically, customers have had little knowledge of the charges that are made for the services they receive, and therefore were less likely to have an expectation of the price they should be paying. Because a customer tends to buy services less frequently than they would buy goods, they are less likely to know how much they should be paying for it. For example, when a consumer goes to buy a pint of milk and the retailer states the cost, the customer knows instantly whether that price is expensive or cheap. That is because the customer has an expectation of the price based on knowledge and experience.

This is not usually the case when people go to buy services. They usually have less experience and therefore have less of an expectation of the charge that will be made. What usually happens is that the retailer tells them the cost and the customer uses knowledge of the service to judge if the price represents good value.

As far as financial services are concerned, many customers have very little experience and very little knowledge of the service they are buying, and therefore only a vague expectation of the price they will be expected to pay. For some products consumers are becoming more educated about such costs and are shopping around, comparing the price charged by different providers. This is true of such things as mortgages, ISAs and life assurance.

However, for many other financial services products and for the services offered by financial services companies, this is not the case.

Because customers often have no realistic expectation of the prices they may be charged, financial services companies have found ways of charging for their services in ways that fit with the customers' expectations. Let us look at some examples.

Customers do not expect to pay for personal banking or for there to be charges for a deposit account.

Most customers expect that they will not be charged for personal banking. However the bank needs to operate at a profit and therefore cannot afford to run accounts with no costs involved. Similarly for deposit accounts, customers would certainly not expect to see a charge made from their account and yet the bank needs to make some money to cover operating costs and profit.

The way this is done is by offering an interest rate to the customer that is lower than the rate the bank receives when it lends that money. The costs are covered and the profit made by the bank taking the difference between the rate that the money is lent at, and the rate they pay the individual customer. This way the customers' expectations are met and the bank continues to be able to cover costs.

Customers do not expect to have to pay for advice that they receive regarding their financial products and services.

Banks, building societies, insurance companies and intermediaries all offer customers advice about the products and services that they sell, most particularly regulated products. While customers may be expecting to pay for the product they buy, few customers currently expect to pay for the advice.

While some advisers charge a fee for their services, there are only a proportion of customers who choose to do business this way (although this proportion is slowly increasing). The rest of the customers would certainly not expect to receive an invoice at the end of the interview.

To accommodate this the companies, who of course have to cover the costs involved in providing such advice, build the charges for the service into the products that are sold. With regulated products, the adviser is the required to disclose to the customer the cost of that advice as covered by the product fees.

What we can see is that customers have expectations regarding the charges made for services. They expect outright charges for some, but not for others, and it is important that the marketing manager understands these expectations, and manages the marketing mix around them.

14.4 Codes of conduct and professionalism

As well as the regulatory requirements that govern the selling of financial services products there are also codes that set out the standards of services that customers can expect from their providers. The two we shall examine now are the Banking Code and the Mortgage Code. Details of each are available from most banks and building societies if you want to look at them in more detail.

The Banking Code

This is a voluntary code followed by banks and building societies in their relationships with their personal customers. It sets standards of good banking practice that are followed as a minimum standard by those companies that subscribe to it. Because it is a voluntary code it allows competition and market forces to operate and therefore encourages higher standards of service to customers.

The standards are encompassed in the eleven 'Key Commitments', and these are shown below. The commitments apply to the carrying out of business for almost all products and services provided by the company in addition to any other regulatory requirements, with the exceptions mentioned below.

Mortgages are covered in more detail in the Council of Mortgage Lenders Code of Mortgage Practice. However not all subscribers to the Banking Code are members of the Council of Mortgage Lenders.

The Banking Code does not apply to the selling of investments or investment activities as defined in the Financial Services Act 1986.

The code provides customers with valuable safeguards and should help them to understand how banks and building societies will deal with them as customers. If in doubt as to whether their provider subscribes to the Banking Code, the customer can check by contacting either the British Bankers' Association, The Building Societies Association, or the Association for Payment Clearing Services.

The Independent Review Body for the Banking and Mortgage Codes monitors compliance by banks and building societies with the code and oversees any review of the code.

The eleven Key Commitments are that any organization that subscribes to the code will:

1. Act fairly and reasonably in all their dealings with their customers.

2. Ensure that all their products and the services they offer comply with the code in addition to their own terms and conditions.

3. Give information to the customers about their products and services that are explained in plain language and offer help if there is anything the customer does not understand.

4. Help customers to choose the product or service that fits their need.

5. Help customers to understand the financial implications of

   ● A mortgage

   ● Any other form of borrowing

   ● Savings and investment products

   ● Card products

6. Help customers to understand how their account works.

7. Ensure that customers have safe, secure and reliable banking and payment systems.

8. Ensure that the procedures the company sets out for its staff to follow reflect the commitments set out in the Banking Code.

9. Correct any errors they make and deal quickly with customers' complaints.

10. Consider cases of financial difficulty and mortgage arrears sympathetically and positively.

11. Ensure that all products and services comply with the relevant laws and regulations.

The leaflets that customers can pick up in bank branches outline the purpose of the Banking Code and the eleven Key Commitments and go on to give further explanations of the standards of service they can expect to receive. It gives additional information about such things as the help they can expect in selecting products, how products will be marketed, how accounts will be operated, and the type of information that they can expect to be given.

It also gives information on what help they can expect if they have financial difficulties and how to make a complaint. It also contains a section outlining where to go for further help, and some useful definitions of everyday banking terms.

The Mortgage Code

The Mortgage Code provides protection for the customer as a borrower. It sets the minimum standards that mortgage lenders and intermediaries have to meet. The code sets out details of how the mortgage should be arranged, what information should be given to customers before they commit to the loan, and how the mortgage should be dealt with once it is in place.

If a lender or intermediary fails to meet the standards of the code and customers suffers as a result, they will be entitled to compensation under a compulsory independent complaints scheme.

The code has ten main commitments. Broadly speaking they say that lenders and intermediaries will:

1. Act fairly and reasonably with customers at all times.

2. Make sure that all products and services keep to the conditions of the code.

3. Give the customers information in plain language and help if there is anything they do not understand.

4. Help the customer to choose a mortgage unless they have already done so.

5. Help the customer to understand the financial effects of having a mortgage.

6. Help the customer to understand how a mortgage account works.

7. Make sure that the procedures staff follow reflect the commitments of the code.

8. Consider cases of financial difficulty sympathetically.

9. Correct errors and handle complaints speedily.

10. Make sure that all services and products meet the relevant law and regulation.

How the lenders or intermediaries keep to the Mortgage Code is monitored independently. Any organization under the code must be a member of a recognized complaints scheme such as the Banking Ombudsman, the Building Societies Ombudsman, or the Mortgage Code Arbitration Scheme. This gives the customer an extra level of protection, as each of these schemes can award compensation of up to £100,00 to a customer who suffers as a result of a lender or intermediary who fails to keep to the code.

15

PRESENTATION SKILLS

After reading this chapter you should

- Be aware of the nature of the presentation skills required for presenting to customers

  Over the telephone

  Face-to-face

  In writing

- Know how to use technology in presentations

- Understand the best use of in-branch displays, seminar opportunities, and other local activity

Salespeople are required to give presentations to customers as part of their everyday work. These presentations can be to groups of people or can be to individuals, and can be written presentations, presentations over the telephone or face-to-face with the customers.

If the seller is to be successful he or she must be confident and competent to make such presentations. We shall, in this chapter, look at the nature of the skills that are often known as 'presentation skills' and examine the ways in which the salesperson can make the best presentations possible. Many of the skills apply in whatever form the presentation is given, while there are other techniques that apply specifically when talking to large groups, for example.

What we need to remember throughout this chapter is that the purpose of a sales presentation is to sell. The purpose of the presentation is also to impart information, and to give the customer the chance to ask questions and have them answered. However the main reason for any sales presentation is to persuade the customer that the products and services being offered by the seller are useful.

15.1   Preparation

If the presentation is to go well it is essential that the salesperson prepares adequately. Good presentations do not happen by chance, they happen because the person giving the presentation has spent sufficient time beforehand thinking about what he or she is going to say and how he or she is going to say it. If the presentation is going to be successful as a sales presentation it must achieve three things:

- It must be interesting. If the customer is bored within the first few minutes the seller will never be successful in persuading the customer to purchase the product.

- It must be meaningful to the customer, who must be able to relate to what is being said and be able to see the benefits.

- It must move the customer to take the required action, i.e. make a purchase. There is no point in giving a sales presentation unless it is aimed at actually getting the customer to buy.

While not always the case, the objective of a sales presentation is generally be to get the customer to make a purchase. It is important that each and every presentation has objectives set. This focuses the mind of the presenter when both preparing and delivering the presentation, and provides some criteria against which we can judge if the presentation has been a success. As well as making a sale, some other objectives of a presentation may be such things as:

- To persuade the customer to continue with a product or service that has already been purchased.

- To show a customer or group of customers the benefits of a particular service that the organization is offering.

- To persuade a customer to have a further discussion with the salesperson, i.e. to sell the benefits of an interview.

Set an objective

Once the objective is set, the salesperson needs to consider this objective all the way through the presentation, and the whole presentation should be geared towards achieving this objective. Having set an objective, the next step is to decide on the message of the presentation. If the presentation is to be successful in achieving what you want to achieve, then the message you are delivering to your audience, be it one person or one hundred, must be clear.

15.2 Know the audience

The message that the salesperson delivers and the way in which it is delivered depends largely on the audience. It is essential that if the presentation is going to be meaningful, i.e. it is going to interest and stimulate the audience, that it is tailored to suit them. This may well be easier on a one-to-one presentation basis, especially in situations where the salesperson has already met the customer. However, even if there is a large audience, the presenter should attempt to find out as much as possible about those people, their ages, their current level of knowledge of the subject being discussed, etc.

This kind of information allows the presenter to deliver the message in a way that the audience can understand and which is relevant to them. The presenter needs to use language that the audience can understand, and to ensure that the information is pitched at a level suitable for their current understanding. The presenter may also need to vary the pace, tone and language of the presentation and all of these need to be considered in advance.

Once the presenter has decided on:

1. The objective of the presentation,

2. The message that will be delivered in order to achieve that objective and

3. The way in which the message will be delivered in order that it is meaningful and interesting to the audience,

then he or she can then begin to prepare the actual presentation.

15.3   Structure the presentation

When preparing the presentation the salesperson must have a basic structure in mind, i.e. the way in which the presentation will take shape. An example of a presentation structure could be something like this:

● *Introduction*

  If the salesperson has not previously met the customers or where the presentation is to a group of people, it may be necessary for the salesperson to start the presentation by introducing themselves. He or she will also need to introduce the presentation, that is to give a brief overview of what is to be discussed in the next few minutes.

● *Opening statements*

  The salesperson may wish to start the presentation with an opening statement explaining the purpose of the presentation and state the objective. For example 'today we are going to look at the benefits of the new home banking service offered by our organization and answer any questions you may have before deciding whether to subscribe to the service'. This tells the audience what they can and cannot expect to be covered in the presentation, and also sets the scene for the 'call to action' later.

● *Body of the presentation*

  In the body of the presentation, the salesperson delivers the message he or she wishes to get across in a way that is easily understood by the audience and which is relevant to them. The salesperson may wish to pick out just three or four main points and deliver those together with supporting material, because there will be a limit to the concentration span of the audience and therefore the amount of information that can be delivered at any one time.

● *Summary*

  At the end of the body of the presentation it will be useful to give a summary of what you have discussed and what the main points/benefits are.

- *Call to action*

  We said at the beginning of this chapter that the main purpose of a sales presentation is to persuade the customer to take action and either buy a product or service, or book an interview, etc. This being the case, it is important that at the end of the presentation the salesperson asks the customer to take that required action.

Presentation aids

If presenting to either a single customer or a group of customers on a face-to-face basis, the presenter may wish to use visual aids to help the presentation flow. These could be in the form of diagrams, charts, sales literature, etc, which are paper-based. Alternatively the presenter may decide to use a video, OHPs, slide show, or laptop presentation. We shall look shortly at the best use of such technology when presenting, however it is an essential part of the preparation that the presenter checks that all the required items are in place and working properly before the presentation starts.

Making the presentation

Once the preparation is complete we are now ready to make the presentation. We shall concentrate for the moment on the skills needed for presenting to a group of people, and then look a little later at the differences that need to be applied when presenting to a single customer or over the telephone.

When customers are attending a presentation, the message that they take away with them, and the impact that that presentation has on them, is based not only on what is said (verbal), but also largely on how it is said (vocal) as well as what they see (visual). For this reason we shall look at the skills required under these three headings.

Verbal

Obviously what is actually said when we present to a large audience is very important. We must have an interesting message for them which, as we saw earlier, is tailored to their requirements and situation. Therefore the skills required to ensure that we are successful verbally is ensuring we can get over our message in a way that is suitable to the audience we have.

Vocal

Presenters need to concentrate not only on what they are going to say, but how they are going to say it. The tone of their voice, the pitch, the clarity and the speed at which they speak all contribute to the customer's perception of the presentation. The competent presenter also needs to consider the following:

- *Intonation*

  Nothing puts an audience to sleep faster than a monotone speaker. The presenter needs to make an effort to ensure that his or her voice is interesting and this involves raising and lowering it and altering the tone. Changes in the voice can also be used to give emphasis to certain points and give meaning, although the presenter needs to ensure that it always appears natural and not forced.

- *Pauses*

  The use of pauses when presenting is indeed a skill. Often nervous presenters feel the need to speak non-stop, because they are uncomfortable with silence. Including appropriate pauses can make it easier for the audience to listen and take in the information that they have been given. In sales presentations especially, pauses can be extremely useful. The customer is being asked to take in information and then make a decision to buy. In order to do this he or she needs at least a few seconds thinking time, and will be able to think only when the presenter pauses from speaking. The competent presenter is not afraid of a short silence, but understands its benefits and uses such a pause to advantage.

- *Fillers*

  Often, before presenters have mastered the skill of using a pause, they have a tendency to 'fill' any gap in their talk. They may fill it with short noises such as 'uuhm' or 'er'. These are all extremely distracting to the audience, and if they happen repeatedly will divert the audience totally from the message the presenter is trying to convey. Often presenters do this without realizing, and if this is the case should make a conscious effort to avoid doing it.

Visual

What the customer sees has a huge impact on the effectiveness of a presentation, and therefore a number of presentation skills revolve around ensuring that the visual effects of the presentation are correct. For example:

- *Formality*

  Some situations require a very formal presentation with the presenter situated behind a podium and working to a very strict script, whereas others are informal with the presenter moving around, ad-libbing and perhaps encouraging audience participation. Either type, or indeed anything in between, can be acceptable, depending on the circumstances. The skill is to judge the audience and the topic and ensure the correct level of formality.

- *Presence*

  If the presenter is to be successful he or she must achieve a 'presence'. What is meant by presence is that such presenters have an 'air' about them; they have a 'quality of poise and effectiveness'. This presence enables them to have a close relationship with their audience. Generally a good stage presence is achieved by a presenter who has mastered all the presentation skills and therefore develops presence naturally. However there are things that presenters can make sure they get right so that they can start to develop visual skills. For example, the clothing presenters wear have an immediate impact on the way the audience view them. The attire should be professional and suitable for the occasion, and anything distracting should be avoided. The way in which the presenter carries himself or herself will also need to be considered. A good posture contributes to the way an audience perceives the presenter who should avoid slouching at all times.

- *Body language*

  An important contribution to the visual skills a presenter needs to develop revolves around the correct use of body language. We can transmit an amazing number of messages through such things as head movements, facial expressions and gestures, sometimes without realizing what we are doing. A skilled presenter should understand such messages and be able to use body language to advantage.

  The presenter should be comfortable with achieving eye contact with the audience, because avoiding eye contact makes members of the audience feel that they are unimportant, or that you are unconcerned about them. Facial expressions are also important because they can convey interest, be serious or smiling, or can make the presenter appear nervous or anxious. Hand movements and gestures also need to be controlled. Although a presenter who never moves at all could well be extremely boring to watch, the presenter should ensure that any movements are not distracting to the audience or detracting from what is being said.

- *Notes*

  Many presenters use notes; in fact it is usually advisable to have at least a small number of bullet points to refer to, to ensure that the presentation is structured. However using notes is another skill that a competent presenter needs to master. If they are relied on too heavily, the presenter will loose the audience's attention. They should never be lifted up or shuffled, because this would be a distraction. Therefore the presenter must be able to glance fleetingly at notes without allowing this to interrupt the flow.

Style

Style is also important, and each salesperson or presenter will develop his or her own presentation style. There are no rules as to what this style should be, although it is preferable to ensure that the presentation style adopted includes the following:

- *Energy*

  There is nothing worse than a lethargic presenter. The audience will feel bored and lethargic themselves and the presentation will seem to drag on for a much greater length of time than it actually takes. Presenters can hardly expect the audience to be interested in what they have to say if they do not appear interested themselves. Often nerves make presenters seem lethargic, so they will need to 'psych' themselves up before they start to speak. In order to appear energetic and enthusiastic they must feel positive and lively all the time they are presenting.

- *Confidence*

  Ideally the presenter should have confidence. While this is easy to say, it is, for a lot of

people, difficult to achieve. This means that many presenters have to fake confidence–
that is, appearing confident even though they may be a little nervous. The best way to
ensure that they are as confident as possible is for them to ensure that they are fully
prepared and well practised.

15.4   One-to-one presentations

Not all presentations are made to large groups of people. The majority of a salesperson's
presentations may well be made on a one-to-one basis between the salesperson and the
customer. However, many of the skills we have discussed for group presentations are just as
relevant in these one-on-one situations.

Preparation

The seller needs to be well prepared for such presentations and all the same principles
apply. The salesperson still needs to have an objective and ideally have a good understanding
of the customer being presented to. The presentation should have a structure in the same
way as a group presentation.

Verbal skills

The message obviously still needs to be interesting to customers in order to retain their
attention and to actually persuade them of the benefits and therefore have them agree to but
the product or service. On a one-to-one basis, it is much easier for the seller to tailor the
presentation to the customer with personalized benefit statements, using information gained
about the customers needs and desires.

Vocal skills

These are also needed in a one-to-one situation, but are likely to come more naturally to the
seller who is making the presentation to a single person rather than a large group. This said,
there is still a great deal of skill in achieving a clever use of pauses.

Visual skills

These are just as important in an interview-type presentation as in a group one. The seller
still needs to judge the desired level of formality and ensure that the type of presentation
given is suitable to the circumstances. He or she also needs to be very aware of body language,
including such things as the seating arrangements. While most formal interviews and
presentations take place across a desk, for some this may appear to be a barrier and therefore
sitting diagonally from the customer may be more appropriate.

Style

Also important. Again, each seller will develop his or her own style, but whatever it is the
seller still needs to have confidence in order to turn the presentation into a sale.

Telephone presentations

To make a sales presentation, or indeed a presentation of any kind, over the telephone requires a great deal of skill. Whereas in a face-to-face presentation there are the three ways in which people will pick up the message, with the telephone, there are of course only the two, vocal and verbal. The lack of the visual can make the situation much more difficult, especially if you consider that people are generally considered to receive over 50% of the message they take away through visual communications.

This loss of the visual communication means that the presenter needs to make up this loss in other areas. Such things as eye contact, nodding and smiling all make customers feel at ease and that the presenter is communicating with them, and telephone presenters have to compensate for these in the words that they use or the way in which they speak.

Another problem with telephone presentations, especially for financial services product that can sometimes seem detailed and complex, is that the presenter is not able to use diagrams or charts, etc. To help with explanations, presenters therefore need to ensure that the way describes things to the customer is extremely clear. Also, of course, the presenter cannot see the customer and cannot therefore judge body language and facial expressions that would otherwise help the presenter to ensure he or she had been understood and was not losing the customer's interest. In order to compensate, the telephone presenter needs to develop excellent listening skills.

As one would expect, with telephone presentations vocal and verbal skills become extremely important, as does the need for the presenter to be very well prepared in advance. What the presenter says should be carefully considered in advance, remembering that the words are now the only method of relaxing the customer, setting the tone of the presentation and delivering explanation, etc. Also the verbal skills are more important. When customers cannot see the presenter, they concentrate more on what they hear and they way in which it is said.

If the presentation is fairly lengthy, making the voice interesting becomes essential if the customer is expected to keep listening. Although presenters still need to use pauses, they should to bear in mind that this can be more difficult on the telephone where there is no visual contact and the timing and length of such pauses needs to be judges carefully. Also the presenter has to be more conscious of the dreaded 'uhm', 'err' and 'OKs' that people tend to use to fill gaps in their speech. These can be irritating when listening to any presentation, and they become especially so over the telephone in a verbal-only presentation.

Written presentations

There are many advantages to making presentations in writing, both for the presenter and for the customer. These include:

● Not only can they be prepared in advance, they can also be checked and reviewed before the customer receives them.

● What the customer receives is always exactly as planned, unlike verbal presentations when bits could be missed or amended slightly in the delivery.

- The presentation can include charts, pictures and diagrams in order to aid understanding.
- Customers can read the presentation at a time that suits them and at their own pace.
- They have a permanent record and can therefore re-read the presentation if there were any parts they cannot remember or want to go over.

However, there are also some disadvantages:

- Not only is there no body language or gestures etc. to help to deliver the message, but there can be no intonation, etc. This means that it is purely the words themselves that must deliver the messages.
- The presenter cannot see or hear customers as they receive the presentation and is therefore unable to see if he or she has correctly judged the level of detail etc. Face-to-face and over the telephone presenters can judge such things and amend the delivery as they go through, but this is not possible with a prepared written presentation.
- A written presentation does not allow the opportunity for the presenter to check understanding or for the customer to ask questions.

What this shows us is that there are circumstances where a written presentation is simply not suitable, but other occasions in which it is an ideal solution. If a written presentation is being used, the presenter must remember the following things:

- The presentation has to be very well structured, because the customers do not have the benefit of a presenter or salesperson to guide them through it.
- A written presentation still needs to have a clear objective, and the presentation itself should be geared to achieving this objective.
- The presentation should be tailored to each individual customer's circumstances and level of knowledge and understanding if he or she is to read and understand it alone, and to be moved to take the required action.
- The words used and the way in which they are used must be clear and jargon-free. Remember the customer does not have the benefit of being able to ask questions if, for example, he or she does not understand a term that is used.
- The way the presentation looks when the customer first opens it is very important. First impressions count! It should look interesting and yet professional. It should be nicely packaged, but well spaced, perhaps with the text broken by charts etc. in order that it does not look too wordy and daunting for the customer when first opened.

Written presentations are often used by the salespeople who sell regulated financial services products. The regulations state that the customer to be given a record of any recommendations the seller makes, even if they are also given verbally. Because of this what often happens is that once the seller has investigated the customer's needs, he or she makes their recommendations in a written presentation delivered to the customer. The seller may well then meet or telephone the customer a few days later to check understanding, answer any questions and complete the appropriate sales.

Let us now look at an example of how such a written presentation could look. Over the next few pages there is an example of the kind of written presentation a financial adviser may send. You will see that, although the presentation is written rather than verbal, many of the skills we have examined so far are still relevant.

There is obviously a great deal of preparation required before the documnet can be issued. The financial adviser will have a great deal of information about the customers and will therefore ensure that the presentation is aimed specifically at them and their circumstances. The structure of the presentation is similar to that of a verbal presentation: there is an introduction, followed by the body of the presentation, the summary and the call to action.

Financial presentation for Mr Neil Watkins

1. Introduction

Firstly I would like to thank you for your interest in our Financial Services and for taking time to discuss your personal financial details with me. The service that I offer will help you to look at where you are now and what you want from your finances in the future, and I will help to make sure that your money works harder for you.

I can help you to plan your savings, ensure that your mortgage is the right one for you, and make sure that you are covered against illness or in the event of death. We can also help you to plan for a comfortable retirement, and give you advice on your investments.

Last week we discussed your retirement planning and your savings. I have outlined in this presentation your current position, and made some recommendations as to how you can achieve the things you want.

You can contact me if you wish to discuss anything in this presentation or if you have any queries. We have an appointment on Friday at 3.00p.m. at which I can run through this presentation and my recommendations, and discuss them with you.

Following that I will remain in touch on a regular basis so that I can monitor progress against the goals we have set, and ensure that you get the very best from your finances.

2. Income and out-goings

Before I can make any recommendations regarding your retirement and other savings we need to consider what money you have available to save. From the discussions we had, I believe that your current situation regarding income and outgoings are as follows.

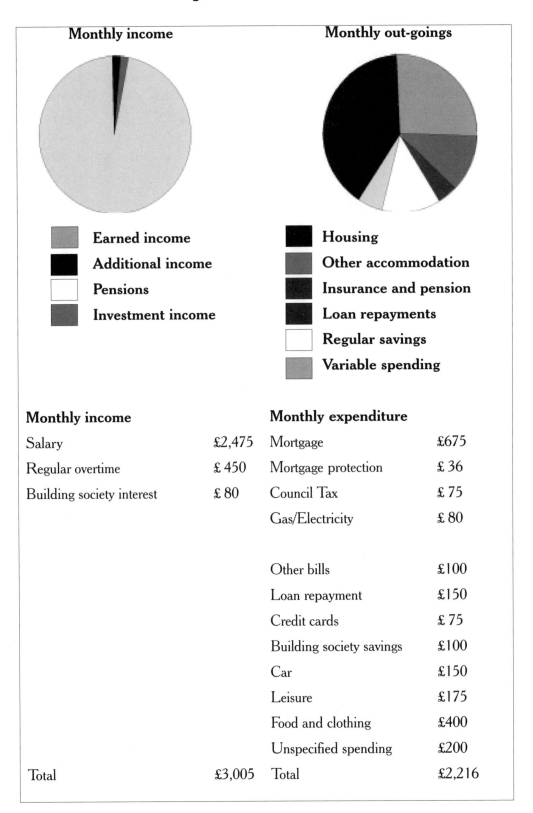

Monthly income		
Salary	£2,475	
Regular overtime	£ 450	
Building society interest	£ 80	

Monthly expenditure	
Mortgage	£675
Mortgage protection	£ 36
Council Tax	£ 75
Gas/Electricity	£ 80
Other bills	£100
Loan repayment	£150
Credit cards	£ 75
Building society savings	£100
Car	£150
Leisure	£175
Food and clothing	£400
Unspecified spending	£200

Total	£3,005

Total	£2,216

Your monthly income available for saving is therefore **£789**.

3. Retirement planning

You told me you want to enjoy your retirement and would like to ensure that you have sufficient funds to do so. You think that you would need approx. 50% of your income once you retire.

You said that you do not feel that the state benefit would be adequate for your needs because you wish to continue to take holidays abroad once you have retired.

You felt that you would like to retire before age 65, ideally at age 55.

Your employer does not have a company pension scheme, but you do have some preserved benefits from a previous employer.

Retirement income

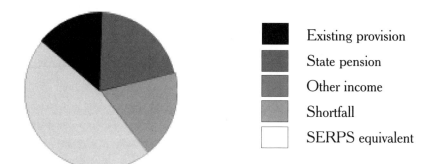

■	Existing provision
■	State pension
■	Other income
■	Shortfall
□	SERPS equivalent

Retirement income	
Income needed = 50% of current salary	£18,000
Less state benefit	£ 3,364
Existing provision	£ 3,178
SERPS benefit	£ 3,091
Shortfall	£8,367
Equivalent at age 55	£38,638

Therefore, if you wish to retire on 50% of your pre-retirement income, you will need to fund for an income of approx. £38,638 p.a.

4. Savings

You currently save monthly into a building society account and use this money for holidays and unexpected expenditure.

You wish to save an additional £200 per month, in order to build a lump sum over the next 5 to 10 years.

You would like to have some flexibility in the payments in order that you could increase or decrease them if necessary.

You would like a tax-efficient method of saving if possible.

Although you intend to save for 5 to 10 years, you would like a savings plan that allows you access to your funds in the case of an emergency or unforeseen circumstances.

5. Recommendations

Following our initial discussions and in keeping with your specific requirements I would recommend the following:

Plan	Premium	Term	Reasons
Personal Pension	£360 per month	22 years	To provide the required level of income in retirement. To build a cash lump sum at retirement for a holiday of a lifetime To provide tax-efficient savings.
Individual Savings Account (ISA)	£200 per month	5 to 10 years	To accumulate a lump sum as desired. To provide flexible savings. To give tax-free growth. To allow access to funds if needed.

6. Summary

I have outlined my understanding of your current situation and your present goals as far as your financial situation is concerned.

I have made some recommendations as to how your goals can be achieved.

I will discuss these recommendations with you further at our next meeting, where I will be happy to answer any questions you have.

Then, if you are in agreement with them, we can proceed on this basis.

I look forward to seeing you on Friday.

Students please note

This presentation is only an example of what could be given. In a real-life situation the seller would be required to give a great deal more technical information regarding the recommended plans and further information as to how those recommendations were reached.

Technology in presentations

We have looked at the skills needed to make a good, effective presentation, and we have seen that visual skills are equally as important as the verbal and vocal ones. This is because what people see is as powerful, than what they hear; if not more so. Anybody who attends presentations regularly will verify that the ones they remember the most are those that contained some impressive visual media.

The use of audiovisuals is one way to ensure that your customers will remember the presentation you give, long after the words have been forgotten.

For this reason, an increasing number of financial services sellers and presenters are using audiovisuals to add interest to what can sometimes otherwise be a fairly dry subject for many people.

Before we go on to look at the type of technology that can be emplyed, we need to remember that any such presentation aids should be used to support the presenter– they are not in themselves the presentation. In a truly effective presentation, technology is simply a very effective form of supporting material.

For any presenter intending to use technology or audiovisuals of any kind there are some simple guidelines that should be considered when planning how they will be incorporated.

- Presenters should find something that fits the type of presentation that is being given, the size of the audience, and the formality of the situation.

- Technology should support both the objective that presenters have set themselves, and the message they are using to achieve the objective. Although technology is useful for getting attention and gaining interest, it should still have a role to play in helping presenters to achieve what they have set out to achieve.

- Any supporting audiovisual material should be used in moderation. Although we have said that it can be extremely good at adding interest to a presentation, it can have exactly the opposite effect if overused.

What to use and why

The use of technology can be done simply to help the presenter, i.e. to make the job of presenting easier. It may be that the audience never sees it because it could be simply for the presenter's benefit only, as in the case of an auto-cue. This can be useful for someone presenting to a large group of people, who wanted to deliver a formal presentation. The auto-cue enables a presenter to deliver a pre-prepared message with little or no deviation and without the need to refer to notes or to memorize the entire thing.

Another reason for using technology may be to reinforce the points being made by the presenter. For example, we now know that customers are far more likely to remember what was presented if they saw it as well as heard it. For this reason many presenters show some written information at the same time as talking about it in order to ensure it is understood and retained. This is especially useful in situations where the customer is being given numerical information to digest.

Let us look at an example. A presenter is talking to a customer about the percentage of people in his profession that retire early from their jobs. Although he or she could just state these numbers, the customer is far more likely to remember and think about them if they are also shown as below:

Percentage of staff retiring early	
1970	5%
1975	7%
1980	11%
1985	16%
1990	23%
1995	34%

This information becomes even more powerful if presented in chart form, particularly if it is in colour.

Figure 15.1: Same data (in colour for customer if possible)

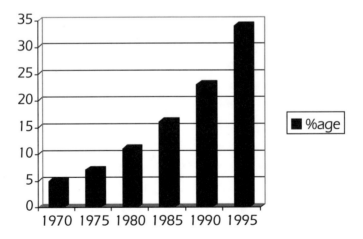

We can see that the first presentation aid is better than using words alone, but that the second is better still. Such a chart could be presented in paper form, but would be more impactful if shown on a large screen via an overhead projector (OHP). The only problem with an OHP is that the presenter needs to pick up the slides, put them on, switch on the OHP, and then remove the slide when it is finished with. This can all be distracting for the customer.

Another method of achieving the same result while looking more efficient would be to have the presentation on a system such as Microsoft PowerPoint. This allows a variety of slides, both words and pictures, to be pre-prepared. They presenter can then move through these, both backwards and forwards, at the touch of a button.

This kind of presentation aid can be used in a one-to-one presentation on a laptop or desktop computer. It can also be used with small to medium groups if transmitted through a powerbeam and projected onto a screen. Another benefit of using such technology rather than the traditional OHP is that such things as the graphs can be built up slowly as the presenter is talking, thereby giving the presentation more interest and a more professional feel. If presenting to a large group, probably the best way of using such technology is to have the visuals projected onto the screen from the back of the room and operated by someone other than the presenter.

It is also possible to add sound to such presentation aids so that either music or some suitable and impactful sound can accompany any visual. This makes the presentation more interesting, and the choice of music or sound can help to reinforce the message being delivered.

Video can also be used in presentations. After all, video is simply a combination of colourful moving pictures and sound. When we think of it in those terms we can start to see why this may also be very effective at delivering a message. A video recorder and television set could be used for presenting to small groups of people, but larger groups would need big-screen projection. Some presentation facilities on both laptop and desktop computers allow for video to be included, and using this can add variety, interest and a professional look.

15.5 Points to remember when using technology

- The placement of any equipment being used should be carefully planned in order that it does not block anyone's view of the presenter. Also ensure that the presenter has somewhere to stand beside the screen where he or she does not block the view.

- Preparation is essential. The presentation aids themselves should to be prepared in advance, and the equipment being used also needs to be in place well before the start of the presentation itself. The presenter should also check that everything is working, and have a full run-through before the start.

- Always ensure that the presentation could still be delivered if the technology fails. Although we can take as many precautions as possible to ensure that it does not happen, there will always be an occasion where we are let down by our equipment. It is important that if this happens there is sufficient back-up material in, say, a printed format to enable the presentation to continue. As we said earlier, the technology should not be the presentation; it should be there to support the presentation. As a result, failure of the technology does not prevent the presentation from continuing.

In-branch displays and seminars

Those financial services companies that have a branch network have an ideal opportunity for displaying and presenting information to customers. These in-branch displays can be used for a number of marketing activities and if used correctly can be extremely effective.

The displays can be on walls within the branch, or can be free-standing units with information on all sides. They can display posters or can contain leaflet and flyers. Because the people who see them are those people who are visiting the branch, they are likely to already be customers of one sort or another. This means that they have already shown a willingness to do business with the company, and therefore brand advertising, and brand awareness campaigns, would probably not prove to be the best use of such opportunities.

The other thing we need to consider is the fact that customers are in the branch for a purpose, i.e. they have something they want to do, and therefore they are unlikely to spend a huge amount of time reading whatever is displayed there. They will simply see the information as they are passing, or while they are in a queue waiting to be served. For this reason the information needs to be eye-catching, easy to grasp and quick to understand.

As a result, most branches use the opportunities provided by the in-branch display units to give customers a brief insight into the other products and services they offer. For example, a bank may well consider that the majority of the people who use its branches are customers with current or deposit accounts. It could decide to use the branch displays to inform those customers that the bank offers other services that could well be of use to them, for example travel insurance, foreign currency, mortgages, or household and motor insurance.

Customers will see the information and over time they will come to think of their bank as a provider of a much wider range of services than those traditionally associated with a bank. Of course, while acknowledging that customers are busy doing something else and therefore only giving the customers brief information, the bank also wants to ensure that there is a method by which customers can easily obtain further information if they are interested.

This could be done by including a call to action such as 'ask at the counter for further details and an application' or by making available, as part of the display, leaflets with further information that customers can pick up, take home and read at their leisure. This will mean that those customers who actually want to find out more or buy the product can do so, and those who do not still see something that is informative and simple.

In-branch displays can also be used for local campaigns, i.e. to present information that is of particular interest to the people within that branch area. This type of use enables the branch to run mini-campaigns for products or services as required to meet its particular sales plan. One advantage of using this method of promotion is that it is relatively cost effective.

We saw in an earlier chapter that many financial services providers are moving their branches into what have traditionally been retail buildings in High Streets and shopping centres. These buildings have large glass fronts and therefore allow the opportunity of a branch window display of a considerable size and impact. The marketing manager should consider carefully how to best use such an opportunity.

The advantage of a window display over an in-branch display is that it will be seen by a far larger number of people, including – most importantly of all – people who are not currently customers of the organization. This means that the best use of the window display would be to advertise whatever product or service the company feels has its best competitive advantage. This could be a hugely competitive interest rate, a unique service, or a product that is better than those on offer from the competition. The window display should be used to give just the headline information, and invite people to call in for further information. (The company may also want to give details of other ways of gaining information, for example, telephone number or Internet address for those people who pass the branch outside opening hours.)

Seminars are another way of presenting information to customers or to potential customers. They involve a number of people attending a presentation given either in the branch or at some other venue such as a hotel function room. A salesperson from the company presents information about a topic of interest involving a product or service offered by the organization. Seminars are often used as an alternative to one-to-one selling, or as an introduction to the one-to-one selling process.

A seminar can be used as a selling mechanism for a product that is fairly simple to understand, but where the seller wants to have the opportunity of explaining the features and benefits to the prospective customers. The salesperson invites people considered as likely to find the product interesting and of benefit, and they listen to the information being presented. They are given an opportunity to ask questions, and then to buy the product if the desired. The obvious advantage to this type of seminar selling is that the salesperson can explain the product to a large number of people at one time, and therefore there are economies of time and effort involved.

Alternatively a seminar can be used to give people an introduction to a product or service and get them interested enough so that they will attend a one-to-one meeting with the salesperson. Some people are reluctant to agree to an appointment with financial services salespeople because they do not fully understand what they do, or the benefits of such a service. However people are less reluctant to attend a seminar as part of a large group of like-minded people. The salespeople simply use the seminar to introduce themselves and the service they provide, explaining the benefits of such a service. The objective is to gain the agreement of a proportion of those attending the seminar to make an appointment to discuss their finances.

16

CREATING A POSITIVE, PROFESSIONAL AND KNOWLEDGEABLE IMAGE

After reading this chapter you should

● Understand the importance of personal style

● Be aware of the ingredients that make a professional salesperson

● Know how important it is for salespeople to be organized in their approach to their selling role

● Be aware of some of the methods of self-organization that a seller can use to improve performance

Introduction

For an individual to be successful in the selling of financial services products to the public, there are a number of things that he or she needs to get right. A little like baking a cake, the perfect result will be achieved only if all the right ingredients are used. If any of these ingredients is missing or below standard, the result will be a less than perfect outcome. The most successful salespeople not only have all the right qualities and skills but are always looking to improve them in order that the results continually get better.

The basic ingredients that lead to the professional seller are shown in the diagram opposite:

Figure 16.1: Ingredients for the professional sales person.

Personal style and attitude

Sales skills

Business and industry knowledge

Company knowledge

Product knowledge

Business knowledge and industry knowledge

These are important if the salesperson is going to be able to converse knowledgeably with people at all levels and instil confidence in customers. The seller should have an understanding of all aspects of finance and be up to date with all topical issues. He or she will need to keep business knowledge up to date and will probably do this well by reading the financial papers, watching the news and finance programmes on television or by listening to such information on the radio.

Salespeople of course need to be particularly knowledgeable about the industry in which they operate. They should be knowledgeable about technical issues in the industry such as taxation and legal issues. Again they need to keep such knowledge up to date, including such issues as the effect of the budget, etc.

They also need to be aware of who their competitors are and what they are doing. This means keeping up to date with the products they offer, the markets and the customers that they deal with, and their promotional activity. They should also be aware of other people and personalities in their industry, and ensure that they know what are the topical issues.

Many companies try to help their salespeople with this aspect of their role by carrying out market intelligence and issuing to their staff press cutting relating to industry matters . This said, professional salespeople would anyway be interested in matters that affect the industry in which they work. They will therefore take the time and effort to ensure that they are aware of anything that either now or in the future could affect them, their customers, or their business.

Company knowledge

Salespeople who wish to appear professional in front of their customers need to know their own company inside out. They need to demonstrate a thorough understanding of the company and how it operates. They need to be up to speed with all company policy and aware of the company's position on all topical matters. They also need to be aware of all the company's advertising and promotional activity, even that relating to products or services they may not themselves sell.

When customers discuss financial business with the company's salesperson they are not thinking of the company in terms of being segmented into different business units. Customers consider the salespeople to be the face of the company. It is therefore important that an individual salesperson does not refuse to deal with matters that are not strictly a part of his or her role. The salesperson must always be helpful and if he or she cannot deal with the query, should know the right place and the right person to direct the customer to.

Salespeople should also always be true ambassadors for the company. They must always be seen to be supporting the company policy, even if there are aspects of it that they do not personally understand. They must always show customers that they are proud to work for the company whose products and services they are recommending.

16.1   Product knowledge

This is essential if salespeople are to look professional in front of customers. They must know all aspects of the products back to front and be able to answer the customers' questions instantly and accurately. This may seem obvious, but there are some salespeople who struggle to deal with customer questions without referring to the product literature. Keeping this knowledge up to date may mean that people for whom selling is only a part of their role or who sell only a particular product on very rare occasions will have to work hard to refresh their product knowledge.

For salespeople who sell regulated products, proving they have the required product knowledge and proving they keep this up to date is a regulatory requirement. The salespeople are required to pass tests to show they have knowledge of all the products they are authorized to sell, and to do so on a regular basis.

All salespeople will be required to pass the test, but those who want to create a positive and professional image ensure that they go beyond the minimum requirements. They will ensure that their knowledge of the product is not simply at the level required to pass the test, but is such that they can deal confidently and competently with any question customers may have.

Nothing is more frustrating to a customer than being faced with a salesperson who does not know in detail the product. Being faced with such a situation, the customer may become very irritated. Not only this, but the customer will lose confidence in that salesperson's ability and will therefore be far less likely to buy.

This can be a particular difficulty in the financial services industry. Many customers lack the knowledge to confidently select financial services products themselves and therefore look to financial advisers for help and assistance. They need the companies' adviser to give them the advice they need, and also the confidence that they have done the right thing, and therefore a competent and professional adviser is of the utmost importance to them. They are extremely unlikely to buy from a salesperson they do not have confidence in.

Sales skills

There are certain skills that salespeople require if they are to be successful in selling financial services products. These are such things as questioning skills, listening skills, and objection handling. These will be examined in more detail in Chapter 17.

Most financial services companies are aware that these skills do not come naturally for most people, even those who appear to be born salespeople. For this reason, selling skills are covered in a salesperson's initial training. They are also included in any on-going training that the salespeople undergo.

This said, even people who have been selling for some time and have had considerable success at doing so can always benefit from a refresher of their skills. The professional salesperson avoids slipping into bad habits, or into a comfort zone, and is constantly be looking to improve sales ratios and volumes. Improving sales skills is one thing that will help to do this.

Personal style and attitude

The purpose of this text is not to argue the rights and wrongs of whether personal appearance should matter to the success of the salesperson, it is simply to state that it does. The professional salesperson needs to look the part. What this means is that sellers need to conform to the dress code for their industry. While jeans and a sweater may be perfect dress for a person selling farm equipment and travelling round farm properties, those people selling financial services products need to look smart and professional.

In almost all cases this means a business suit. Those advisers who work in the branch of a bank or building society may well have a uniform to wear, similar to other branch staff. Other companies have purposely asked their advisers not to wear the staff uniform in an attempt to differentiate them from other members of staff and therefore increase their professional profile. Either way, the adviser must look well-dressed and successful.

The adviser needs to be well groomed and fairly conservative. This does not mean that salespeople should not dress to reflect their personality, but that they should always be aware of the image they are projecting to the customer.

Attitude is also extremely important if the sellers are to succeed in making the sale. They should be confident in the manner in which they deal with customers, but should always appear willing to help. They should also show that they are happy to be dealing with the customer and that the customer's requirements are paramount. People want to deal with someone who cares about their requirements and their needs.

The salesperson should also be extremely confident in front of the customer without appearing arrogant. People like to deal with people who know what they are doing and who are not fazed by questions and queries.

16.2   Communication

Professional sellers also need to develop the ability to communicate effectively with people at all levels. They need to be equally at ease talking to a person with an in-depth knowledge of the industry and products as they are with someone with little or no knowledge.

This ability is a skill that the salespeople have to master and develop. They need to be able to speak to people with little knowledge without using jargon. They must be able to explain the products and concepts in way that customers will understand without talking down to them. They must also develop the ability to explain difficult matters in a way that appears simple to customers without patronising them or making them feel uncomfortable.

They also need to be able to judge the level of a customer's knowledge and if that knowledge is considerable, they need to communicate in a way that shows they have acknowledged this. Often this ability to adapt to the way in which they communicate to the type of customer they are dealing with will come with experience.

Self-organization

All of the things we have looked at so far in this chapter are the basic qualities and attributes that are required by the successful, professional seller. However it is possible that two people who have exactly the same level of industry knowledge and company knowledge, and the same sales skills, can have different levels of success.

The difference comes down to how well planned they are and how well they organize their activity. People work in different ways. Some people like the pressure of deadlines and enjoy being busy. Others need a much calmer approach to their work and like to plan in advance. Whichever way the seller works naturally, everybody needs to be organized to some extent if they are to appear professional and make the most of their selling potential.

People find their own ways of planning their workload and organizing their efforts, but we shall now look at some of the things they can do to help themselves to become better at self-organization. This includes:

● Forecasting the workload and planning

- Knowing when they are able to work best

- How to avoid wasting time

- Controlling interruptions

- Using a diary to best effect

- Delegating

16.3   Forecasting the workload and planning

The first step to self-organization is to know the amount of work there is to be done and to plan in advance for the busy times. If there are times when the salespeople know they will be particularly busy, they should ensure that they allocate time to do these tasks and leave their diary clear for these times. During quieter times they should catch up on the less important work so that these tasks do not get left until the busier periods.

Of course this will be possible only if the adviser is always aware of the tasks and jobs that must be done. One way of ensuring that all tasks get completed and that nothing gets missed is for the salesperson to use a 'to do' list. This is a simple tool that requires the salesperson to spend a few minutes at the beginning of each day thinking about what needs to be done. They then write them on the list and tick them off as they are completed.

Figure 16.2: 'To do' list

Day Monday		
To Do	**By when**	**Done**
Submit last week's sales figure	10 a.m.	
Make next week's appointments	Thursday p.m.	
Write report on branch promotion activity	Wednesday 5p.m.	
Prepare training session for branch counter staff	Thursday 10a.m.	
Telephone Mr Andrews to report progress of his application	11a.m.	

This type of 'to do' list is often used to help people see the tasks they must complete and ensure that nothing is missed. Although it does show the time and the day that the task must be completed by, it does not rank those tasks in terms of importance.

Including the urgency of the task would ensure that the salesperson tackled the tasks in the right order, and that the most important jobs always got done. The diagram below shows a 'to do' list segmented into quadrants, where the tasks would be entered into the appropriate section depending on the urgency and importance. The tasks are to be attended to in order, starting with those in quadrant number 1.

Figure 16.3: Ranked to do list

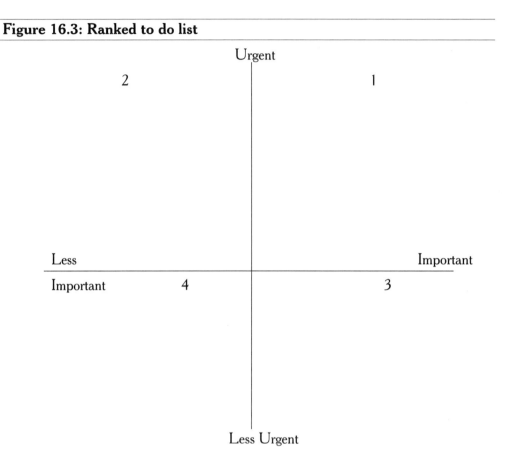

Know when you can work best

Different people naturally work better at different times of the day. Some people like to start work very early in the morning and find that this is the time they have most energy and are most able to concentrate. Other people are not 'morning people' and find it difficult to start very early. They prefer to start a little later in the day and work until later in the evening. Other people concentrate better if they have breaks throughout the day, and some prefer not to stop for lunch.

The skill for salespeople is to recognize when they are at their best and plan their workload around those times. Although the time of their working day may to a great extent be dictated to them, they can still plan to do the jobs that require the greatest level of concentration at the times they are best able to do them. In order to know when these 'best' times are, the salesperson should keep a record for a few days of his or her energy levels and see if there is a pattern. For example:

Figure 16.4: Energy levels throughout the day

Energy and

Concentration

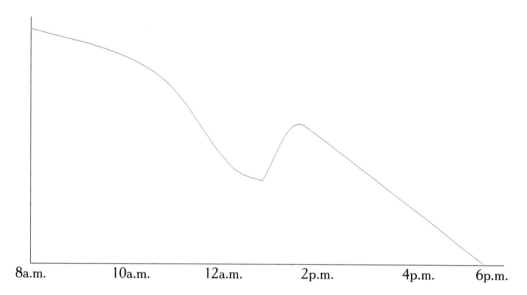

8a.m.   10a.m.   12a.m.   2p.m.   4p.m.   6p.m.

Do not waste time

This seems so obvious that it should go without saying, but if people actually looked at what they do each and every minute of the day, they would probably be amazed at the amount of time that is wasted. Often the reason for this waste is that people tend to find other things to do to put off having to start difficult or tedious jobs. Here are a few tips a salesperson could consider in order to avoid wasting any time:

● Where there is more than one job of equal importance to do, do the difficult or boring jobs first.

● Always finish one job before starting another.

● Set a definite time to start a job and stick to it.

● Allocate the amount of time a job should take and thereby set a deadline and to try to work to the deadline rather than letting jobs linger on.

Controlling interruptions

Interruptions are a common cause of self-organization problems. Some interruptions are of course necessary, the skill the seller needs to learn is how to differentiate between the necessary interruptions and the unnecessary ones.

The necessary interruptions are those that help the salesperson to achieve objectives; for example, he or she may be in the middle of writing a report when interrupted by a call from a customer asking about products or services. This is a necessary interruption as that call could lead to further business towards the salesperson's target.

Unnecessary interruptions are those that distract sellers from their task and prevent them from achieving their objectives. The way to avoid these is to do the following:

- Try to set aside time for staff to discuss work issues. This will limit the number of times they interrupt because, if they have something they need to speak about, they can wait until that allocated time.

- Deal with interruptions later if they are not important rather than allowing them to break the flow of the task in hand

- Salespeople should set aside time each day when they really cannot be disturbed and ensure that everybody knows this is the case.

- Ask someone else – a secretary, personal assistant or a member of the branch staff – to screen the interruptions and allow through only the urgent or necessary ones.

Use a diary effectively

Every salesperson should have a diary and needs to use it in order to book appointments for interviews with customers. However, simply having a diary does not mean that the salesperson is organized. Some people use their diaries effectively, others do not. The seller who wants to create a positive and professional image needs to learn how to get the very best use of a diary.

Most salespeople have other staff booking appointments into the diary on their behalf; this is all the more reason to ensure that the diary is well organized in advance. Here are some basic rules of that will help the seller to get the best use of this organization tool:

- If other people will be booking appointments into the diary, pre-mark appointments for them to fill.

- Ensure that these slots are long enough for each appointment, so that there will never be any need to cut them short or keep people waiting

- Allow sufficient space between appointments to allow for the completion of any paperwork that will need to be done after the customer has left, and for the preparation that will be needed for the next customer.

- If the salespeople interview customers in their own homes, they should book the slots with sufficient travelling time allowed in order that they can get from one appointment to the next.

- Mark in the diary times when you are not available to see customers because you will be doing administration tasks and dealing with post, etc. While this should not take up too much of your time it is important, especially if selling regulated products, that the administration is all up to date.

Let us look at how a salesperson's diary may look:

Figure 16.5: Diary

Monday		Thursday	
9	Post & Prep.	9	Post & Prep.
10	App. No. 1_____	10	App. No. 1_____
11	Admin. & Prep.	11	Admin. & Prep.
12	App. No. 2_____	12	App. No. 2_____
1	Admin. / Lunch	1	Admin. / Lunch
2	App. No. 3_____	2	App. No. 3_____
3	Admin. & Prep.	3	Admin. & Prep.
4	App. No. 4_____	4	App. No. 4_____
5	Admin.	5	Admin.

Tuesday		Friday	
9	Post & Prep.	9	Post & Prep.
10	App. No. 1_____	10	App. No. 1_____
11	Admin. & Prep.	11	Admin. & Prep.
12	App. No. 2_____	12	App. No. 2_____
1	Admin. / Lunch	1	Admin. / Lunch
2	App. No. 3_____	2	App. No. 3_____
3	Admin. & Prep.	3	Admin. & Prep.
4	App. No. 4_____	4	App. No. 4_____
5	Admin.	5	Admin.

Wednesday		Saturday	
9	Post & Prep.	9	Post & Prep.
10	App. No. 1_____	10	App. No. 1_____
11	Admin. & Prep.	11	Admin. & Prep.
12	App. No. 2_____	12	App. No. 2_____
1	Admin. / Lunch		
2	App. No. 3_____		
3	Admin. & Prep.		
4	App. No. 4_____		
5	Admin.		

Delegation

This is one of the most important skills for people who wish to ensure they make the best possible use of their time. Most people find that they need to both delegate work to other people and be able to take work delegated by others. While being aware of the need to delegate, most people fail to do so, or fail do so effectively. Only those people who are able to delegate effectively feel the real benefit. Those who delegate badly simply end up chasing work and probably completing it themselves, thereby creating more work than they were trying to save. The art of good delegation involves:

* Delegating in plenty of time so that the recipient of the delegated work has a reasonable time in which to complete the task.

* Giving a clear and concise briefing to the person who is to carry out the work, including details of the priority it is to be given, the timescales involved, the exact nature of the task, and the resources required.

* Review the progress that has been made before the deadline and ensure the task is underway. Never rely on other people's memories.

* Try to delegate whole tasks rather than just sections of a job because other people will find this much more interesting and fulfilling and will be happier to do this.

* Once delegated, leave them to it. Although you will need to review progress, you should not be constantly hovering over the person who is doing the work.

* Say thank you once the task is completed. People who feel appreciated are far more likely to accept further work in the future.

The examples given above are just a few of the ways in which the salespeople can become more organized in their daily working and thereby improve their performance. The more organized they become, the more they will be able to do in the time that they have available, and therefore the more likely they are to meet and exceed their sales targets.

17

COMMUNICATIONS

After reading this chapter you should

● Understand how to plan and structure a customer interview

● Know how to record the information gathered in that interview

● Understand how to recognize customers' needs from the information gathered

● Know how advisers formulate solutions to those customers' needs

● Know how to deal with stressful situations, including handling customer complaints

17.1 Planning and structuring a sales interview

We saw in Chapter 10 the benefits of planning sales activity in advance. We looked in detail at the way in which good planning enables salespeople to ensure that they have sufficient resource, and to plan their actual activity in order that they can achieve their objectives. Planning also enables them to monitor their progress towards their objectives.

Once the salesperson has the discipline of working with a good planning process and has seen the benefits of planning, he or she will be able to bring this into everyday working practices. The benefits of planning apply equally to a salesperson's everyday working life as they do to the annual planning process.

When a salesperson is conducting an interview with a customer, the probability of that interview being a success and resulting in a sale will be far greater if the structure and content of the interview is planned in advance. This will produce the following benefits:

● Because they know what they will be discussing in the interview they will be able to ensure that they have everything they need in advance in terms of paperwork, brochures, customer details, etc.

● They will know how much time is required and can therefore ensure that they do not need to cut the interview short to see another customer.

● They will know what they want to achieve from the interview and will therefore have an objective. The interview will be focused on achieving that objective.

● They will have a structure. The customers will feel that they know what is going on and what is expected of them.

● They will appear far more organized and professional to the customer.

The first stage in the planning process is to have an objective for the interview. Of course some interviews will be carried out at the request of the customer without any specific reason being given, but in most cases the interviewer will have a fairly clear understanding of what the interview is about. From this he or she can set a goal, an objective to be achieved, and then measure the success of the interview against this objective.

The objective and the structure of the interview will depend largely on the nature of the product or service being sold. Let us look at an example and use it to show what the structure of the interview may be. The example is a salesperson who is selling regulated products such as pensions and investments. Other types of interview will follow broadly the same structure, but will be tailored depending on the individual circumstances.

When considering the structure of the sales interview we need to remember the customer's buying pattern and look at how the salesperson can match behaviour to this. We looked in detail at the customer's buying behaviour earlier in this text, but just to recap, we said the stages that customers must progress through before they would buy are as follows:

1. Recognition that they have a need and a desire to satisfy that need

2. Evaluation of the different options available to satisfy that need

3. Making a decision to buy

4. Questions to gain reassurance that they have done the right thing

When salespeople are planning the objective for an interview or the structure and content, they must always be aware of the customer's buying pattern and work with it. This means that the objective should be to help the customer to progress through the stages of the buying process to some degree or other.

For some simpler products and services, the customer may well make a purchase in a single interview. This is likely to be true for the type of product where the customer passes through the first stage without any assistance from a salesperson, such as a personal loan sale.

With such a product customers have already seen the need for the product themselves– they know that they want to borrow some money before they approach the financial services company. They meet the company's salesperson only when they are at the second stage of the buying process, i.e. they are evaluating the different options available to them. In this case the objective for the interview would be to find the most suitable loan product for the customer's circumstances and have the customer agree to take it.

However, with some products customers are not always aware of exactly what their need is, or the real extent of their need, and therefore when they meet the salesperson they are in a position of not having passed through the first stage of the buying process. The salesperson's objectives and structure therefore need to take account of this.

This would be the case for something such as a pension sale. A customer may be aware that he should really be saving for retirement, but not aware of the amount that he should be saving or over what period. Similarly many people know that they really should have some life assurance, but have not reached the point of understanding the need sufficiently that they want to do something about it.

For these cases, the skill of the salesperson is to help the customer through the recognition of needs and therefore that is where the interview should start. If the salesperson is to cover the entire sales process, he or she may well need to see the customer more than once and will plan to carry out two interviews.

If this is the case, the salesperson will have an objective and structure for the first interview and a different objective and structure for the second. The objective for the first may well be to simply gather as much information as possible about the customer and his or her circumstances. This would enable the salesperson to gain a clear understanding of the customer's needs and the extent of those needs, and explain them to the customer. The seller would then arrange a second interview where the objective would be to show the customer the best way to satisfy those needs and gain their agreement to those solutions, i.e. the sale.

Once the objective is set then the structure of the interview becomes apparent. Let us look at our example of the salesperson selling regulated products. There is an interview booked for a customer who wants to discuss savings and investments. The seller will set an objective for this interview as discussed above, and book a second interview in order to make recommendations and the sale. The structure of that first interview would look like this (please turn to page 262):

Figure 17.1: Structure of a first interview

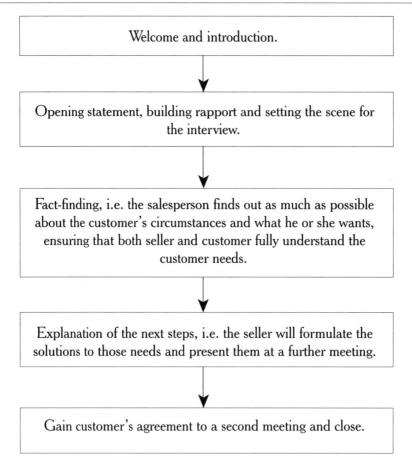

Welcome and introduction.

Opening statement, building rapport and setting the scene for the interview.

Fact-finding, i.e. the salesperson finds out as much as possible about the customer's circumstances and what he or she wants, ensuring that both seller and customer fully understand the customer needs.

Explanation of the next steps, i.e. the seller will formulate the solutions to those needs and present them at a further meeting.

Gain customer's agreement to a second meeting and close.

At this interview the salesperson has started to build the rapport and the trust that is necessary for the customer to feel comfortable buying financial services products. The seller has also helped the customer through the first stage of the buying process. The seller has discussed the customer's circumstances and helped the customer to see the need to save some money on a regular basis. The customer has also seen the need to move investments to a product with the possibility of greater returns and is looking for a solution to that need.

In between the first and second interview the seller will have time to re-examine the customer's requirements and formulate the best solution to those needs. He or she will then plan how best to present these solutions to the customer and gain the customer's agreement to the sale. The structure of the second interview will look like this:

Figure 17.2: Structure of a second interview

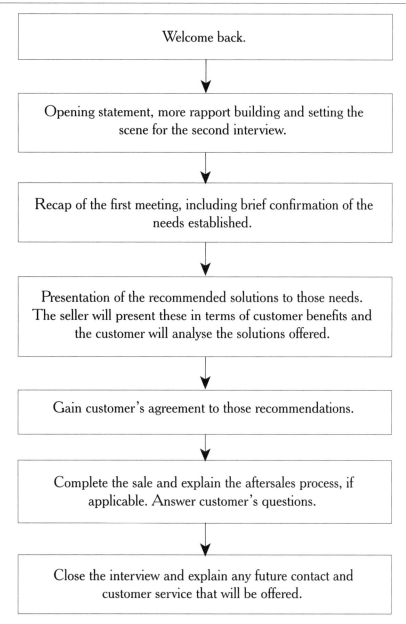

17.2 Recording the interview and the information

Throughout the interview the salesperson will be asking questions of the customer and gathering information about him or her. The extent of the information gathered will depend on the nature of the products and services being sold, as well as the nature of the sales process involved.

If the customer knows exactly what to buy and simply comes into the branch to make the purchase, the seller is likely to record only the information needed to make that sale. However, if we take our example salesperson who is selling a full range of regulated financial services products and advising the customer about needs and requirements, the seller will need to gather a huge amount of information about the customer and record it.

If an interview is conducted over the telephone, many financial services companies record the call as a record of what was actually said. If this is the case, the customer must be told that the conversation is being recorded. However, if the interview takes place face-to-face this is unlikely to be the situation. The information gathered has to be recorded by the seller in order that he or she can accurateley assess the customer's needs and recommend solutions.

As the information is given by the customer throughout the interview, the salesperson either writes it down, or uses a laptop or desktop computer to record the facts and figures. Because the salesperson will ask similar questions in each interview and gather similar information from each customer seen, it is usual to have a pre-prepared form to complete the information on. This form is often known as a fact find, and helps the salesperson in two ways:

1. It ensures that he or she remembers to ask the customer for all the information required by prompting with the relevant questions.

2. It gives a standard format for recording the information and a permanent record of the facts given to the seller by the customer.

The questions contained in such a fact find are those the salesperson would need to know the answers to before he or she can fully assess the customer's needs and formulate solutions. It also contains the questions that the seller needs to ask in order to offer a tailor-made solution to that customer, and we will examine exactly how the seller goes about doing that later in this chapter.

Firstly, let us look at the kind of information that a salesperson needs to know before making recommendations to the customer, and the way in which he or she may record the information. As we saw earlier, some companies use a paper-based fact find, and others have far more advanced versions which are computer based. They also vary in detail. Some adviser ask for far more specific information than others, depending on the nature of the service they offer. The version shown on the next page gives an idea of the basic information that may be gathered during such an interview:

FACT FIND FOR: ....

SELF	**PARTNER**
Name:	Name: ....
Address:	Address:.................................
....	....
....	....
Tel. No.:	Tel. No.: ....
Date of Birth:	Date of Birth: ....
Marital Status:	Marital Status: ....
Dependants Yes/No*	Dependants Yes/No*
Name:	Name: ....
Date of Birth:	Date of Birth: ....
Employment Status:	Employment Status: ....
Occupation:	Occupation: ....
Employer's Name and Address:	Employer's Name and Address:
....	....
Work Tel. No.:	Work Tel. No.: ....
Income:	Income: ....
Bonus:	Bonus: ....
Other Income:	Other Income: ....
Total Income:	Total Income: ....

* Cross out answer that is not appropriate

EXPENDITURE

	SELF	**PARTNER**
Mortgage/Rent	£	£ ....
Household Bills	£	£ ....
Food	£	£ ....
Insurances	£	£ ....
Pension	£	£ ....
Loan Repayments	£	£ ....
Hire Purchase	£	£ ....
Credit Cards	£	£ ....
Savings	£	£ ....
Car/Travel	£	£ ....
Leisure	£	£ ....
Clothing	£	£ ....
Unspecified	£	£ ....
Total	£	£ ....

RETIREMENT PENSION

	SELF	PARTNER
Do you have an occupational pension?	Yes/No*	Yes/No*
Type of scheme:	Money purchase/ Final salary*	Money purchase/ Final salary*
Accrual rate:	....	....
Employer contribution:	....	....
Your contribution:	....	....
Date of joining:	......./......../.......	......./......../.......
Retirement date:	......./......../.......	......./......../.......
Do you have a personal pension?	Yes/No*	Yes/No*
Start date:	......./......../.......	......./......../.......
Monthly contribution:	£	£ ....
Retirement date:	......./......../.......	......./......../.......

What pension arrangements
do you have from previous employers?

* Cross out answer that is not appropriate

SAVINGS AND INVESTMENTS

	SELF	PARTNER
Current account	£	£ ....
Deposit account	£	£ ....
Unit trusts	£	£ ....
Bonds	£	£ ....
PEPs	£	£ ....
ISAs	£	£ ....
Shares	£	£ ....
Other	£	£ ....
Do you save on a regular basis?	Yes/No*	Yes/No*
How much do you save a month?	£	£ ....
What are the things you would like to save for in the future?	....	....

* Cross out answer that is not appropriate

PROTECTION

	SELF	PARTNER
Do you have life cover?	Yes/No*	Yes/No*
If Yes, please give details	....	....
	....	....
	....	....
Do you have critical illness cover?	Yes/No*	Yes/No*
If Yes, please give details	....	....
	....	....
	....	....
Is your income covered in the event of illness or unemployment?	Yes/No*	Yes/No*
If Yes, please give details	....	....
	....	....
	....	....

* Cross out answer that is not appropriate

In addition to this factual information, the salesperson will need to gather information of a non-factual nature. This might involve such things as the customer's opinions about certain aspects of financial planning, plans for the future and likes and dislikes. These, together with the factual information, will enable the salesperson to build a full picture of the customer's needs and ensure that the recommendations are tailor-made to suit.

Interview skills

Conducting a sales interview requires certain skills if the interviewer is to do the job effectively and efficiently. When recruiting people into the sales role, the manager will look for individuals who have these skills or whom they consider can be trained to have such skills. While knowledge can be gained during an induction programme, interview skills take time and practice to acquire and perfect. Because of this skills training should be an on-going event for all sellers.

The types of things that are often refferred to as 'selling skills' include the following.

Interpersonal skills

Sellers need to be able to talk to people at all levels from the very financially sophisticated to those with little or no knowledge of the subject. They need to be able to explain things in a way that customers can understand and that will help them to make decisions.

Customers are often uneasy about discussing their financial affairs with people they do not know because they consider it to be a very personal subject. The salesperson needs to be able to put people at their ease and make them feel happy to give them details of their income and other matters. People often lack confidence when dealing with complex financial matters and feel much happier buying from someone they feel comfortable with and someone they trust. The successful adviser needs to build good relationships with the customer in a relatively short space of time.

Questioning skills

We have seen that sellers have to ask the customer a large number of questions because they require a great deal of information to offer the customer solid recommendations as to their financial needs. While this would at first glance seem like a fairly straightforward thing to do, there is skill in asking these questions. They have to be asked in a way that will prevent the customer from getting bored or from feeling interrogated.

A skilled salesperson asks open questions in order to get customers to talk more about themselves, to gather more information while actually asking fewer questions. For example, the salesperson might want to know about the individual's job. The unskilled adviser will ask the following questions:

> *"Where do you work?"*
>
> *"What is the nature of your job?"*
>
> *"How much do you earn?"*
>
> *"Do they provide a pension scheme?"*
>
> *"Do you get sick pay?"*

The skilled interviewer will say to the customer:

> *"Please tell me about you job and the benefits package you get."*

As a result of asking the customer this one question rather than the five above, the salesperson will get more information from the customer, who has been encouraged to 'chat'. Not only will this help to build rapport with the customer and allow him or her to feel at ease, but will give the interviewer an insight into the customer's preferences.

The way in which customers answer the question will also show the seller the type of things they consider to be important to them. This helps the salespeople to ensure they offer the right solutions to customers' needs and enables them to present the solutions in terms of benefit statements.

The benefit of such a style of questionning is that customers feel that they have been given the opportunity to talk and that the salesperson is genuinely interested in them. If this is the case and customers feel that the salesperson understands them, they are far more likely to buy.

Listening skills

This initially seems like something that people do all the time, and therefore not something that we should really consider as a skill, or something that requires training. However, while we think we listen to people every day, active listening is something quite different. By active listening we mean really listening to what someone is saying and how he or she is saying it.

Active listening is especially difficult if the salesperson is trying to make notes or complete paperwork at the same time as hearing the answer to questions. The reason it is so important for the salesperson to be able to listen to the way people give the information they give, is because often the emphasis people put on things, or the order they give things, tell the seller as much as the actual words.

If sellers are to successfully match the products and services offered to the customer's needs they need to know as much as possible about the customer and therefore need to listen to everything the customer has to say.

Analytical skills

The salesperson needs excellent analytical skills. This is because the customer's circumstances can often be complex and the salesperson has to be able to quickly understand them and analyse them. He or she has to be able to assess different solutions against these needs and weigh up the benefits of each option. While some situations can be straightforward, others, particularly those relating to regulated products, can require careful numeric analysis.

17.3   Recognizing customer needs

With many products, particularly those outside the financial services industry, the customer is well aware of the need before they go to the company or retailer to make purchase. In Chapter 12 we looked at the buying process and we saw that the first stage is the customer's recognition of a need. If customers do not recognize they have a need they will never progress through the other stages.

With some financial services products such as credit cards or personal loans, for example, customers have already passed through this stage of the process and recognized a need for a product. They are attending the interview because they are at the second stage of the process— that is, they are assessing the different options available to them and assessing the merits of each. Alternatively they may have assessed the merits of different products themselves and be visiting the provider simply to complete the purchase.

However, with other financial products and services, customers are less able to recognize that they have a need or the true extent of the need that they have. The role and indeed the skill of the salesperson is to help the individual through this stage of the buying process.

Customers are likely to have recognized to some degree that they need advice or that they have a need of some sort that has led them to attend an interview with the seller. However, before they can progress to the point of agreeing a solution and making a purchase, they will require the salesperson to help them to understand the exact nature of those needs.

The fact find that we looked at earlier in this chapter will help the adviser to see the customer's current situation and asses the needs that the customer has. The adviser will look for needs in terms of savings, investments, borrowing, retirement provision, and protection in the event of death or illness. While some needs are easy for the customer to see, others require more complex analysis before the true extent of the need becomes clear.

If the interviewer is using technology to assist in carrying out the interview, it may also help in assessing the area and the extent of the customer's needs. For example, it may well prompt the adviser to ask certain questions and then measure the answers against certain models built into the system. It could use the information input to provide the adviser and the customer with facts as to the extent of the shortfall in the customer's current financial provision. This will help the customer through this initial stage of the buying process.

Let us look at how this may work.

The adviser (let us assume it is a woman) asks the customers about levels of income and records the information. She also asks about the level of regular expenditure that the customers have and who pays what. This information is recorded. The advanced technology used by some financial services advisers is then able to show the customers the shortfall in income they will suffer if one of them were to be unable to work due to illness, or if one were to die. This will help the customers to recognize that they have a need for life assurance and income protection insurance.

We saw in Chapter 15 when looking at presentation skills how much more effectively the information is conveyed when in tablular or pictorial form. This is also true when helping the customer through the recognition of needs stage of the buying process. For example, if the customers have a need for life assurance to replace lost income if one of them dies, it could be presented like this:

Figure 17.2: Analysis of income and expenditure

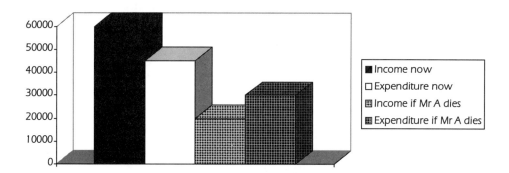

Showing the current income and expenditure in the chart form above allows the customers to see that currently income is greater than the level of expenditure and hence they are probably able to save at the current time. However, what the graph also shows is that if Mr A were to die, although the expenditure would fall (there may be no mortgage payments if there is life cover on the mortgage, for example) the income of Mrs A would be considerably lower than they are currently enjoying.

We can see in fact that the income would fall below the level of her expenditure, leaving a shortfall each month. Faced with this information the customers can see that unless they are happy to face a dramatic drop in their standard of living, they will need to have some life assurance in order to replace Mr A's income in the event of his death.

While technology can help in the recognition of customer's needs, skilled salespeople will themselves be able to recognize these needs and help the customer to see them, with or without the use of such technology.

17.4   Formulating solutions to a customer's needs

Once the adviser fully understands the customer's needs, the next stage is to present the customer with the solutions to those needs. The complexity of deciding on the right solution depends on the nature of that need and the product or service that satisfies it. The adviser will be able to use his or her understanding of the customer's needs to assess the product or service that will best satisfy them, and ensure that the product is tailored to exactly meet that individual customer's specific need.

Let us look at a couple of example of how this might be done.

If the customer's need is to find the best method of investing a lump sum, the adviser will have a range of products that will do this. He or she will then use the information gathered from the customer to recommend the one that most suits the customer. In order to do this accurately the adviser will need information such as:

- How much does the customer wish to invest?

- Is he or she investing for income or for growth?

- What is the customer's income tax and capital gains tax position?

- How long is the customer investing for?

- Does the customer require any access to the money during this period of time?

- What is the attitude to risk, i.e. would the customer risk capital for the opportunity of greater returns?

It is the answers to these questions that will determine the recommendations the adviser makes. The adviser will use his or her knowledge of the products to select the one that exactly matches the customer's requirements, and then sell it to the customer by explaining the features in terms of personal benefits as seen in Chapters 7 and 12.

Other customers' needs may require more complex calculations to be done to ensure that the right solution is offered. Let us look at an example of a customer whose need is income in retirement. The adviser will have asked the customer questions about those requirements and will therefore know the product that will most suit the customer's needs. If the adviser feels that a personal pension plan is the solution, he or she needs to know how much the customer would need to save each month to have the necessary retirement income. In order to do this the adviser would need to go through the following steps:

Step 1   Understand the level of income required in retirement in today's terms, e.g. £15,000.

Step 2   Calculate the equivalent of this level of income at the date the customer wishes to retire, i.e. £56,000 at that date would be the equivalent of £15,000 now.

Step 3   Calculate the lump sum that would be needed to provide this level of income at the retirement date.

Step 4   Using stipulated levels of assumed investment growth, work out how much the customer would need to save each month in order to have accumulated the required lump sum at retirement.

Step 5   Ensure that this level of monthly saving is within the customer's budget.

Again when this has been done the salesperson will need to explain the recommendations in terms of personal benefits. For example:

"You said you wanted an income in retirement; this product will provide the level of income you required from your 55th birthday, the date you said you wanted to retire."

The method of formulating the solution depends on the nature of the need and the product that solves that need. This will of course vary between customers. However what we can see from these two examples is that in order to do this job effectively, the salesperson requires all the skills that we looked at earlier in this chapter. The seller will need to know the customer and his or her circumstances well. The more information the seller collects about the customer, including likes and dislikes, the more accurately will he or she be able to formulate the solution to exactly match those requirements.

17.5   Handling a customer's complaints

No matter how hard a company works to ensure that it offers the best products at the best price and the best service possible, there will always be something that goes wrong and leads to a customer complaining. What we need to consider now is how we should deal with those complaints.

Customer complaints should be taken seriously by the organization. For every person who takes the time and trouble to complain, there could well be another ten, or even twenty, who are equally dissatisfied but who have not felt able, for whatever reason, to make a complaint. In the same way as satisfied customers tell their friends and family how happy they are with their provider, dissatisfied customers also tell people.

Obviously all complaints need to be treated with speed, efficiency and courtesy. This said, the best way to ensure that customer complaints are handled in the most efficient and effective way possible is to help all members of staff to see complaints in a positive light. At first the idea that complaints are a positive thing may seem a strange view to many people, but can be explained as follows:

- There is nothing as satisfying as turning an irate and unhappy customer into one who leaves feeling happy with the product or service they have bought and thanks you for your help.

- By complaining, customers are showing you what parts of your products and services need to be improved and therefore helping you to become more competitive in the marketplace.

- Complaining customers often compare the product or service they have received with those that they have seen offered by other providers. This gives the company a great deal of information about the ways in which other companies are gaining competitive advantage.

When we are faced with an irate customer, especially one who is snapping or shouting, and particularly if it is happing in the branch in front of other staff and customers, the situation can be very stressful for the person who is trying to deal with the complaint. To avoid making the situation worse we need to ensure right from the start that the situation is handled very carefully.

We have seen throughout the chapters on marketing and selling the amount of time, effort and expense involved in attracting new customers to the company. We have also discussed the merits of ensuring that once a customer is on board, that relationship is maintained and developed in order to ensure that the customer remains with the organization throughout their lives rather than switching between providers. If a company is to follow this method of relationship building in order to retain their customers, the way in which they deal with those customers when something goes wrong becomes extremely important.

Let us look then at a few basic rules for ensuring that the situation is dealt with properly and to the satisfaction of both the company and the customer.

- If the customer has made an appointment to come in and discuss the complaint, make sure you are punctual and do not keep them waiting because this will only irritate them further.

- Welcome them and thank them for taking the trouble to bring the problem to your attention, and for allowing you the opportunity to discuss it.

- Ask the customer to explain the problem. Allow plenty of time to go through the grievance so that he or she gets a proper hearing. Never interrupt the customer during his or her account of the situation.

- While the customer is going through the details of the complaint, ensure that you look interested and attentive even if you have heard the details many times before. If the customer feels you do not care enough to listen, this will make the situation much worse.

- Always be sympathetic to the customer's issues and the problems encountered. Financial services companies need to be particularly so, because any problem with finances are usually seen as fairly serious by the customer, and can, in some circumstances, cause great difficulty and/or embarrassment.

- If the company is at fault, apologize to the customer. It does not matter if it was not your fault; the customer sees you as being the face of the company and will therefore expect you to take responsibility for whatever went wrong. Never blame someone else within the company or try to pin the blame on technology. If there was a technological error, it is still the company's fault and the customer is therefore right to expect an apology.

- Once the problem is understood and you have apologized, explain to the customer what will be done to put the problem right. You must accept responsibility for correcting the error even if you need to refer to another part of the business once the customer has gone. Again the customer deals with you as the face of the company and will therefore expect you to deal with his or her concerns, rather than be passed around the company to other departments.

- If you do tell the customer that you will sort out problems, ensure that you do. Follow up to ensure that the required action has been taken and write to the customer to confirm this has happened.

- If the company is not at fault and the complaint is due to the customer's own misunderstanding, explain this to the customer in a calm and polite manner.

- If you are dealing with the complaint over the telephone, exactly the same principles apply as when dealing with the complaint face to face.

- Many customers choose to make their complaint by letter; again the rules for dealing with the problem are exactly the same.

- While we should always be polite to customers, unfortunately they are not always polite themselves. Allthough we should do everything in our power to remain calm and therefore calm the customer, or rare occasions some customers become abusive. No member of staff should have to accept this conduct and you should calmly and politely tell the customer that you can no longer deal with the matter until they are calmer, and end the conversation. However, if the member of staff follows the guidance given above, this should ensure that the situation always remains pleasant and ends with everyone feeling happy with the outcome.

Regulated products

Companies that sell life assurance, pensions and investments, regulated by the Financial Services Authority, must adhere to the rules put in place by the regulators for dealing with customer complaints. This does not mean, however, that the above advice does not apply equally to these complaints, it simply means that in certain circumstances the complaint must be handled in accordance with the regulator's rules.

The types of complaint that need to be dealt with in this specific manner are those relating to the sale of regulated products. While it is not possible to list all types of sales complaints, the following list gives some examples of complaints that could be received:

- A customer may complain that the product or service he was sold by the company was inappropriate to meet his needs.

- A customer could complain that the terms of the product sold were inappropriate, for example, too high a sum assured on a life policy.

- A customer may complain that he was incorrectly advised to cancel another policy that he had with another provider and replace it with a new one (churning).

- A customer could complain that he was given sales literature that contained information that was misleading about the product.

- A customer could complain about the ability or competency of the salesperson who sold him the product.

If such a complaint is received by an adviser or by any other member of the company's staff, he or she should immediately send it to the compliance department which would deal with it. It will acknowledge the complaint and register it. It would then need to conduct a thorough investigation to see if there was a genuine reason for the complaint. It would then write to the customer stating its findings.

If the company finds that there was no error on the part of its employee, the customer can, if he or she wishes, take the complaint further. When the company writes to the customer stating the results of its investigation, it will explain that if the customer is not satisfied with the outcome, he or she can complain to the Ombudsman.

The Personal Investment Authority Ombudsman Bureau provides an efficient and user-friendly complaints resolution service that is a comprehensive but cost-efficient alternative to taking action through the courts. It investigates complaints made against financial services organizations regulated by the PIA and the FSA.

The customer can only approach the Ombudsman for help once the company has investigated the complaint and given the customer notification of its findings. The customer then has six months in which to ask the ombudsman to make further investigations. The Ombudsman will request all the relevant information from the company and will make an assessment of the complaint.

If the Ombudsman considers the customer's complaint should be upheld, he will write to the customer to inform them of this decision, and will outline an appropriate remedy, including an amount of compensation to be paid if this is deemed necessary. Cases are usually dealt with within six months.

18

BALANCING THE NEEDS OF THE CUSTOMER WITH THOSE OF THE ORGANIZATION

After reading this chapter you should

- Understand the issues the business will face when prioritizing the needs of the customer and the needs of the organization

- Be aware of the issues relating to how different companies within a group compete for business, and how different branches within a network can compete for the same customer

We saw in Chapter 5 that any financial services company must operate to make a profit if it is to be a viable business in the longer term. This need to make a profit will affect the decisions that the management team takes and the strategies that they adopt. However at the same time we have also seen that unless the company takes into consideration the needs of the customer and ensures it meets those needs, the business will fail.

Let us remind ourselves again of the definition of marketing.

The management process responsible for identifying, anticipating and satisfying customer needs profitably.

When we consider the definition it becomes obvious that there are going to be many instances where a careful balance is required between the needs of the customer and the needs of the organization. Not only in the marketing of financial services products does there need to be balancing, but also in the sales and servicing of such products.

We will now look at some examples. Probably the best way to see the balances that are required is to consider situations that will occur in terms of the elements of the marketing mix, i.e. product, price, place and promotion.

18.1   Product

The balancing required in terms of the actual product offering can be summarized as shown in the diagram overleaf.

Figure 18.1: Balance between customer and company requirements

| Customers want individually tailored products, designed specifically for their needs | Company wants simple products that are easy to administer. |

If the company were to consider only the needs of the customer then it would sell products that were 'all things to all men'. That is it would ensure that the products it offered were designed with individual customer's needs in mind and in such a way that they could be tailored to suit each individual customer who bought the product.

However this would mean huge amounts of work for the company both at the time of sale and throughout the life of the products. This is because if each product it sold was different in order to cater for different customer's needs, each would need to administered differently throughout the term of the product.

This would be both costly and time consuming – even if possible. For this reason, the company is likely to prefer a simple product that is easy and cheap to administer and which is exactly the same, no matter who buys it.

In reality the financial services products offered today show that companies have considered both their needs and the needs of their customers and found what they consider to be a balance. The products are clearly designed with the customers' needs in mind. The companies spend a great deal of time, effort and money researching the needs of their customers and ensuring that they can offer a solution that is tailored to those needs. However the company will offer those products that it feels will satisfy the needs of the majority of the customers, not necessarily every single one.

These products usually have some options available on them, allowing the product to be tailored to some extent to match the needs of the customer. But these options will be predetermined and limited.

We can see that the majority of the financial services companies today are selling products that have found the balance between the needs of the customer and the needs of the organization.

18.2 Price

This is also an area where compromise is needed between the needs of customer and seller. At its most basic level it could be viewed as shown opposite:

Figure 18.2: Balance between price and profit

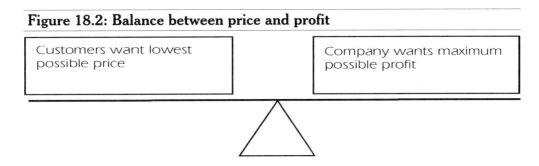

Of course in reality it is not as simple as this. There are many other factors to consider in the setting of prices, including such things as those considered in Chapter 2, i.e.

- Actual costs
- Competitor pricing
- Customers' willingness to pay
- Brand values
- The company's pricing strategy, etc.

This said, we know that careful consideration of both the customer's and the company's needs will have to be carried out if the pricing is to be successful. Too great an emphasis on the needs of the customer and the organization will not make sufficient profit to survive; too great an emphasis on the needs of the business and the customers will go elsewhere.

18.3   Place

Most financial services companies operating today distribute through a variety of different channels. They may well sell through intermediaries and brokers as well as through their own sales force. They might operate a branch network and a telephone call centre, and many companies now also distribute through the Internet.

For the ease and simplicity of the company's administration capabilities, it would be far easier for the provider company to look at each of these distribution channels in isolation, and indeed many companies do. They have different parts of the organization set up to deal with each of these, with different marketing departments, different sales teams and different administration units. It would be far easier therefore if customers could be restricted to using only one distribution channel for all their dealings with the company.

However customers want to deal with the company; they do not see the divisions within it and therefore do not follow any 'rules' regarding their point of entry to the company. They may well purchase a product from one branch, but then expect service from another. Alternatively they could purchase their account from a branch, but want to deal with certain transaction over the telephone.

Customers want flexibility in the way in which they deal with the organization, even though this may not necessarily be the easiest thing for the company to achieve. The diagrams below highlight the different ideals of both the organization and the customer.

Figure 18.3: Company would like each customer to select just one distribution channel

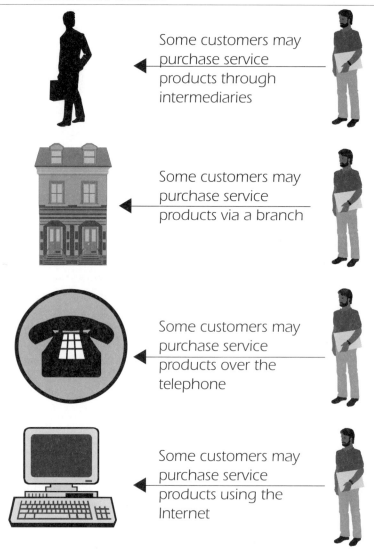

Some customers may purchase service products through intermediaries

Some customers may purchase service products via a branch

Some customers may purchase service products over the telephone

Some customers may purchase service products using the Internet

Figure 18.4: The customer would like to choose from all distribution channels

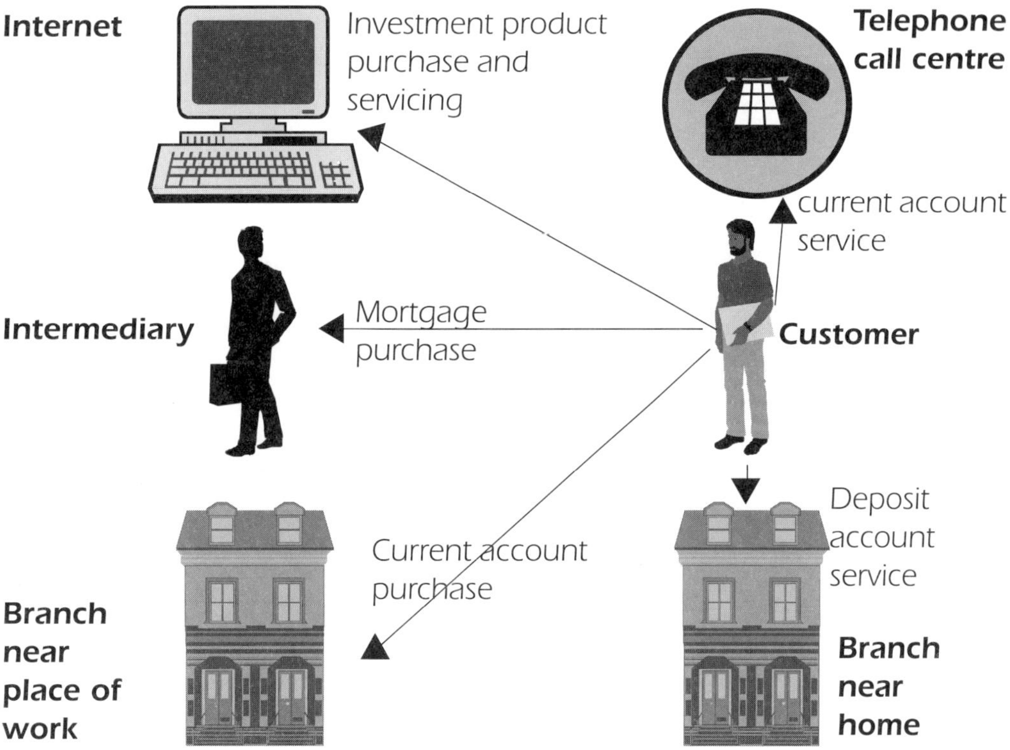

This flexibility required by the customer may cause problems for the organization. For example:

- If the customer uses more than one branch, which branch will actually 'own' that customer?

- If a sale starts in a branch but is then completed over the telephone, who should be remunerated for the sale?

- If the customer buys the product from one branch and it is paid for that sale, how will the company deal with the fact that another branch or distribution channel is expected to service that business and therefore incur the costs of providing the service?

- If the costs of the different distribution channels are significantly different, the organization may want to make different charges depending on the channel used. For example it may offer a discounted rate to customers who purchase their mortgage over the Internet. How will they ensure that the customers who receive such a discount are restricted to using the lower-cost channels?

These are just a few examples of why the needs of the customer may not fit well with the needs of the organization. Again, if the company is to survive and prosper it must find a balance between giving customers exactly what they want, and ensuring the business operates at a required level of profit.

Of course this type of debate is not restricted solely to distribution. Exactly the same applies to the different companies that often operate within the 'group' organization. Many large companies are subdivided into smaller companies dealing with specific products. For example, the group business may consist of one company that operates the banking products such as mortgages and deposit accounts etc. and another company that offers the investment products such as unit trusts and ISAs. If this is the case it will be likely that each will be run as a separate business unit with its own objectives and sales targets, as well as its own accountabilities and responsibilities.

It is quite conceivable that customers could find themselves dealing with both parts of the group at the same time, and the customers need will be for a service that covers both companies, i.e. a consolidated 'group' approach. They may well find that they are in a situation where they are deciding between two products offered by different companies within the group – a deposit account or an investment product, for example.

Customers will expect the company to be able to offer advice and guidance as to which is the most suitable for them. The last thing customers will expect is for different parts of the same company to be in out-and-out competition with each other and fighting over their business. In order to get a balance acceptable to both customer and company, there may well need to be rules of engagement set between the different parts of the group to ensure that there is a seamless appearance in front of the customers and therefore prevent any difficulties arising.

The group will need to balance customers' needs with those of the organization and find a way of dealing with customers which shows no signs of any internal division, while allowing the companies to continue to operate as separate business units.

18.4   Promotion

Figure 18.4: Balance between customer and company promotion requirements

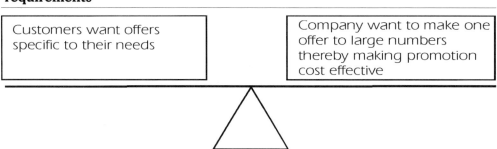

Customers want offers specific to their needs	Company want to make one offer to large numbers thereby making promotion cost effective

Customers do not want their financial services provider to send them 'junk mail'. However they do generally want to know about new products and services that they will find useful and which will fulfil their needs. They want to be treated as individuals and therefore only offered things that match their particular needs.

The company, on the other hand, would ideally like to promote one offer to as many people as possible. They also want to gain the maximum possible response. A balance is therefore needed.

For this reason financial services marketing departments use segmentation techniques in order to try to find groups of like-minded people who have similar needs. This allows the company to mail a large number of people with the same offer, and all of the customers receive an offer that is suitable and applicable to them.

18.5   Communication

Figure 18.5: Balance between customer and company use of communications

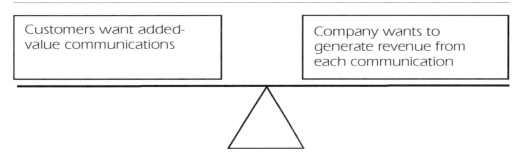

This is another area where there may need to be a balance between the needs of the customer and the needs of the organization. The customer will want interesting and informative communications from their financial services provider sent at regular intervals. The company will wish to keep in touch with their customers, but only in order to generate revenue and profit. Therefore a balance is needed between the two positions.

The balance that is often found is something like this. The company issues regular communications to its customers giving information about the products and services that they currently hold. It may also send the 'added value' type communications that the customer would like to receive, such as newsletters and customer magazines.

However in order to meet the organization's need to make profit, it will include in such communications direct marketing offers for other products and services that will be of interest to the customers. The business generated should cover the cost of the communications. Therefore the situation will be of benefit to both the customers who get the communications they require, and the company which gains additional business and increased customer loyalty.

These are just a few examples of how the marketing, sales, and service managers within a financial services organization will find themselves having to continually balance the needs of their customers with that of the organization in which they work. The successful manager will be able to understand the needs of both parties and find a win/win solution whereby the needs of both are met.

19

CONTROLLING DELIVERY AND FOLLOW-UP ACTIVITY

After reading this chapter you should

● Know how to allocate responsibilities to ensure that service is delivered

● Be more aware of the systems and records required for servicing financial services business

● Understand the importance of internal communications

● Know how to gain support from colleagues in order to maximize the service delivery

Introduction

So far in this text we have looked at the ways in which organizations can best market their products and services to the potential customer. We have also looked at the different ways that, once they have attracted the customer, they can make the sale. What we will consider here is the next step, i.e. what happens once the customer has agreed to buy the product and made the application.

Although the most visible part of the process of adding new business to the books may well be the marketing and sales, that does not mean that the follow-up activity is not extremely important. While getting the customer to sign the application may well be the end of the sales process as far as some are concerned, the truth is that this is far from being the end of the matter. If the promises made in the advertising campaigns and the interview with the salesperson are not kept, customers will very soon take their business elsewhere.

The follow-up activity is the delivery of the product that was sold via the marketing and sales activity and could therefore be considered as the most important part of the chain. We shall now consider the way in which an organization allocates responsibility for the follow-up activity, and the systems and records that need to be in place. We shall also consider the importance of regular communication between the different internal departments, and the best ways of working together to improve service.

19.1   Allocation of responsibilities

So far the allocation of responsibility has been a fairly clear-cut issue. The marketing department is responsible for all marketing activity such as segmentation, customer selection, advertising, promotional campaigns, etc., and the sales force is responsible for turning the enquiries generated by the marketing activity into sales. Once the sale is made, however, it becomes far less apparent where responsibility should lie.

Before the company can start the sales process it is important that it gives careful consideration to this issue and plans all the activity that will be required once the customer agrees to make a purchase and that it allocates such responsibilities to specific individuals or departments.

To see how this may work, we shall look at an example and consider the elements that make up the follow-up activity. Let us imagine that the company is selling life assurance policies. The sale and some of the follow-up activity are shown in the diagram on page 288:

Figure 19.1: Process for sale and follow-up

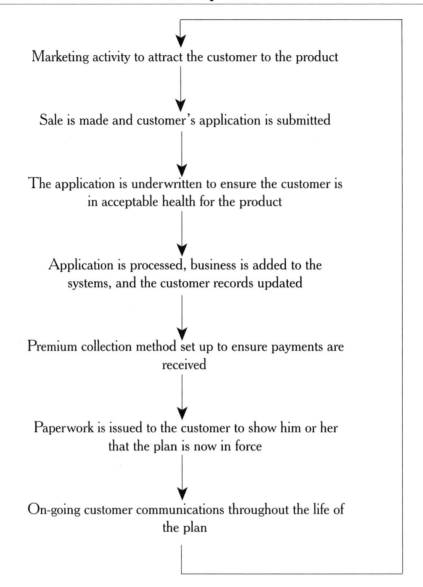

Marketing activity to attract the customer to the product

Sale is made and customer's application is submitted

The application is underwritten to ensure the customer is
in acceptable health for the product

Application is processed, business is added to the
systems, and the customer records updated

Premium collection method set up to ensure payments are
received

Paperwork is issued to the customer to show him or her
that the plan is now in force

On-going customer communications throughout the life of
the plan

This diagram shows that although the marketing and sales activity are essential, the work cannot stop there. However, the setting up of the plan is clearly not the responsibility of the marketing or sales teams. Their roles are clearly defined as attracting customers and making sales. They quite clearly need to be able to hand over the business to other people once the application is submitted, and allow them to take responsibility.

For this reason every financial services company has teams of people whose jobs are to carry out the follow-up activity needed to convert the sale into actual business. Although we need to bear in mind that each company is organized in a slightly different manner, here is an idea of the different departments that may exist within a financial services organization and the responsibilities they have.

The examples shown refer particularly to an insurance company, but banks and building societies are similar. It may be useful to check out the responsibilities of the departments in your organization and compare them to these.

Department	Responsibilities
New business team	These people ensure that all the correct paperwork is received and set up the application as a new plan. They ensure that the systems are up-dated to show that this business exists and set up or amend the customer records accordingly. They ensure that there is sufficient medical information for the underwriters to do their job and issue the customer with the correspondence that shows the policy is set up and in force. They also ensure that there is an acceptable method of payment and that premiums will be collected.
Underwriting	The underwriters assess the customer's health and decide if this is an acceptable risk for the company to take. They may decide that the health of the customer poses an increased risk of claim for the company and they in that case decide on an increased level of premium that the customer should be charged.
Existing business	Once the policy is set up and premiums are being collected, responsibility for the case is handed over to an existing business team. They ensure that the customer receives on-going information about the plan and deal with any amendments to the plan. They may also be responsible for such things as cancellations and maturities, and death claims.
Customer services	Customer services are responsible for dealing with any queries that the customer may have throughout the term of the policy and deal with both written and telephone queries. They also deal with minor amendments such as change of address or change of name, for example.
Legal and compliance	These people ensure that all the procedures used in marketing, sales and the follow-up activity are within the rules applicable to that type of business. They are responsible for ensuring this is the case for both new and existing business.

IT (information technology)	The IT teams are responsible for all the technology that the business uses. They ensure that the sales people have everything they need to produce the quotations etc. and that the new business teams have the systems they require for setting up the policy. They are also responsible for maintaining the systems that hold the existing business records and customer information, and ensuring that the customer services team have access to customer and policy information to enable them to deal with customers' queries.
Finance	The finance team needs to monitor the amount of business being sold to ensure that business projections are being met and the company remains profitable. They have input into the pricing decisions with the marketing team and are involved in such things as salary and bonus structure debates with the human resources team.
Operations	It is likely that the company has a group of people known as the operations team, or business process team. The role of these people is to ensure that the entire process for dealing with business is set up and coordinated. They are also pro-active in looking for better ways of processing business in order to save time and money, and may therefore suggest new processes and more efficient ways of operating.
Human resources	This team of people are responsible for ensuring there are sufficient suitable and appropriate staff to enable the company to carry out its business. They deal with all nature of staffing issues, including pay and conditions and grievance handling.

We can see that once a sale is made, the follow-up activity required necessitates the involvement of a large number of people and departments, each with their part to play and with specific tasks for which they are responsible. If the follow-up activity is to be effective and efficient, these departments all need to be working together in a coordinated and organized manner.

The operations department is there to ensure that this happens and that the processes laid down to deal with the business after it is sold are all working to plan. Periodically they are likely to carry out a review of the operating procedures to see:

1. That they are currently working as planned.

2. If they could be improved to enable the business to be run more productively and more cost effectively.

3. If they are as customer-focused as possible and providing the service that the customer wants.

19.2   Maximizing internal communications

We saw at the start of this chapter how many people from numerous departments within an organization are involved in the entire process, from marketing to sales and then to actual delivery. If the customer is to be delivered a good level of service and the company is to run efficiently, it is absolutely essential that all areas of the business are able to communicate with each other effectively.

To see how important it is we shall look at an example showing how a decision taken in one department can effect all other areas of the company, and why they need to have such a decision communicated to them quickly.

Decision	The sales manager decides that in order to meet targets for the coming year he will need to increase the size of the sales force by 10%. Let us look at who will need to have such a decision communicated to them if the business is to continue to run smoothly.
Human resources	This department needs to know of the decision because they will be required to recruit these people and establish terms and conditions, etc.
Training	The new recruits will need training and this has to be planned and developed by the training team, who also needs to ensure they have the resource available to do it.
IT	The IT department needs to know that the new recruits are being taken on because they need to supply them with the appropriate point-of-sale technology and install it in time for them to start selling.
Marketing	The marketing department needs to know that the sales force is increasing in size by 10% because they are likely to be required to supply the sales force with 10% more leads. This involves increased activity for them and may have staffing implications.
New business	The new business teams need to know because they will have to ensure they are sufficiently well prepared for dealing with the additional business that the increase in the size of the sales force will mean for them.

We can see from this very simplified example that the actions of one department can have effects on almost every other department within the company. If there is no communication between the departments, the actions of one could well mean that another finds it difficult to operate or suffers a dramatic fall in performance level. Communication between different departments is essential.

We also know that many financial services companies are in fact made up of a group of many smaller companies. Some of these companies are product manufacturers and some are product distributors. The distributors are likely to distribute products from each and every one of the manufacturers, and the manufacturers will distribute their products through all channels. The diagram below shows how this could work.

Fig19.2: Make-up of a financial services 'group' business

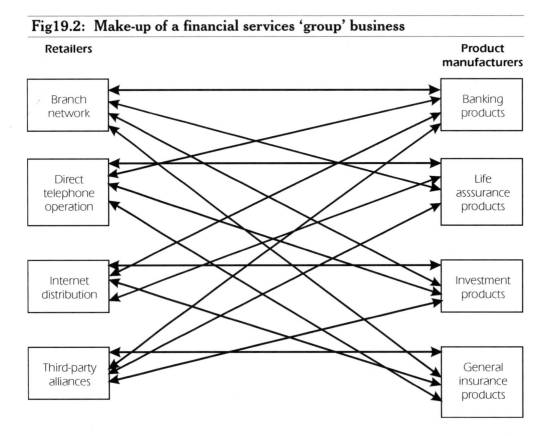

When a financial services group is set up in this manner, it is not only the departments within each group that need to communicate with each other, but also the different companies within the group. Customers are not aware of the structure of the company and nor do they really care. They see the company as a single entity and therefore that is how the company must ensure it works. When a company is made up of such a complex arrangement, the only way it will be able to perform is if it is able to communicate effectively. Let us look at some of the ways a company can improve the communications between departments and companies.

Establish agreements

The companies within the group should start the year with agreements as to what each will be doing and what they expect from the other. This is particularly important between product manufacturers and retailers. For example, the product provider could be planning a new product for part way through the year, or alternatively could be planning to withdraw a product. The retailers who are responsible for promoting these products need to be aware of this so that they plan their promotional activity around such decisions.

The manufacturer and retailer would therefore need to have agreements as to which products were being promoted and the amount of notice that would be required for any changes to the product range, etc.

Share plans

As well as the high-level plans, departments within the company also need to share their detailed plans with any other departments that may be affected by them. For example, the marketing department would have details of when it was planning its campaigns throughout the year. Both the sales force and the customer services departments would need to know these dates so that they could ensure their staff were sufficiently trained and prepared for the increased level of enquiries at those times.

Meet regularly

Regular meetings are essential in order that people can discuss what they are doing and how it will impact on other areas. While they may have shared their plans at the start of the year, plans will inevitably change and therefore discussion is essential. Managers from different departments within the company need to meet to discuss the business, and so do managers from different companies within the group.

Internal magazines

There should also be some form of communication that goes to all members of staff at all levels. While the managers are sharing plans and meeting regularly, it is beneficial for staff throughout the company to have an understanding of what is going on elsewhere. We saw in the chapter that looked at sales skills that the effective salesperson needs to be well-informed about all areas of the company and its activity if he or she is to appear efficient in front of the customer.

There are many ways of doing this. One method is to ensure that all managers are briefed on the items of interest to staff and that they cascade this through their departments, as shown on the next page.

Figure 19.3: Cascade of information

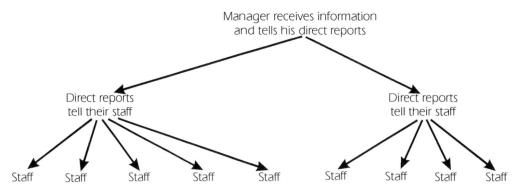

The advantage of this method is that it is quick and cheap to do; the disadvantage is that it cannot be guaranteed that everybody will receive the communication, or that the messages will not get distorted by the time they reach the end receiver.

Another method of communicating with staff is via a staff magazine, and many financial services companies produce one. The benefit of such a magazine is that it ensures that a consistent message is sent to every member of staff in an informative and yet interesting way. The staff can read the communication at a time that suits them, and it should ideally be a mix of information about what is going on in the group, and staff issues of interest to them.

The disadvantage of such a method is that it is both timely and costly to produce. This said, many companies still use staff magazines, especially as a method of communication between head office and staff at remote locations, i.e. branches. Other methods of communication used by some financial services companies include issuing sales staff with audio cassettes to listen to in their cars, and the use of business television to broadcast news around different work sites.

Technology

Technology can certainly help the staff from around the company to keep in touch with each other. Having an internal electronic mail system that is fast and efficient encourages people to communicate. This allows messages to be sent to people at all geographical locations simultaneously. It saves both time and money and ensures that everybody is kept up to date.

19.3   Systems and records

The systems and technology used by the company is the responsibility of the IT department. They ensure that everybody has the systems they need in order to carry out the tasks that they are required to perform. However the job of delivering the products to customers and servicing those products can be made much easier by the use of such systems around the company.

For example, the new business team will set up customer records and details of how the product application is progressing. It will be useful if the salesperson can have access to view that record so that he or she can keep customers informed of how their application is progressing. Such an arrangement also benefits the new business team, who will not be inundated with requests for such information from the salespeople and can therefore get on more quickly with the job of processing the business.

Another example of where systems can help the business to provide excellent service would be with existing business. If details of existing business and customer records are available throughout the company and can be accessed by different people, it enables customers to get accurate and timely information no matter where they direct their query. Branch staff, customer services staff and head-office departments are all able to access the records and see what is happening, and give information.

It also helps if, for example, staff throughout the group can have access to just one set of customer details. That way if the customer changes address, anyone from the company can access the records and make the change without having to check to see if the customer has dealings with other areas in the group and change their records accordingly.

These are just two brief examples of how technology can help. There are many ways in which having the right systems and records in place can help the staff to reduce their workload and prevent the same task having to be repeated in different parts of the company. This enables the company to deliver excellent customer service and therefore increase customer satisfaction and retention.

19.4   Security and confidentiality

Although we have spent some time now looking at the positive aspects of communicating with everybody in the organization and ensuring everybody is aware of what is going on, we should take just a short look at what could possibly be a disadvantage.

If all the company's plans for the coming year are made available to all members of staff, there is an obvious risk that they will be leaked to competitors who will take advantage of such knowledge to gain a competitive edge. The only way to ensure that there is absolute security and confidentiality is to keep all plans and activity secret; however, we have seen that this is not a sensible route if the company wishes to perform effectively.

Therefore the only solution is to find a balance between the level of communication that is desirable for an efficiently working organization, and the level of secrecy that is required for the plans to remain confidential. Finding this balance probably involves the following:

Selecting the staff carefully

Deciding who to communicate with needs to some extent to be on a 'need to know' basis. If the business plans or other information do not effect staff, the company may decide to limit the security risk by not telling them. Of course all staff will be interested in the things that are going on around the company, and in order to maintain morale the company should keep people informed. However, if piece of information is considered to be confidential it should be shared only with select people.

Timing

The timing of communications needs to be carefully considered. Staff should be given information in plenty of time to take any action that is needed of them. However there is little point in giving them the information any sooner than they need it, particularly if it is of a sensitive nature. Ensuring that information is distributed in a timely manner also cuts down the security risk.

Grading information

Another way of ensuring that information remains confidential is to grade the information as it is communicated. Staff could be told which pieces of information are, for example, highly confidential and therefore cannot even be discussed with other people within the company, market sensitive and can therefore be shared only with other people within the company, or not confidential at all and therefore pose no risk.

This ensures that staff can be given the information they need in order to do their job effectively, but know how to treat the information they receive, thereby cutting down on the security risks.

19.5   Gaining support from colleagues

Often when departments within a company want to change their plans or implement new ideas they find themselves in the position of needing help and support from their colleagues in other areas of the business.

On some occasions they are extremely willing to help, but other times, the support that is being requested causes them difficulties, interrupts their own plans and causes them additional work and disruption. If the plans are to progress the manager has to find a way of gaining support from colleagues, even in these difficult times.

Some of the things that help in this task are:

- Remember to involve other people from the start. If they are involved in the initial planning stages and have contributed to the ideas stage, they are far more likely to be supportive when it comes to implementing the new plans.

- Always ask for help rather than expect it. When dealing with their own staff, managers can simply tell people what they expect of them and have it delivered. When dealing with colleagues from other areas of the business that do not report to them, the approach needs to be rather different. Nobody likes to be told what to do by somebody from another area of the company, and if this happens they are likely to react less favourably than if they were politely asked for assistance and to lend their expertise to a situation. The way the request is delivered can make all the difference.

- Explain the benefits of the support that is being requested. People are more likely to agree to give their support if they can see the benefit to the company of what they are being asked to do. It is also useful if they are shown exactly how their contribution fits in to the overall plan and they can see the direct benefit of the support they will be giving.

- It may help the situation if there is a formal request at the start of the project which sets out the exact nature of the support requested and the resource that this is likely to entail. Such a document should also explain the benefits as outlined above, and show which other areas of the business are also giving support. An example of such a request form is shown in Chapter 1.

- Try to offer your support to colleagues when they request something of you. If you are seen to be helpful and supportive and a real team player, other people will be more inclined to help out when you want their assistance.

20

EVALUATING CHANGE TO IMPROVE CUSTOMER SERVICE

After reading this chapter you should

- Know what sources of information are available to judge the current effectiveness of service standards
- Understand how to evaluate such information
- Know the lines for reporting service standards
- Understand how to present proposals for improving service standards

Introduction

Before we can look at the importance of service, and how it impacts on the product offering, marketing and sales, we need to understand what we mean by 'service quality'. In providing financial services to the public there is an interaction between that customer and the organization and its staff. Service quality encompasses the delivery of those products to that customer, at all stages of the relationship and throughout the life of that product. It can also be used to describe relationships between different areas of the organization that supply services to each other in order that the end-product or service can be delivered to the customer.

In the past decade financial services organizations have become increasingly customer focused, as the environment has become more and more competitive. This has meant that the organization's strategic marketing plans no longer focus solely on the company's response to business and economic conditions, government legislation and technological advances. They now also concentrate on the customers' needs, attitudes and behaviours.

As the market has become more competitive, and new entrants appear in the market, organizations must find ways to maintain a competitive advantage. In many industries this can be done with product differentiation, or pricing. However, we have already seen, in a heavily regulated area such as financial services product differentiation is more difficult to achieve. Although pricing competitively is still an option, there is still often little to choose between providers. However, with pricing being highlighted and somewhat dictated in products such as CAT standard ISAs and the soon-to-be-launched stakeholder pensions, some companies are now looking to their service quality as a way of achieving a competitive advantage. High levels of customer services are seen as a way to pursue a differentiation strategy and sustain a competitive advantage without cutting product price.

20.1   Maintaining and developing customers

Customers have become increasingly aware of the range of financial service providers and the products that are available to them. When faced with such a plethora of suppliers, customers' expectations rise. They begin to see that they can shop around and move their business to another provider if they are not totally happy, and therefore they become more critical of the service they receive.

We have seen many times in previous chapters how important it is for an organization to maintain the customers it has. It is considerably more expensive to recruit a new customer than it is to retain an existing one, and therefore many organizations are actively seeking to improve the service they provide to their customers as part of their strategy to develop long-term customer relationships. With a focus on service quality, an organization seeks to build customer loyalty through satisfaction, which will in turn bring reduced costs and improved customer retention.

We also saw earlier how satisfied customers become advocates for the business, telling family, friends and colleagues about the excellent service they received. In this way the organization may well attract new business and new customers from this positive endorsement.

Excellent service could well lead to a reduction in costs and an increase in production. If sales improve so will the profitability of the organization. For this reason, many companies have seen that any money they have spent on increasing the level of service they provide is an investment in the business, and can often be measured against an increase in market share and the performance of the business.

Staff

If a company is to have a strategy of excellent service and hopes to increase business because of it, it needs to consider the quality of its staff. High levels of service quality are only achieved by having good-quality, well-trained staff which is highly motivated. In recent years many financial services organizations have undergone mergers and takeovers, and this had lead to reorganizations and in many cases to a reduction in the number of staff required. Such changes need to be carefully managed; otherwise they can have a detrimental effect on staff morale and motivation.

Commitment to staff and communication with those staff will benefit the organization in terms of increased morale and motivation, better job satisfaction, and staff who feel greater loyalty to the company. These will all contribute to reducing staff turnover and thereby avoid the costs of recruiting and training replacements. Also, committed competent staff make fewer mistakes and provide better levels of service that will lead to greater customer satisfaction and fewer complaints.

If a company is to deliver service quality to a level that will enable it to retain and develop customers, it must have an understanding of the interactions between itself, its staff and the customers. The first step is therefore to identify the key elements of service quality as perceived by the customer, taking into account those customers' needs and preferences. The next stage is to measure the importance of service quality in different areas of the interactions and measure how the current service offered measures up to these customer requirements. This will then show the business where there are service quality 'gaps'.

Identifying service quality gaps enables the customer services manager to put together a service quality plan. This plan should include such things as:

- Ensuring the services offered fully meet the needs of the customers

- Introducing systems and procedures that are both customer- and employee-focused

- Maintaining a suitable delivery environment

- Maximizing the use of technology to increase speed, efficiency and accuracy of service delivery

Once the customer services manager has identified and assessed the key elements that will lead to excellent service, he or she must convert those elements into standards and processes. The manager will also need to recruit and train, and of course motivate, the required staff in order to ensure delivery takes place.

Potential failure points must be noted and where necessary service guarantees must be developed (for example, in line with mortgage and banking codes of practice). The manager must also ensure that procedures are put in place for service recovery if they are ever needed.

It is also important to monitor the implementation of the plan and ensure that the objectives are met. This involves the manager in selecting methods to research and measure customer satisfaction and employee performances. Although it is important at the implementation stage of any changes to the service delivery, it should ideally be done as a rolling programme rather than on an ad hoc basis, because this will allow the company to spot any slippage in service standards and take remedial action quickly.

As with all activities undertaken by a large organization, the development of service quality is not possible without management support. The organization may require cultural changes to achieve the customer focus among its staff, thereby ensuring that the end customer becomes the focus for everybody's activities. Change needs to come from the senior management, who have to show that they are committed to both the staff and the customers alike.

20.2   Defining service and service quality

A service can be described as the way in which we deal with our customers each time they have a 'service encounter'. This encounter is the direct interaction between the organization and one of its customers and can occur in one of many ways. For example, a bank customer who wishes to draw money from his account can do so in one of many ways. He can go to a branch and request the money from a cashier, he can go into the branch and use an ATM, or he can use an ATM situated in a remote location away from the branch of the bank. Each of these is an interaction with the organization, and the way in which the customer is dealt with during that interaction is important to the customer and the way he or she feels about the service.

Each time customers come into contact with the organization or a member of its staff, they judge the service they receive and form an opinion of the company and the overall level of service provided. For example, if the customer visits the ATM and finds it out of order, this could well leave him with very negative feelings towards the bank, particularly if it happens more than once. On the other hand, a helpful friendly cashier will leave the customer with a positive image of the company. Because these interactions have such a high level of impact on customers and their view of the organization, ensuring that each encounter is of the highest possible quality is an important element of any plan to improve the service experienced by customers.

These service encounters also have an impact on staff in relation to their motivation and morale, as well as their level of job satisfaction. No member of staff can be expected to remain highly motivated all the time if he or she is constantly dealing with dissatisfied customers. Therefore, financial services organizations must manage their service encounters successfully for the benefit of both customers and staff.

There are a number of approaches an organization can take when looking at the level of service it should offer, but any decision should revolve around the need to meet the customers' expectations and needs. It should examine in detail what service standards the customer would expect to receive and ensure that what is actually delivered meets those customer expectations. This is because customers always make judgements about service standards that result in a comparison of the service they actually receive and that they would ideally like to receive.

Sometimes there is a gap between the level of service customers received and what they would ideally like to have. If this is the case it will lead to customer dissatisfaction. We can start to understand why such a gap may exist if we look at the service quality model developed by Zeithaml et al. 1990, as shown in the diagram on the next page. This identifies five reasons that a gap in service quality may exist.

Gap 1	Exists because there is a difference between the levels of service that the customer expects to receive, and the company's understanding of the level of service it believes a customer expects to receive.
Gap 2	This could be caused because the management is unsuccessful at translating the customer's requirements of service into service quality standards for the organization and its staff to adhere to.

Gap 3   Exists because the actual delivery of service, either pre- or post-contract, has failed to meet the standards set.

Gap 4   This would exist if the levels of service were not properly communicated to the customer.

Gap 5   This exists if the customer's perception of the service that is being provided falls short of what he or she had hoped for.

Figure 20.1: A model of service quality, Zeithaml et al. 1990

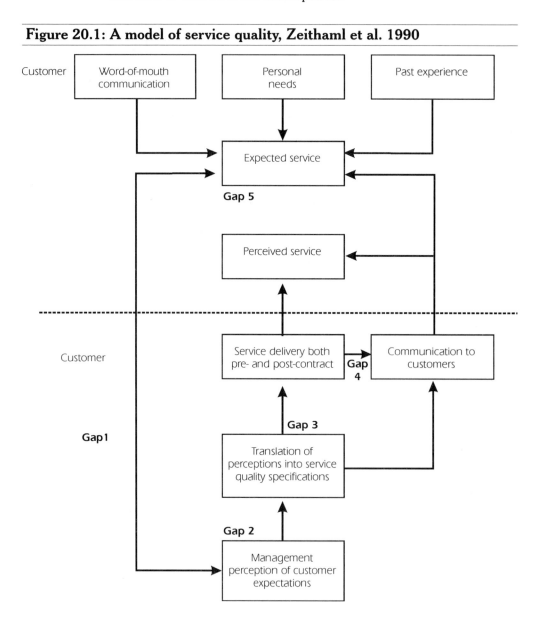

Customer care

Having defined the service quality it becomes obvious that the major element is the customers' expectations of service and the way in which they perceive the service they are receiving. However, understanding these are key to an organization because they set the service standards and thereby the minimum levels of customer care. When looking at exactly what customers expect to receive in terms of service and customer care, it is probably best to examine their expectations by breaking down the service into its basic elements as follows:

Physical features and facilities	Customers often feel that these items are important in their overall assessment of the organization. They often comment on such things as branch locations, privacy and equipment available. They are also influenced by the appearance of both the staff and the building.
Reliability	All elements of reliability are important to customers. They want their financial services organization to get things right first time, from accuracy of transactions, ability to keep promises, to staff competency and capability.
Staff	As would be expected, the staff that the customer encounters have a large impact on customers' view of the service they receive. The staff need to be honest and reliable but also discreet. They also need to be friendly, especially if the organization is attempting to build relationships with customers and develop customer loyalty.
Responsiveness	This is a major issue for customers. They want the staff to be ready and willing to respond to their requirements, and they want their issues dealing with as quickly as possible. Slow service can be one of the major factors that lead to a customer having a perception of poor service from a bank or building society.

Providing levels of service that fall short of customer expectations carries the risk that customers will take their business elsewhere. It is well documented that there is a great deal of customer inertia when it comes to changing financial services providers. However, banks such as First Direct have capitalized on the growing customer dissatisfaction in respect of responsiveness to needs and have successfully recruited large numbers of customers away from their competitors.

Customers may well accept service standards that fall short of their expectations in one or two areas if they feel that the rest of the service they receive meets or exceeds their requirements. However, companies must not become complacent because in an increasingly competitive market they will be risking the potential loss of custom. Organizations must also be aware that simply meeting their customer's expectations of service quality may not always be enough to retain business. The customers' expectations can be always be exceeded and competitors may well attempt to do this if they are using service as a way of attracting new business.

20.3 The role of the branch in delivering service quality

Once customers' needs and expectations have been identified, analysed and turned into the appropriate service systems and standards, and staff have been recruited and trained, the next step is to ensure that these 'promises' are delivered.

Advertising and promotion are used to communicate the service to customers. This then sets a level of expectation. It is therefore important to ensure that the levels of service being communicated can be delivered. Branches are an important part of the service delivery because they are the representatives of the whole of the organization from a customer's perspective. The customer's perception of the service standards offered by the organization are likely to be formed following a service encounter at branch level that shapes his or her view of the organization as a whole.

It is in this delivery that the branches of a bank or building society have most impact. The key element of the branch impact are through the customer facing staff and the back-office support staff. Ensuring that the delivery of service matches the specifications is dependent on the performance of these staff, who must be both able and willing to deliver the required levels of service.

The contribution made by branch staff in ensuring customers' expectations are met is paramount. The successful delivery of a service strategy therefore depends on the development of adequate personnel policies for staff recruitment, training, motivation, reward and recognition. Before the organization can sell the service proposition to its customers, it must first 'sell' it to staff. Explaining to the staff what the service standards are, what they will achieve and why they are so important ensures that the staff have bought in to the idea of quality service and will therefore be much more likely to ensure it is delivered.

Recruiting and selecting the right staff for service delivery is very important. Some key characteristics, which may indicate a person's ability to carry out the role effectively, may be:

- Interpersonal communication skills i.e. an ability to talk effectively to people at all levels

- Flexibility and adaptability

- Empathy with customers

- Process and technical skills

Developing a service strategy and the ability to deliver service quality at the required level may well lead to the identification of training needs for both new and experienced staff. This is likely to cover areas such as technical training to ensure staff are able to deal with most queries satisfactorily themselves and interpersonal skills to ensure that the customers are dealt with in the same manner whichever branch they visit and whichever member of staff deals with their needs.

Making sure that the branch delivers excellent service depends on ensuring the following:

- All of the branch staff working as a team. This is demonstrated by a caring management and by committed and involved staff.

- Getting the right people for the job. Dealing with customers all day and performing this role to a consistently high standard takes a certain type of person.

- Making sure that the staff have all the right tools they need to do the job. This means they must have all the knowledge and the technology.

- The staff must be empowered to deal with all but the most serious of complaints.

- The management should ensure that the branch staff are very clear as to what their role is and what is expected of them. They should know how their performance is to be measured and how it will be rewarded.

- Staff also need to be clear on their role in dealing with customers and how this interacts with their responsibilities to the organization to ensure that any conflict is avoided.

Branch staff require supervision and a process for evaluating their performance. Some financial services providers have reward and recognition schemes for branch staff who have performed particularly well.

One of the most difficult things for branches to manage is the reconciliation of the resources that they have available to them with the service delivery promises made at a head-office level and then communicated to customers. Branch managers are often faced with difficult decisions regarding the importance to customers of individual aspects of the service promises. For example, if a manager has a staff shortage, is it more important to have sufficient staff at the cashier's desks during the busy periods, or is it more important to have those staff answering the telephones and dealing with customers telephone queries?

Another important role for branches in the delivery of service quality is that of gathering information. They are in an ideal position to elicit comments regarding the service from customers who visit the branch. Any commonly made comments or any trends in customers' expectations can be passed on to the appropriate department for action. An organization that has a true service culture encourages staff to put forward suggestions as to how it can enhance customer care and service delivery.

20.4 Measuring and monitoring service quality

Service quality is not easily measured, particularly as the measurement relies on customers' perception. However, it is important to have some form of measurement if the company is to understand not only the customers' expectations but also whether the customer feels the organization is currently meeting those expectations.

There are several ways in which the organization can choose to measure the quality of its service, and each method has advantages and disadvantages. The one most commonly used is the *SERVQUAL questionnaire*.

SERVQUAL is a 22-item scale based on six dimensions: tangibles, reliability, responsiveness, assurance, empathy and recovery. The first five categories were established by Parasuraman et al. (1988) after factor analysis and testing had taken place. The sixth dimension, recovery, was added by Gronroos (1988) following further work.

The questionnaire is formatted into 22 pairs of Likert-style scales. The first 22 questions seek to establish the customers' expectations of service. The second 22 aim to measure the perceived level of service as currently being provided by the organization.

The SERVQUAL questionnaire is felt to be both reliable and valid, and is often used by researchers investigating service quality in many industries. It can be used to track trends in service quality, categorize customers and compare the service offered by one company with that offered by its competitors. It can also be used to compare the standards of service being offered by different branches of the same organization.

The limitation of the questionnaire is that it can be used only for current and previous customers, because the respondents must have knowledge and experience of the organization in order that they can answer the questions.

In the questionnaire, customers are given a number of statements to read and then asked to mark how they feel about that statement on a scale that goes from strongly agree, through to strongly disagree. An example is shown below:

Figure 20.2: Example of SERVQUAL questionnaire

Service expectations

'Customers should not have to queue'

Strongly agree	1	2	3	4	5	6	Strongly disagree

'Customers should be able to trust bank employees'

Strongly agree	1	2	3	4	5	6	Strongly disagree

'Banks should have up-to-the-minute equipment'

Strongly agree	1	2	3	4	5	6	Strongly disagree

'Banks should tailor personal loans to suit a customer's needs'

Strongly agree	1	2	3	4	5	6	Strongly disagree

Perceptions

'I do not have to queue at my bank'

Strongly agree	1	2	3	4	5	6	Strongly disagree

'I can trust the employees of my bank'

Strongly Agree agree	1	2	3	4	5	6	Strongly disagree

'My bank has up-to-the-minute equipment'

Strongly Agree agree	1	2	3	4	5	6	Strongly disagree

'My bank tailored my personal loan to suit my needs'

Strongly Agree agree	1	2	3	4	5	6	Strongly disagree

There are some service managers who have criticized the questionnaire and this will happen with all methods of quality measurement. The main criticisms lodged against the SERVQUAL are as follows:

● The variables are not weighted as to their importance. The services being tested will by their very nature vary in importance to the customer.

● Some of the statements contain negative wordings, and these can be confusing to some customers.

● Asking the same thing from the two perspectives can seem repetitive to customers.

● There is no allowance made for the timing factor i.e. when did this customer most recently experience the service?

It has also been suggested that the questionnaire incorporates only the desired levels of service and not that level which the customer would find acceptable or adequate. In order to incorporate this the wording can be changed so that it tests what would be expected from an organization that would like to claim to have excellent service. For example:

'Banks should have up-to-the-minute equipment'

Strongly agree	1	2	3	4	5	6	Strongly disagree

The addition or omission of the word 'excellent' allows the organization to test both acceptable levels of service as well as aspirational service quality. The completion of such a questionnaire shows instantly where there are gaps between the service standards the customers would like or expect to see and those being provided by the organization. The company can then develop a plan to close those gaps.

Monitoring

Of equal importance to measuring is monitoring, and any organization concerned with its level of service must have systems in place to carry out this task. Methods of monitoring include research and evaluation among customers and staff using surveys, focus groups and discussions. Mystery shopping exercises can also provide information. Collecting and analysing customer complaints and letters also forms a useful monitoring exercise.

Many organizations offer service guarantees either as a permanent part of their service strategy or as a tactical promotional tool. These must be monitored to provide key performance indicators regarding service delivery. While the use of such service guarantees is not currently widespread among financial service providers, the increasingly competitive environment may lead more organizations to introduce them.

UK banks and building societies do, however, have codes of practice for both banking and mortgages. The aim of these codes is to outline to customers their consumer rights and provide information to customers about customers' service and complaints. In other words, they are designed to explain to customers the minimum levels of service quality they should expect from an organization.

If a financial services organization is to pursue a strategy of service excellence as a way to attract customers, it may well decide to offer service above and beyond that outlined in the code and introduce service guarantees. If it does so it will need to consider the following points.

A good service guarantee should be:

- Unconditional
- Easy to understand
- Simple to communicate
- Easy to invoke and collect on
- Meaningful to the customer

Complaints

Customer complaints form a valuable source of data regarding the level of service being experienced by customers. They should therefore be seen as such and collected and analysed on a regular basis. Most organizations are aware that a large proportion of the customers who are dissatisfied with the service they receive never take the time and effort to make a complaint, but instead simply tell other people about the problems they encountered. This means that even a small number of complaints could indicate that there is a larger number of unhappy customers.

There are a number of reasons why unhappy customers may be reluctant to make a formal complaint, for example:

● They may simply consider it to be too much trouble, especially if they have busy lifestyles.

● They may fear that there will be 'hassle' if they make a complaint and may prefer not to get involved in this.

● They may expect the organization to be indifferent to the feelings of their customers regarding service standards, and this will lead them to believe that actually making a complaint will be fruitless.

● They make not know how to make their complaint or who to complain to.

Although an organization may feel that it does not want to encourage these people to go ahead and make their complaint, they should consider the following. There is evidence to show that customers who complain to an organization and then have that complaint dealt with to their satisfaction, show a greater level of loyalty to that company. They are likely to become an advocate of the company and engage in positive word-of-mouth communications. Although it may not be pleasant receiving complaints, it is better to have heard the complaint and be left with a satisfied and loyal customer, than not to have it raised and have an unhappy customer spreading the word about the poor service received.

All financial services organizations attempt to get things right first time and employ sophisticated techniques and rigid processes in order to ensure that this is the case. However there will always be times when this goes wrong, for example the company may make incorrect debits, unwarranted charges, etc. The challenge is to recover the situation as quickly as possible and ensure that it does not happen again.

Service recovery is an important element of the organization's service delivery and should be a planned process that ensures the customer who is dissatisfied or irritated is returned to a state of satisfaction as soon as possible. Service recovery has economic value for the organization because, when successful, it engenders loyalty and therefore customer retention. When we consider the cost to the organization of acquiring new customers, we can see that it is well worth investing some time and money to ensure that the existing customers are retained.

Service recovery also helps the organization to recognize problems and improve the service it offers, not just for the customer who complained, but for all existing and new customers.

If and when something does go wrong, the customer will have expectations as to how the organization should correct the situation. He or she will expect things to be put right, receive an apology if the organization was at fault, be treated efficiently and politely and, if appropriate, expect to receive compensation. This means that from a customer's point of view, service recovery is both a physical and emotional repair. It is not only the problem that needs to be fixed, but also the customer's view of the company and its staff. The organization needs to attend to both the customer's as well as their problem.

An important success factor in service recovery is the empowerment of the customer facing staff. These staff have to have the incentive, the responsibility and the authority to identify, empathise with and solve the customer's issues and complaints. Knowing that the management has the confidence in them to do this will allow the customer-facing staff to carry out this role with enthusiasm and confidence.

Empowering them to deal with the situation gives the staff a better attitude towards management and this will show in their attitude towards the customers. Also the improvement in staff morale that this brings will lead to the staff performing their jobs more effectively and therefore reducing the level of complaints received.

Service recovery is not just about fixing things that have gone wrong. It should focus on the critical service encounters that customers are saying are important to them, and help the organization to develop a long-term customer service strategy.

20.5   Other sources of information

We have already looked at some of the ways in which an organization can measure the levels of service it is providing. However it is worth considering if there are other sources of information that a company could use to assess the service standards it currently provides and therefore find ways of improving its customer care.

20.6   SERVQUAL questionnaires

These can be used, as discussed earlier in this chapter, to identify the expectations customers have regarding service levels. They also show how well the organization is currently performing against these expectations.

Customer satisfaction surveys

These can be used by the company instead of, or in addition to, the SERVQUAL questionnaires. An organization may well use a customer satisfaction survey to test a certain element of its service delivery by issuing them to customers who have recently used that particular service. They could also be used to measure any increase or decrease in satisfaction following the implementation of any changes in service. In order to do this, the satisfaction surveys would need to be issued both prior to and post implementation of the new service and the results compared.

A customer satisfaction survey could also be used to measure the importance that a customer places on the existence of certain service elements. This would allow a manager to prioritize which of the elements of the service he or she should concentrate resource and effort to improve. It could also be used at an individual branch level to check that customers at different branches have similar service standards and similar expectations of service. If not, it will enable individual branch managers to tailor the service they provide to meet the specific expectations and requirements of their particular customers.

A great deal of thought and consideration has to go into the planning and preparation of a customer satisfaction survey if it is to be successful in meeting the objectives as described above. The questions need to be:

- Clear and concise, so that the customer knows exactly what is being asked.

- Neutral, i.e. they should not try to steer the customer towards a particular answer.

- Sufficient in number to achieve a meaningful amounts of information, but not so many as to put the customer off completing the questionnaire.

- Easily answered, i.e. a tick box or a simple rating system is quicker for customers than if they are expected to write a full answer, and therefore customers are more likely to complete the survey. This also make data capture and analysis much easier.

The questionnaire can be posted to the customer or can be completed over the telephone. Telephone surveys may well receive a greater response. This is because many customers are willing to answer a few simple questions over the telephone, once they have answered the call. However this is only the case if the type of customer being surveyed is the type who is comfortable using the telephone as a means of communicating with a financial services company. Some customers find business telephone calls to their home intrusive and therefore these people would respond better to a postal survey.

If using a postal survey, the costs may well be greater and the response rate lower. In order to increase the response rates the company should ensure that the customer can see a benefit in completing the questions. There are two ways of doing this. The company could take the time to explain to the customer the reason for sending the survey, and the improvements in service it expects to make following analysis of the results. Alternatively, the company could simply offer an incentive for the customer to take the time to complete the form. This incentive could be in the form of a reward such as entry into a competition to win a holiday.

20.7   Management information

If an organization wants to improve the service it offers, it needs to be able to collect and analyse information from many sources and present this in a clear and concise manner. It can collect meaningful information about the number and nature of complaints it receives as was highlighted earlier in this chapter.

There should be some central point of collection for this information because complaints may well be received in different parts of the organization as well as throughout the branch network. Collating such information enables the company to see if there are any patterns of complaints or trends, and then to react accordingly.

There are also lots of other sources of management information that could be interrogated if the company is serious about improving its level of customer service. For example, an insurance company could look at the average length of time that customers hold their policies, even comparing this to similar statistics for other providers because this would give an indication of customer satisfaction.

They could also examine the number or proportion of their customers who, after buying one product, go on to buy a further product or service from them. This again would give an indication of how happy customers are with their original purchase.

Another possibility open to motor insurers, for example, would be to compare the renewal rate of customers who had made a claim in the previous year and therefore experienced the claims service, compared to those who had not. This would show whether the current levels of customer service were leading to increased customer loyalty or not.

Alternatively the company could try direct marketing further products and services to their existing customers who had just used some particular aspect of the service. It could compare the results of this attempt to cross-sell, with the results of a similar offer made to customers who had not experienced the service. Again the comparison would gauge the level of satisfaction with the service and show if it is building customer loyalty.

There may also be management information available to show how well the company is measuring up to the standard it sets itself. For example, if the company uses technology to deal with customer service it may well be able to provide information on such things as time delays. It could show the average length of time between receipt of a customer query and the answer being delivered or such things as the average length of time a customer is kept waiting before a telephone call is answered. It is important that the manager finds out exactly what type of information is available and makes use of it.

20.8   Branches

We have already seen that the staff at the branches have an important role to play in both the marketing and sale of financial services products. They are also a crucial part of the delivery of those products and services. One particularly useful part of their role is that they can send back information they receive from customers regarding the expectations they have of service standards.

Although the managers at the organization's head office will have carried out extensive research before developing a service proposition, they will always benefit from information received directly from customers. During the lifespan of a product customers' expectations may well change. Branch staff, with their daily contact with the customers, are in an ideal situation to see the development of customer expectations and alert managers when they see this happening.

Branch staff are also able to feed back information they receive from customers regarding the service standards customers say they are receiving from other companies, i.e. the organization's competitors. This will help the company to judge whether they have a competitive advantage as far as service is concerned and should therefore be marketing this, or whether they are likely to lose business to other companies whose service appears to be better.

Branch staff are also able to tell the company if they are currently losing business because of the service customers are receiving from them. They are in an ideal position to discuss this with customers when they come in to close accounts and withdraw their business. They are also in a position to report back on any new business sales they have lost because of service, either theirs or that of the competition.

20.9   Research

A company will also want to carry out research into the service standards provided, both by themselves and by other companies who are in competition with them. One of the most common ways to do this is the use of a 'mystery shopper' exercise as described earlier. As we saw, this involves a member of staff or an individual employed by the research agency posing as a customer and reporting back on the service received.

This is an extremely good way for a company to test the level of service being offered by its staff compared to that available elsewhere in the industry. This is because it is the same person commenting on the service offered by the different providers and he or she is therefore be able to make direct comparisons. If the person is from a research agency or from another third party, he or she will be able to take an independent view of the service received.

Mystery shopping is most useful for measuring and comparing pre-sales service and query handling; it is more difficult to measure post-sales service in this way. In order to do this the involvement of an actual customer may well be needed.

20.10 Presenting proposals for improving service

We looked in Chapter 15 at the skills needed in order to make successful and effective sales presentations. All of those skills apply equally if presenting proposals for improving customer service. The presentation, whether verbal or written, needs to be thoroughly planned in advance.

One of the major considerations when planning such a presentation is to decide on the audience, i.e. who the presentation should be made to. If the proposals are for a minor change in the systems used, or a simple change to a process already in place, them these may only need to be presented to the customer services manager. He or she will be able to examine them, make a decision, and implement the changes if considered worthwhile.

If the proposals involve a major change from the current procedures, then it will be necessary to present them to senior management. We said at the start of this chapter that creating a service culture within an organization where all the staff become customer-focused and service-orientated can involve a major change for staff at all levels. This type of change would impact on large numbers of people around the organization and would be the type of decision that could be taken only at high level. It would need senior management to give the go-ahead, and would need their full and visible support if it were to be successfully implemented.

Once the audience is decided, the next stage is to prepare the actual presentation. It is reasonable to follow the same structure as was outlined in Chaper 15, i.e:

- Introduction and objectives
- Opening statement
- Body of the presentation
- Summary
- Call to action

20.11 Introduction and objectives

The individual who is giving the presentation will need to set a clear set of objectives, i.e. exactly what he or she is trying to achieve in giving this presentation. For example, the objective could be:

> *To gain senior management agreement to re-train the customer service staff in complaint handling in order to increase the level of customer satisfaction and therefore increase customer retention.*

Another example could be:

> *To gain agreement to introduce a new system for dealing with after-sales service, including the purchase of new equipment and the employment of additional staff.*

Whatever it is, presenters must be clear as to exactly what they are aiming to achieve by presenting their proposals. When introducing the presentation they may want to outline their objective in order that everybody is clear as to what the desired outcome is and what is expected of them.

20.12 Opening statement

In the opening statement presenters may well wish to outline briefly what it is they are proposing to change, why they are proposing the change and what the benefits will be, both to the customer and to the company. For example:

'I am proposing that we introduce a new process for dealing with customer queries received over the telephone. The reason for this is that I feel we can achieve a competitive advantage by doing so, thereby attracting additional new business. The benefit to the customer would be a faster and more efficient service, the benefit to the business would be additional customer satisfaction through a service far superior to that offered by the competition and therefore additional business, which I estimate would be valued at approx £x per annum.'

The opening statement is the equivalent of the executive summary of a written presentation, and sets the scene for the bulk of the presentation that follows.

Body of the presentation

This contains the detailed information to back up the recommendation presented in the opening statement. It could contain such things as:

- An outline of the current service standards and how these compare to those offered by the competitors.

- Details and findings of any research carried out.

- A brief outline of all alternatives considered for the improvements in service and the reasons why those portions not recommended have been discounted.

- Details of exactly what changes are being proposed, including details of any new equipment needed, costs, impact on staffing levels, timings, etc.

- An explanation of the improved position following implementation of the proposed solution, including how this will compare with the service offered by competitors.

- A detailed explanation of how the benefit case was arrived at, i.e. potential profit vs. costs.

If it is a verbal presentation there will also need to be an opportunity for the audience to ask questions or to request further information for clarification.

Summary and call to action

The presenter then needs to summarize what has been presented in a similar way to the opening statement. He or she should then ask for the action required in their objective. For example:

> *You have now seen the position regarding the current service capability, and the benefits that would be gained from the introduction of the proposed new processes. Can I have your agreement to proceed on this basis?*

Of course the answer will not always be yes. The managers may require further work to be done, or may agree to part rather than all of the recommendations. However, what we can be sure about is that the chances of gaining a positive result will be enhanced by a thorough, well-planned and well-presented case.

21

MONITORING AND IMPROVING PERFORMANCE

After reading this chapter you should

● Know the criteria that can be used for measuring performance

● Understand the ways in which performance can be improved

● Understand the uses and methods of self-assessment, and assessment by others

● Be aware of the ethical issues of marketing and selling financial services

● Be aware of the social responsibilities of financial services companies

Introduction

Financial services companies are keen to become more efficient in order to continue to succeed in the increasingly competitive market. In order to do this they ask their marketeers, their salespeople, and their service providers to increase their performance. The salespeople are under pressure to produce better results each year with the same, or indeed reduced, resource.

In this chapter we shall look at the things people can do in order to improve their own performance and therefore that of the organization. While it would be ideal to think that there would be a simple single effort that could improve the performance of an organization as a whole, the truth is the company's performance depends wholly on the performance of the individuals who work there, as shown on the opposite page.

Figure 21.1

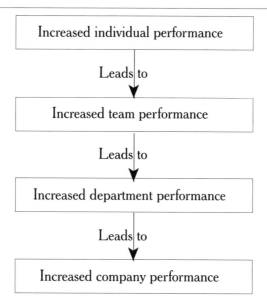

Companies can be reactive to the need to increase performance and look only for ways of doing this when their performance decreases and leads to problems. Alternatively they can be pro-active, and continually look to improve their performance and ensure that all the right tools are in place to allow the company to monitor and increase the performance of all staff, both individually and as their part of the team and department in which they work.

21.1   Increasing individual performance

There are many things a company can put in place to ensure that the environment in which its people work is a performance-focused one, with emphasis on standards and output. We shall look briefly as some of those including:

·· Objective setting

·· Understanding company goals

·· Ensuring team spirit

·· Delegating and allocating work

·· Monitoring and reviewing performance

·· Giving feedback

·· Performance-related pay

Objective setting

This is an essential part of any task carried out by the marketing staff or salespeople and should be the starting point of any work, as shown here:

Figure 21.2: The value of setting objectives

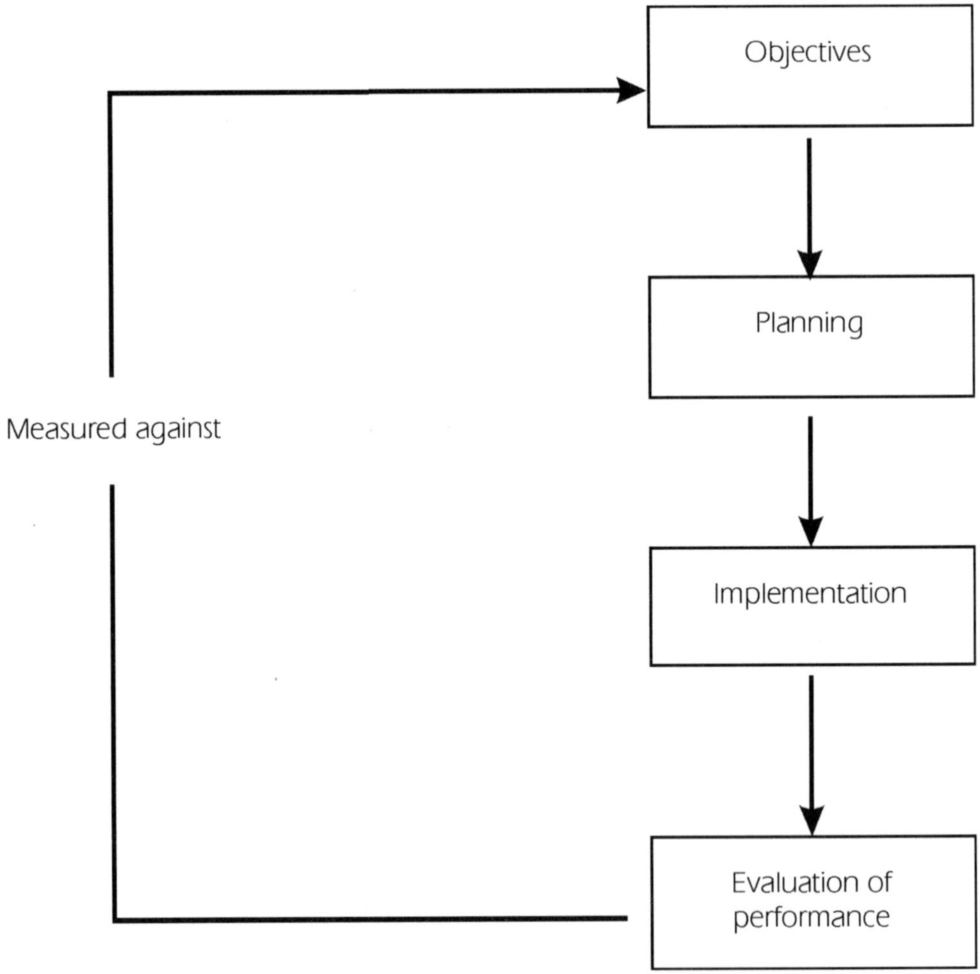

```
                                           ┌──────────────────┐
                                           │    Objectives    │
            ┌─────────────────────────────▶│                  │
            │                              └────────┬─────────┘
            │                                       │
            │                                       ▼
            │                              ┌──────────────────┐
            │                              │    Planning      │
            │                              │                  │
            │                              └────────┬─────────┘
  Measured against                                 │
            │                                       ▼
            │                              ┌──────────────────┐
            │                              │  Implementation  │
            │                              │                  │
            │                              └────────┬─────────┘
            │                                       │
            │                                       ▼
            │                              ┌──────────────────┐
            │                              │  Evaluation of   │
            └──────────────────────────────│  performance     │
                                           └──────────────────┘
```

It is important to set people objectives, stating what level of performance they should be aiming to achieve. If no targets are set, then people have no aspirations and no target to try to reach. The objectives should be clearly defined and understood. They should set targets that are aimed at achieving either:

- Quality
- Quantity and volume
- Efficiency and value for money
- Contribution to strategic objectives or

● External and internal customer objectives

They should be measurable in order that the results of the activity can be monitored and the results compared directly to the targets that had been set. The targets need to be achievable so that people do not get disheartened, but challenging enough to stretch their ability and ensure that they give their very best.

Understand the company's goals

Another way to ensure that individual workers perform to the very best of their abilities is to give them a feeling of belonging to the company, and a belief that they are contributing to the performance of the company as a whole. To do this the company should ensure that each and every employee understands the goals that the organization has set itself. Most have a mission statement and objectives, and the company could print this mission statement and display it around the building on notice boards, etc. It also helps people to know how their objectives will contribute towards the objectives of the company and therefore the company's profitability.

Ensure team spirit

Another way of ensuring improved performance is to make sure that all the people who work together are *actually* working together. Often people who work in the same team are so busy working towards their own objectives that they are unaware of how they could be helping others. There is often duplication of effort because individuals are unaware of what other people around them are doing.

A sharing of ideas and pooling of resource can often lead to increased performance for little or no increased effort. A team always performs better if everybody is pulling in the same direction and aiming for the same ultimate goal.

Delegate and allocate

People can increase their performance by ensuring that where possible they delegate or allocate the work that can better be done by somebody else. There are times when best results are achieved by allocating the task, that is by giving it to somebody and telling him or her exactly how it should be done. There are other times when better performance is achieved by delegating, i.e. giving people the task and allowing them to decide themselves how to achieve it, giving them authority and responsibility.

Giving people responsibility for tasks and the responsibility for the results can often increase their performance. Trusting people to do a job encourages commitment and responsibility. Dramatic improvements can be achieved when individuals are given autonomy.

When delegating tasks, they can either be given to someone who is known to be able to do the job, or to someone who has not previously tackled such a task. There are obvious advantages to giving tasks to people with a proven track record, for example, they are likely to complete it more quickly and possibly more accurately, but they may well get bored doing the same jobs all the time, and their knowledge will never grow. Also there will be crossover of skills among the team members and therefore there could be problems if people are away or leave.

If tasks are given to people who have not completed them before they may be slower and will need the help of a more experienced person for a while, but there will be long-term improvements in performance. This is because they will be more motivated if they have a variety of tasks to do and are able to learn new skills. It will also ensure that the team is multi-skilled and therefore there is always someone available who is able to do the work required. Supporting the staff as they try new skills will give them the freedom to develop and learn and improve their performance.

Monitor and review performance

If people are to increase their performance then, as well as setting objectives, they will need to have their performance against those objectives monitored, and reviewed against those objectives at regular intervals. Throughout the period of the job, the progress should be checked so that the manager can see if they are on target for achieving the goals that have been set, and take remedial action if necessary.

When the task is completed there should also be a review of performance against objectives, aimed at establishing the following:

● Was the task completed?

● Where the objectives met?

● What went well?

● Why?

● Can the things that went well be repeated elsewhere?

● What went badly?

● Why?

● How could things be improved for the next time the task is done?

When reviewing performance the important thing is to see what lessons can be learned from the experience to ensure that the next time a similar task is completed it will be done better, more efficiently and therefore with better results.

Performance-related pay

One way to ensure that staff have a focus on their performance is to amend pay according to that performance. Most salespeople are already paid on this basis and we saw in Chapter 13 that there are many ways of rewarding salespeople, and most of the methods involve some degree of performance-related pay.

The benefits of such pay structures apply equally to those people who work in the marketing and service functions as they do to the sellers, that is it will:

● Focus the reward people are given on the contribution they make

● Improve motivation and commitment

● Encourage acceptance of, and participation in, changes to procedure and processes

● Encourage individuals to be pro-active in improving their own performance

Many financial services companies are now rewarding their entire workforce on this basis because of the benefits it brings. For staff who are not involved in sales, there needs to be some other method of calculating bonus, and this is another reason why objective setting and reviewing performance against those objectives is so important.

Staff can be rewarded either for their own individual performance, for the performance of the team or department against the departmental objectives, or for the performance of the company as a whole. Rewarding staff at the team or department level is aimed at encouraging people not only to try to improve their own performance, but also to ensure people will help others within their teams to improve as well.

In reality, many organizations use a combination of these. For example, they may pay their staff a basic level of pay with a bonus depending on their individual performance against objectives. In addition they could pay an annual bonus if the company performs well.

Giving feedback

Reviewing performance can be done by individuals themselves, or by their manager or another member of the team. While it is important for everybody to regularly review their own performance, it is also helpful to have feedback from other sources, particularly more experienced members of the department.

Receiving feedback from others is an important factor in improving performance, and most people will, as part of their working practices, both give and receive feedback. Giving feedback is important because:

● It informs people what is expected of them

● It helps people to improve their performance for the future

● It shows people that others are interested in what they are doing and how well they are doing

● It motivates people and builds commitment

The way in which the feedback is given is also important. It should be a fair mix of positive feedback as well as negative, i.e. do not only speak to people when they are doing something wrong or badly, also tell them when they are doing a good job and what they are doing well.

However it is necessary to give people negative feedback if their performance is to improve. If they are never told what they are doing badly, they will never do it better. The important thing here is the way in which the negative feedback is given. It needs to be expressed in a constructive manner if it is to help the individual to improve. Rather than saying 'you're not doing well enough' it will be better so say 'I think you would do better if you did this differently'. If the negative feedback is not constructive, it will have exactly the opposite of the desired effect and de-motivate people, thereby reducing performance.

Appraisals

Because of the importance of feedback and the recognized benefits of reviewing performance and giving such feedback, most companies have a formal method of doing this. Almost all financial services companies have a formal appraisal system for ensuring that every individual is given a chance to sit down with the manager and review performance over the last year. The reason so many companies are keen to have this in place is because it will:

- Motivate the staff

- Ensure everybody is praised for good performance

- Give people a chance to recognize any problems they have and an opportunity to plan how they can be overcome

- Identify any training needs and ensure remedial action is taken

- Provide a framework for setting each individual objectives for the coming year

It is important that both the individual and the manager appraise the performance. People receive as much benefit from looking at their own performance and seeing what they did well and badly, as they do from having someone else comment on it. The appraisal system ensures that the individual has to take time out to consider his or her own performance, as the process of appraisals often looks something like this:

Figure 21.3: Appraisal process

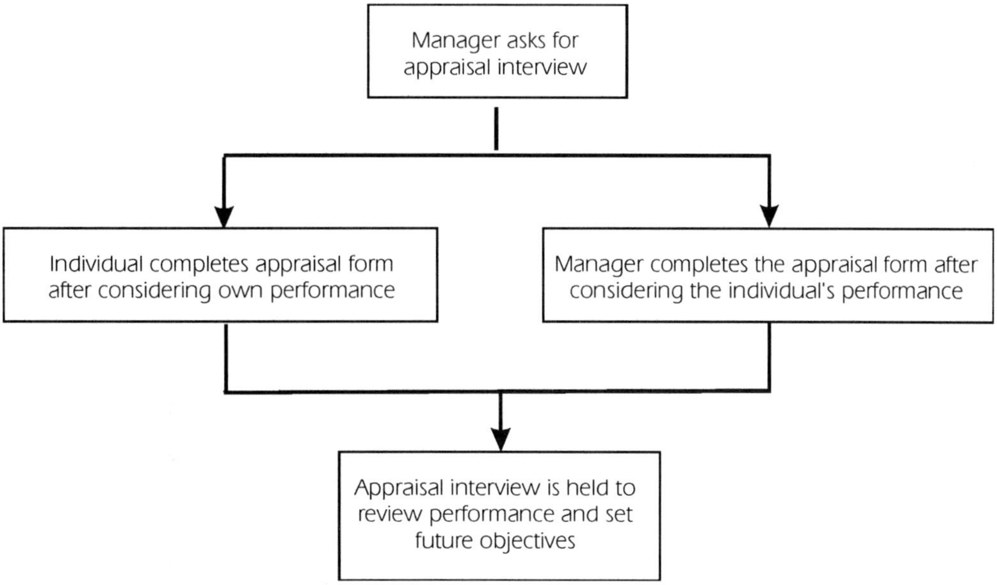

```
                    ┌─────────────────────┐
                    │   Manager asks for  │
                    │  appraisal interview│
                    └─────────────────────┘
```

| Individual completes appraisal form after considering own performance | Manager completes the appraisal form after considering the individual's performance |

```
              ┌──────────────────────────┐
              │ Appraisal interview is held to
              │ review performance and set
              │   future objectives      │
              └──────────────────────────┘
```

Usually the interview follows a standard format and the company provides forms for the individual and manager to complete which provides the basis of the conversations. An example of an appraisal form is shown on page 324:

PERFORMANCE APPRAISAL

Record of appraisal held on ....

Name of staff member		Staff No.
Department/region/area		
Date of last review meeting	January 1998	
Date of interim review		
Job title		

Summarize the job holder's performance and progress over the last 12 months

Previous year objectives

Objectives	Measurement	Results achieved

Objectives for next 12 months

Objectives	Measurement

TRAINING AND DEVELOPMENT REVIEW

The space below is provided to record any newly identified needs and development achieved in the interim period.

Development required/achieved	Agreed action	Target date

Additional comments (if any)

Date: .... Signature of appraiser: ....

Additional comments (if any)

Date: .... Signature of staff member: ....

1. After initial completion and after any revisions or reviews, ensure that the appraiser and the staff member have up-to-date copies.

2. The appraiser should retain this document for at least two years.

21.2   Ethics

Before we can understand what role ethics plays in the marketing of financial services products, we must first understand what the term means. The dictionary would give the following definition:

Ethics

The science of morals, that branch of philosophy concerned with human character and conduct.

Or

of or involving morals', 'a moral principle or set of principles'.

Ethical it describes as meaning 'morally correct' or 'honourable'.

Generally ethics is a term used to describe what is morally right from what is morally wrong. Marketing managers from any organization have a duty to ensure that the activities they undertake are ethical, that is that they do not violate human decency.

Although a great deal of the financial services industry is highly regulated, the rules and regulations deal with those clear rules that can actually be enforced. Ethical issues are generally not covered by regulation. Although it is true that some unethical activity would also be illegal, there is a great deal of behaviour that while totally legal, would still be considered to be against ordinary decency.

All salespeople and marketeers need to consider the ethical issues of what they are doing in order to ensure that it is not causing offence to any of their customers, or the public in general. This said, the issue of ethics and financial services is a complex one.

Basically we can see that ethical means a general view of right against wrong and the way in which such judgements are made. A business has to make judgements every day and needs to consider the way in which these are made, asking itself if those decisions would be judged to be 'ethical' by the public. Managers, marketeers and salespeople need continually to assess what they are doing in order to be sure that they do not do anything that would violate ordinary decency or promote or condone such behaviour.

Because ethics relate to morality, which is an individual judgement, people's judgement of what is and is not ethical differs and marketing managers may find that they are sometimes accused of unethical behaviour by a very small number of people. While this is not ideal, it may not be possible to work within every single person's view of what is and is not acceptable. The manager's judgement may well need to be concerned with what the vast majority of people would find acceptable.

In theory this sounds fairly straightforward, but in practice can be extremely complicated.

Marketing and selling financial services products means that such managers are not involved in such ethical debates as to whether the product is itself harmful, and therefore not sold at all. These allegations could well be directed at the marketing managers of such products as tobacco, alcohol, or even motor vehicles. The manufacturers of medical and beauty products may face allegations of immorality over such things as animal testing, etc. The strength of public feeling towards such issues can be judged by the success of such organizations as the Body Shop, which has built its business on the basis of ethics and social responsibility.

While it would therefore seem at first glance that the financial services industry would escape such problematic decisions, this is not the case; there are still a great number of issues that need to be considered.

Let us then look at a few examples of the types of decisions that could have ethical implications.

Ethical dilemma No. 1

What level of profit is it acceptable to make from the public?

Financial services institutions could well be accused of unethical behaviour in their profit margins. These organizations make huge levels of profit from their business each year, and yet each year hundreds of small businesses go out of business and many more struggle with cash problems while paying the banks charges for their services. This is legal, but is it right?

Ethical dilemma No. 2

Should these companies invest their and their customer's money in unethical companies?
Financial services organizations invest billions of pounds a year on behalf of their customers, and much of this money is invested in companies that manufacture some of the products we mentioned above, such as tobacco and alcohol. While the public is obviously looking to receive a good return on investments, should this be at the expense of their principles? Many customers have expressed concern to financial institutions as to the way in which their investments are handled, and as a result, many financial services organizations offer *ethical investments* or an *ethical fund*. These guarantee not to invest in companies that manufacture or promote harmful products, etc. and have proved to be extremely popular.

Ethical dilemma No. 3

Should companies be allowed to charge more for ethical investments?

The offering of ethical investments does in itself throw up another dilemma. People whose morals lead them to invest only in such ethical funds are likely to be willing to pay a little extra for the peace of mind of knowing where their money is invested. Should financial services companies be allowed to profit from this by charging more for this particular fund, or would this be considered to be exploiting those people with a conscience and therefore judged to be unethical?

Ethical dilemma No. 4

Financial advisers are expected to give their customers the best advice for their needs. Should they be paid commission for making sales?

Some people would argue that if financial advisers are paid to make sales they might be tempted to sell those products even if the customer does not really need them.

Ethical dilemma No. 5

Should advisers be paid different levels of commission for different products?

These advisers should recommend the most suitable product from those available. Is it therefore unethical to pay them more commission for selling one product than selling another?

Ethical dilemma No. 6

A product/service is re-priced at a cheaper rate to attract new customers. Should this new price be offered to existing customers?

Often financial services companies have a price reduction in an attempt to attract new customers and increase market share. If this price is not offered to those customers who have previously bought the service, and shown loyalty to the company, is this ethically correct?

These kind of issues face marketing manager and salespeople each day and they need to ensure that the decisions they take are carefully thought out. They need to base those decisions on the following factors:

- They should reflect their professionalism and their ethics; i.e. they should never take decisions that will knowingly harm people.

- They should, where possible, be honest and fair to all parties, including new and existing customers, employees, the public, and the company.

- All products offered should be safe and fit for their purpose and represent good value for the customer.

- They should avoid false or misleading claims about the product and services they offer.

- They should disclose the full cost of the product or service to the purchaser.

- They should not exploit the customer's needs, or their lack of expertise in their marketing and selling processes.

- They should not exert undue pressure on salespeople to sell particular products.

It is now common for a business to develop its own ethical code of conduct based on factors such as those shown above. Some have even gone as far as to publish their code so that customers and potential customers can see the standards to which the business operates.

21.3 Social responsibility and the role in the community

Ethics, as we said, deals with morality and a personal judgement as to what is right and wrong. Ethical decisions are often taken by individual managers, and if those decisions cause offence they will do so against the individual's beliefs. Social responsibility is concerned with the corporate image and the company as a whole and the expectations of society at large as to how that company will behave. Society expects that a large organization such as a financial services institution will make some contribution to society and will act in a way that is not irresponsible and will not harm the general public.

Once again the issues of social responsibility would initially seem to pose a greater problem for industries other than that of financial services. For example, should a company that is manufacturing a medicine which cures a life-threatening illness be expected to donate that medicine to those who cannot afford to buy it?

However, the financial services industry does need to concern itself with matters of social responsibility, as research has shown that there is an increasing view within this country that a business should be considering the needs of the community in which it operates. There is also evidence that people do consider a company's record in matters of social responsibility when deciding if they want to do business with it, and therefore there may well be an effect on the profits of the business if the company does not take this matter seriously.

A company can display its social responsibility on two levels:

- Stakeholder responsibility
- Societal responsibility

Stakeholder responsibility

This involves ensuring that the company has obligations to those people who are a part of that company in some way. This would involve such people as employees, suppliers, distributors and customers. This means that they would always consider their actions and ensure that they were not acting in a way that would ever harm those people, or cause them any distress.

Societal responsibility

Societal responsibility relates to the organization's responsibility to society in general, and its attitude towards the general public, i.e. those people who are not a part of the company in any way. This kind of social responsibility would manifest itself in such things as the organization supporting ecological matters, and its supporting environmentally friendly products, for example.

Many financial services companies are now very large organizations and therefore form a significant part of the community in which they operate. They may well employ a large proportion of the workforce in that area and therefore be responsible for its financial stability. When this is the case, such an organization has a role to play in the community.

21.4   Creating an image of social responsibility

We have seen that financial services companies have some level of social responsibility and need to consider themselves to be a part of the community in which they exist. They therefore need to consider the outcome of their decisions and the effect those decisions will have on that community. In an attempt to promote their organizations as socially responsible, many have taken actions that show they wish to give something back to the communities that have enabled them to be so successful and produce such profits.

Let us look firstly at the stakeholder responsibilities. Most financial services companies are very conscious of their responsibility to their staff, and in order to create an image or social responsibility endeavour to show that they support those staff and their families. Many companies provide sports and leisure facilities for their staff, and some even provide such things as a crèche for young children, allowing parents to return to work. These could be argued to be simply perks for the staff in order to attract and retain good quality people and therefore the company does it for a commercial reason. This may well be the case, but if so, the additional benefit that the company gets from such actions is that the staff will tell people about such benefits. The company will soon develop a reputation as a caring employer, one that looks after its staff, and cares about the people who work for it.

Let us now look at how a company can create an image of having societal responsibility. Many financial services companies have a budget set aside for supporting good causes in their areas by way of donations and sponsorship. Many also associate themselves with certain charities and support those charities by sponsorship or simply by donations. While this obviously carries a large cost for the company, the benefits are great in terms of its image, and there could even be a commercial benefit of the company's socially responsible attitude.

Other companies link the sale of their products to a charity or good cause and thereby raise money for that good cause. For example, a large number of organizations offer charity-based credit cards by means of which a donation is made to the charity every time the card is used.

Other companies promote a charity and make a donation to that charity each time a product is bought. Examples of this are such things as the recent promotion by a pet-food manufacturer who made donations to an animal charity for each can of cat food purchased, or the company that promoted Red Nose Day '99 by making a donation for each box of washing powder bought. With this method of socially responsible attitude, the company both increases its sales as well as promoting its image and raising money for the charity.

Another way of showing that a company has a socially responsible attitude is for it to promote environmentally friendly products and by ensuring that customers understand that the company cares about environmental issues. It is now commonplace to see financial services companies' literature printed on recycled paper, and for this to be explained to the customers so that they can see the company is being socially responsible in its actions.

Another way of promoting the company's image of social responsibility is for the company to be seen to be giving something back to the community in which they operate while gaining nothing in return, i.e. for no commercial benefit. This could involve them in donating equipment for schools or creating play areas for children, for example.

Another example is Scottish Power, which has run television advertisements explaining how it has undertaken a programme cleaning rivers and ponds to allow wildlife to flourish. While this has cost the company money both to carry out the work and to advertise the fact that they have done it, it ensures that they build a reputation as a company that cares about the environment. It shows that the company is willing to give time, money and attention to its social responsibilities.

Appendix 1

EXTRACTS FROM THE BRITISH CODES OF ADVERTISING AND SALES PROMOTION

The Committee of Advertising Practice is the self-regulatory body that devises and enforces the Codes; CAP's members include organizations that represent the advertising, sales promotion and media businesses.

The Advertising Standards Authority is the independent body responsible for ensuring that the system works in the public interest. The ASA's activities include investigating complaints and conducting research.

Introduction

The Codes apply to:

a   advertisements in newspapers, magazines, brochures, leaflets, circulars, mailings, catalogues, follow-up literature and other printed material, facsimile transmissions, posters and other out-door media

b   cinema and video commercials

c   advertisements in non-broadcast electronic media

d   view data services

e   databases containing consumers' personal information

f   sales promotions

g   advertisement promotions

h   advertisements and promotions covered by the Cigarette Code

The following definitions apply to the Codes:

a   a product encompasses goods, services, ideas, causes, opportunities, prizes or gifts

b   a consumer is anyone who is likely to see a given advertisement or promotion c   the United Kingdom rules cover the Isle of Man and the Channel Islands (except for the purposes of the Cigarette Code)

d   a claim can be implied or direct, written, spoken or visual

e   the Codes are divided into numbered clauses

The following criteria apply to the Codes:

a   the judgement of the ASA Council on interpretation of the Codes is final

b   conformity is assessed according to the advertisement's probable impact when taken as a whole, in proportion and in context. This will depend on the audience, the medium, and the nature of the product and any additional material distributed at the same time to consumers

c   the Codes are indivisible; advertisers must conform to all appropriate rules

d   the Codes do not have the force of law and their interpretation will reflect their flexibility. The codes operate alongside the law; the Courts may also make rulings against matters covered by the Codes

e   an indication of the statutory rules governing advertising and promotions is given in the Legislation section; professional advice should be taken if there is any doubt about their application

f   no spoken or written communications with the ASA or CAP should be understood as containing legal advice

g   the Codes are primarily concerned with advertisements and promotions and not with terms of business, products themselves or other contractual matters

h   the rules make due allowance for public sensitivities but will not be used by the ASA to diminish freedom of speech

i   the ASA may decide that it is not qualified to judge advertisements and promotions in languages other than English

j   the ASA does not arbitrate between conflicting ideologies

Advertising Code

Principles

All advertisements should be legal, decent, honest and truthful.

All advertisements should be prepared with a sense of responsibility to consumers and to society.

All advertisements should respect the principles of fair competition generally accepted in business.

No advertisement should bring advertising into disrepute.

Advertisements must conform to the Codes. Primary responsibility for observing the Codes falls on advertisers. Others involved in preparing and publishing advertisements such as agencies, publishers and other service suppliers also accept an obligation to abide by the Codes.

Any unreasonable delay in responding to the ASA's enquiries may be considered a breach of the Codes.

The ASA will on request treat in confidence any private or secret material supplied unless the Courts or officials acting within their statutory powers compel its disclosure.

The Codes are applied in the spirit as well as in the letter.

Substantiation

Before submitting an advertisement for publication, advertisers must hold documentary evidence to prove all claims, whether direct or implied, that are capable of objective substantiation. Relevant evidence should be sent without delay if requested by the ASA. The adequacy of evidence will be judged on whether it supports both the detailed claims and the overall impression created by the advertisement.

If there is a significant division of informed opinion about any claims made in an advertisement they should not be portrayed as generally agreed.

Claims for the content of non-fiction books, tapes, videos and the like that have not been independently substantiated should not exaggerate the value, accuracy, scientific validity or practical usefulness of the product.

Obvious untruths or exaggerations that are unlikely to mislead and incidental minor errors and unorthodox spellings are all allowed provided they do not affect the accuracy or perception of the advertisement in any material way.

Legality

Advertisers have primary responsibility for ensuring that their advertisements are legal.

Advertisements should comply with the law and should not incite anyone to break it.

Decency

Advertisements should contain nothing that is likely to cause serious or widespread offence. Particular care should be taken to avoid causing offence on the grounds of race, religion, sex, sexual orientation or disability. Compliance with the Codes will be judged on the context, medium, audience, product and prevailing standards of decency.

Advertisements may be distasteful without necessarily conflicting with the above paragraph. Advertisers are urged to consider public sensitivities before using potentially offensive material.

The fact that a particular product is offensive to some people is not sufficient grounds for objecting to an advertisement for it.

Honesty

Advertisers should not exploit the credulity, lack of knowledge or inexperience of consumers.

Truthfulness

No advertisement should mislead by inaccuracy, ambiguity, exaggeration, omission or otherwise.

Matters of Opinion

Advertisers may give a view about any matter, including the qualities or desirability of their products, provided it is clear that they are expressing their own opinion rather than stating a fact. Assertions or comparisons that go beyond subjective opinions are subject to the first column after the title Substantiation above.

Fear and Distress

No advertisement should cause fear or distress without good reason. Advertisers should not use shocking claims or images merely to attract attention.

Advertisers may use an appeal to fear to encourage prudent behaviour or to discourage dangerous or ill-advised actions; the fear likely to be aroused should not be disproportionate to the risk.

Safety

Advertisements should not show or encourage unsafe practices except in the context of promoting safety. Particular care should be taken with advertisements addressed to or depicting children and young people.

Consumers should not be encouraged to drink and drive. Advertisements should, where appropriate, include a prominent warning on the dangers of drinking and driving and should not suggest that the effects of drinking alcohol can be masked.

Violence and anti-social behaviour

Advertisements should contain nothing that condones or is likely to provoke violence or anti-social behaviour.

Testimonials and endorsements

Advertisers should hold signed and dated proof, including a contact address, for any testimonial they use. Testimonials should be used only with the written permission of those giving them.

Testimonials should relate to the product being advertised.

Testimonials alone do not constitute substantiation and the opinions expressed in them must be supported, where necessary, with independent evidence of their accuracy. Any claims based on a testimonial must conform to the Codes.

Fictitious endorsements should not be presented as though they were genuine testimonials.

References to tests, trials, professional endorsements, research facilities and professional journals should be used only with the permission of those concerned. They should originate from within the European Union unless otherwise stated in the advertisement. Any establishment referred to should be under the direct supervision of an appropriately qualified professional.

Prices

Any stated price should be clear and should relate to the product advertised. Advertisers should ensure that prices match the products illustrated.

Unless addressed exclusively to the trade, prices should be shown inclusive of VAT and other non-optional taxes and duties. If advertisements are likely to be read by both companies and consumers, the quotation of any VAT inclusive and exclusive prices should be shown with equal prominence.

If the price of one product is dependent on the purchase of another, the extent of any commitment by consumers should be made clear.

Free offers

There is no objection to making a free offer conditional on the purchase of other items. Consumers' liability for any costs should be made clear in all material featuring the offer. An offer should be described as free only if consumers pay no more then:

a   the current public rates of postage

b   the actual cost of freight or delivery

c   the cost, including incidental expenses, of any travel involved if consumers collect the offer.

Advertisers should make no additional charges for packing and handling.

Advertisers must not attempt to recover their costs by reducing the quality or composition or by inflating the price of any product that must be purchased as a pre-condition of obtaining another product free.

Availability of products

Advertisers must make it clear if stocks are limited. Products must not be advertised unless advertisers can demonstrate that they have reasonable grounds for believing that they can satisfy demand. If a product becomes unavailable, advertisers will be required to show evidence of stock monitoring, communications with outlets and swift withdrawal of advertisements whenever possible.

Products, which cannot be supplied, should not normally be advertised as a way of assessing potential demand unless it is clear that that is the purpose of the advertisement.

Advertisers must not use the technique of switch selling, where their sales staff criticize the advertised product or suggest that it is not available and recommend the purchase of a more expensive alternative. They should not place obstacles in the way of purchasing the product or delivering it promptly.

Guarantees

The word 'guarantee' should not be used in a way that could cause confusion about consumers' legal rights. Substantial limitations should be spelled out in the advertisement. Before commitment, consumers should be able to obtain from advertisers all conditions imposed by the guarantee.

Advertisers should inform consumers about the nature and extent of any additional rights provided by the guarantee, over and above those given to them by law, and should make clear how to obtain redress.

Comparisons

Comparisons can be explicit or implied and can relate to advertiser's own products or to those of their competitors; they are permitted in the interests of vigorous competition and public information.

Comparisons should be clear and fair. The elements of any comparison should not be selected in a way that gives the advertisers an artificial advantage.

Denigration

Advertisers should not unfairly attack or discredit other businesses or their products.

The only acceptable use of another business's broken or defaced products in advertisements is in the illustration of comparative tests, and the source, nature and results of these should be clear.

Exploitation of goodwill

Advertisers should not make unfair use of the goodwill attached to the trademark, name, brand, or the advertising campaign of any other organization.

Imitation

No advertisement should so closely resemble any other that it misleads or causes confusion.

Identifying advertisers and recognizing advertisements

Advertisers, publishers and owners of other media should ensure that advertisements are designed and presented in such a way that it is clear that they are advertisements.

Features, announcements or promotions that are disseminated in exchange for a payment or other reciprocal arrangement should comply with the Codes if the advertisers control their content. They should also be clearly identified as such (see first paragraph after the title legality above).

Mail order and direct response advertisements and those for one-day sales, homework schemes, business opportunities and the like should contain the name and address of the advertisers. Advertisements with a political content should clearly identify their source. Unless required by law, other advertisers are not obliged to identify themselves.

Index